Images of Modern America

ERIE COUNTY FAIR

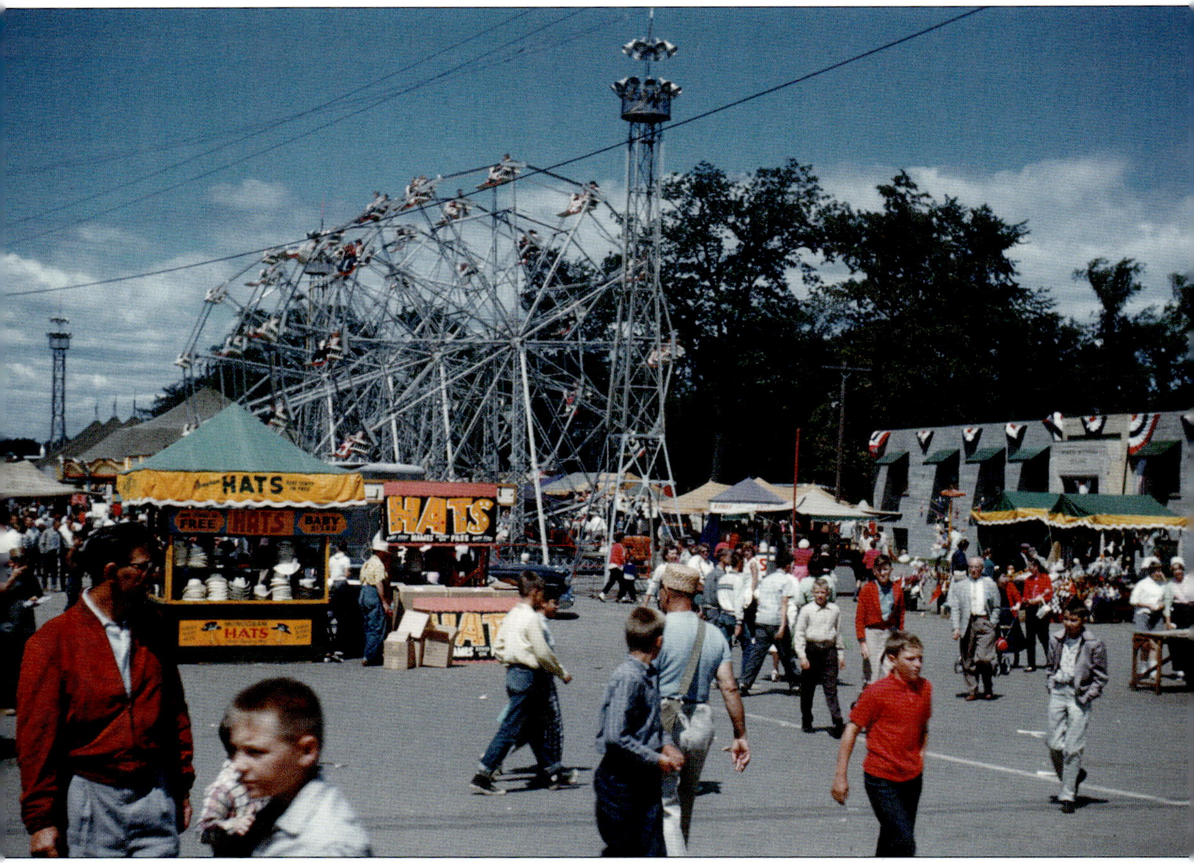

The James E. Strates Shows has been part of the Erie County Fair tradition since 1924. In 1957, the show's signature four-abreast Ferris wheel welcomed fairgoers to its mile-long midway. (Courtesy of the Erie County Agricultural Society.)

FRONT COVER: The glow of the James E. Strates Shows midway transforms the Erie County Fairgrounds into a magical city of excitement where memories are made. (Courtesy of the Erie County Agricultural Society.)

UPPER BACK COVER: Tootsie's Fried Dough Stand along Broadway was owned by Rene Piche. (Courtesy of the Erie County Agricultural Society.)

LOWER BACK COVER: Scenes from the annual Erie County Fair include (from left to right) Fair Bear, the popular Strates Shows Wave Swinger, and competitor Leila Richmond. (All, courtesy of the Erie County Agricultural Society.)

Images of Modern America

ERIE COUNTY FAIR

Martin Biniasz
on behalf of the
Erie County Agricultural Society

ARCADIA
PUBLISHING

ISBN 978-1-4671-1709-8

Published by Arcadia Publishing
Charleston, South Carolina

Printed in the United States of America

Library of Congress Control Number: 2016930932

For all general information, please contact Arcadia Publishing:
Telephone 843-853-2070
Fax 843-853-0044
E-mail sales@arcadiapublishing.com
For customer service and orders:
Toll-Free 1-888-313-2665

Visit us on the Internet at www.arcadiapublishing.com

To those past, present, and future who "think big." It is your legacy and vision that keeps the Erie County Fair growing strong decade after decade.

Contents

ACKNOWLEDGMENTS

Sincere appreciation goes to all who have contributed to the preservation, documentation, and sharing of the Erie County Fair's history. The efforts by George B. Abbott and George G. Sipprell during the early and mid-20th century laid a strong foundation of information. Under the direction of the Erie County Agricultural Society, the late Ellen Taussig continued to chronicle the fair's achievements. Thank you, to Dee Zeigel and Jolene Hawkins for assisting in the organization of the society's extensive archives and to Dennis Lang, Jessica Underberg, and the Board of the Erie County Agricultural Society (ECAS) for allowing me to complete this project on their behalf. Erie County Agricultural Society staff members Holly Smyczynski, Amanda Cammarano, Concetta Sciolino, Russ Marquart, Jeff Horbowicz, and Jackie Cammarano assisted greatly in proofreading and provided colorful stories about the fair's modern history.

Special appreciation goes to James Barrett, who shared his extensive collection of Erie County Fair memorabilia for this and other projects through the years. Carnival historian Bill Pfeifer contributed valuable information about the fair's midway and ride equipment used over the decades. Images from the 2000s were taken by Tom Wolf. All images are from the archives of the Erie County Agricultural Society.

Introduction

In 2014, the Erie County Agricultural Society celebrated the 175th Erie County Fair by welcoming a record-breaking 1,220,101 visitors to its fairgrounds in Hamburg, New York. When the tradition of agricultural fairs in the region began in 1820, the total population of the village of Buffalo was only 2,100 people. With the opening of the Erie Canal in 1825, the Niagara Frontier began a period of meteoric growth that lasted well into the 20th century.

Early settlers to Western New York State discovered an area accommodating for agricultural success. Despite long winters, the region provided sunny, dry summers with sufficient rain for vegetation. Fertile lands benefited from the cooling effects of Lakes Erie and Ontario. Microclimates along the lakeshores provided frost and heat protection for delicate crops like fruit trees and grapes. The Great Lakes also provided an important transportation route to the center of a quickly expanding United States.

By the early 1800s, pioneers from eastern New York and New England began to arrive. Just as settlements in the region began to take hold, the village of Buffalo became embroiled in the War of 1812 and was burned to the ground by the British in December 1813.

In 1819, as the region was just recovering from war, optimistic pioneers looked to form an agricultural union with the goal of educating farmers and sharing information. On August 5, 1819, when the present Erie County was still part of Niagara County, a Buffalonian by the name of Joseph W. Moulton sent a letter to farmers proposing the founding of a county agricultural society. The response was well received, and at a meeting on September 14, 1819, at the courthouse on Buffalo's Lafayette Square, a society was founded. Dr. Cyrenius Chapin was elected president, with a directive to organize and sponsor a fair. The first fair was held in October 1820 at a site near Terrace and Main Streets in an area of modern downtown Buffalo known as Canalside.

According to a history of the Erie County Agricultural Society edited by H. Perry Smith in 1884, as the day for the first exhibition approached, Dr. Chapin realized that if there was to be a fair, he would have to provide it. Fortunately, he owned five farms in the vicinity of Buffalo that were stocked with fine flocks of sheep and herds of cattle. He notified his tenant farmers to begin driving in selected specimens of stock the day before the fair. On the morning before this big event, the doctor became worried. To make sure everything was proceeding according to plan, he sent out his protégé, 17-year-old Orlando Allen, to check on preparation. On horseback, in company with another youth, Allen first went to Dr. Chapin's farm in Hamburg. He found his employer had grounds for his fears. The farmer had done nothing at all about starting the livestock toward Buffalo. So, Allen rode herd on 20 head of cattle and sheep, driving them though forest, wilderness, and bogs to Buffalo. It was breakfast time on the morning of the fair when Allen finally ended his tour of duty driving cattle to Buffalo. He spent all that day at the fair and that night, dressed in a brand-new suit of clothes, he had a fine time dancing at the ball that ended the exhibition. Writing about the first fair, Allen commented, "The day was fine, the entries quite numerous and everything passed off to the satisfaction of all concerned."

In 1821, the greater part of Niagara County became Erie County, and the society's name was changed to the Erie County Agricultural Society. The second fair, held on October, 30, 1821, was affectionately referred to in the *Republic Press* newspaper as a "Farmers' Holiday." The fair's agricultural ball was held at the Rathbone Hotel following a day of plowing competitions and the awarding of premiums.

A combination of a poor economy, transportation logistics, and perhaps the community's attention focused on the building of the Erie Canal, meant enthusiasm for an annual agricultural exhibition faded, so after only two years, the county fair idea was dropped. Two decades later, on August 14, 1841, a group of county citizens formed another Erie County Agricultural Society. Lewis F. Allen of Buffalo was the first president of the new organization, which held its first fair on the grounds of the Erie County Courthouse at Lafayette Square, in October 6, 1841. The following year, in 1842, the fair was held on the grounds of Dr. Ebenezer Johnson's estate on Delaware Avenue at Johnson Park.

As the city of Buffalo expanded, the fair was moved to sites closer to the agrarian community. Many of these sites were locations of driving parks or harness racetracks. The year 1850 began the era of the "traveling fair" that saw the annual event being held in Aurora (1850), Lancaster (1851), East Hamburgh–Orchard Park (1852), Buffalo–Cold Springs (1853), Aurora (1854) East Hamburgh–Orchard Park (1855), South Buffalo–West Seneca (1856–1864), Buffalo–Cold Springs (1865), and Springville (1866–1867).

In 1855, New York State looked to standardize the organization of agricultural societies through an act of state legislation, and the Erie County Agricultural Society was technically dissolved and immediately reorganized under the act.

The frequent moving of the fair around the county became a costly endeavor for the agricultural society, as larger crowds demanded more permanent and sanitary amenities. On January 9, 1868, Luther Titus of Hamburg addressed the agricultural society with an offer, on behalf of the Hamburg Driving Park Association, for the use of its new half-mile track and grounds with office buildings and seats free of charge for holding the next annual fair. By a vote of 18 to 17, the fair moved to Hamburg and held its first exposition in 1868. In a few short years, the site adjacent to the corner of McKinley Parkway and Clark Street would become the permanent home of the Erie County Fair.

In the 1880s, the modern fairgrounds as it is known today began to take shape. The society began to purchase the driving park property outright along with adjacent parcels in 1881. The construction of elaborate barns and exhibition halls began, including the first Grandstand in 1884 and the Women's Building, known as the Octagon Building, in 1885. As it was located only 12 miles from downtown Buffalo, urban dwellers could access the fairgrounds via train service through the village of Hamburg. Trolley service from downtown Buffalo via Orchard Park and Hamburg was inaugurated in 1896, and in 1907 the short-lived Buffalo & Susquehanna Railroad opened a line between Buffalo and Olean with a station location on the fairgrounds near the site of the current Hamburg Gaming. Public transportation to the fairgrounds became a key element in the growth of the Erie County Fair after the turn of the century.

Despite the large crowds from Buffalo, a distinctly rural aura still pervaded the fair during the 1900s. "The grounds were occupied chiefly by country people," reported the *Commercial Advertiser*, "most of who were sitting about quietly visiting. The annual fair brings together a great many who never met at other places, and the renewing of old friendships is always one of the features of the first days." As the day wore on and trains from Buffalo arrived, "it would have been hard to imagine a more cosmopolitan crowd. Country people and city people, businessmen and farmers, ladies in silk and women in calico, Indians and white men, mingling indiscriminately and enjoying themselves equally."

One

The 1950s

Bigger, Better, Longer

By the middle of the 20th century, the Erie County Fair had successfully integrated rural, agrarian and urban cultures into one single, must-attend regional celebration. Just seven years earlier, the short-term future of the Erie County Fair was in doubt as the 1943 fair was postponed due to wartime rationing. By 1950, the success of the fair directly reflected the postwar prosperity and optimism experienced by Western New York. The population of the neighboring city of Buffalo peaked at 580,132 in 1950, when it was the 15th-largest city in the United States. Western New York was a leader in grain milling and aircraft, automobile, and steel production as well as a major transportation and transshipment hub focused on railroads and Great Lakes shipping.

From 1950 to 1959, the fair gradually expanded to a full eight days and featured expanded agricultural competitions, national grandstand entertainment, and a growing collection of midway attractions provided by the James E. Strates Shows. Daily television broadcasts originating from the fair provided by WBEN-TV (Channel 4) brought the fair's excitement into homes located in the nearby cities of Rochester and Jamestown and as far away as Toronto, Canada. By 1955, the fairgrounds included over 55 buildings and occupied a 135-acre tract in Hamburg.

The taste of the fair changed forever with the introduction of signature chicken dinners by Eden-based farmer Bert Weidner in 1956. Thomas and Eleanor Chiavetta's barbecue chicken, added in 1957, featured their own "Italian twist" of spices and seasonings. Vendors Felix Coniglio and Salvatore Butera introduced many suburban and rural Western New Yorkers to pizza for the first time.

Pari-mutuel harness racing, brought to the fairgrounds in 1942 by Buffalo Raceway, began a pattern of growth that lasted through the following decades. Robust rent revenue from racing allowed the fair to set its sights on the future. It was during the 1950s that initial planning took place for increased fairgrounds acreage, new exhibit buildings and barns, dedicated parklands, and landscaped pedestrian promenades.

In an honor usually bestowed exclusively for the New York State Fair, New York governor Averill Harriman visited the Erie County Fair in 1957. This was the first visit to the fair made by a governor while in office since the 1903 visit of the then governor Benjamin O'Dell.

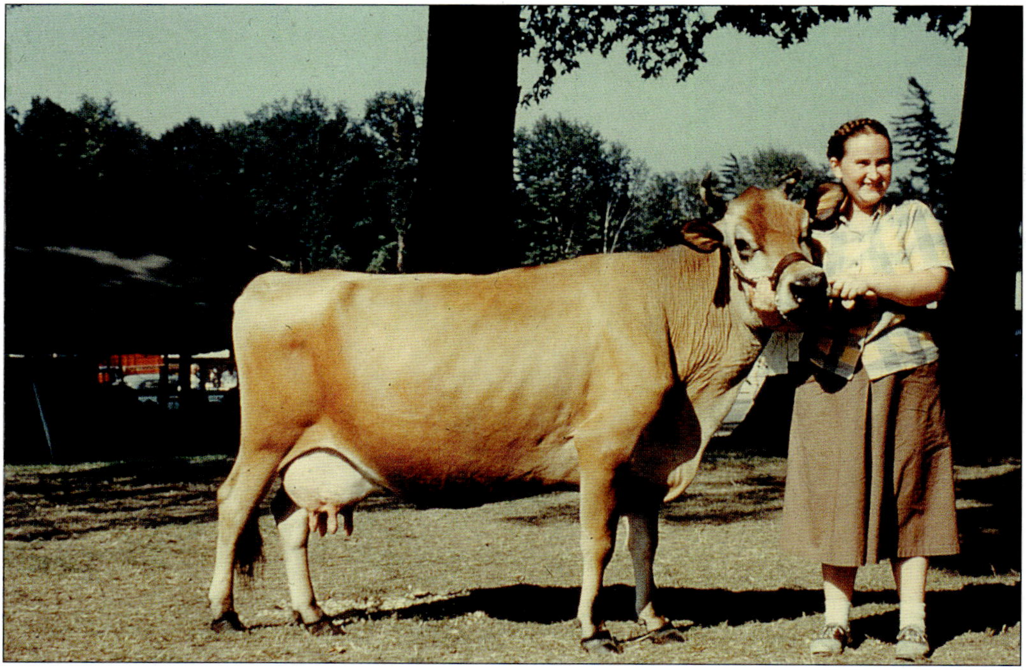

A Western New York 4-H Club competitor shows off her prized Jersey cow during the 1956 fair. The seven-day 1956 Erie County Fair had a total attendance of 122,367.

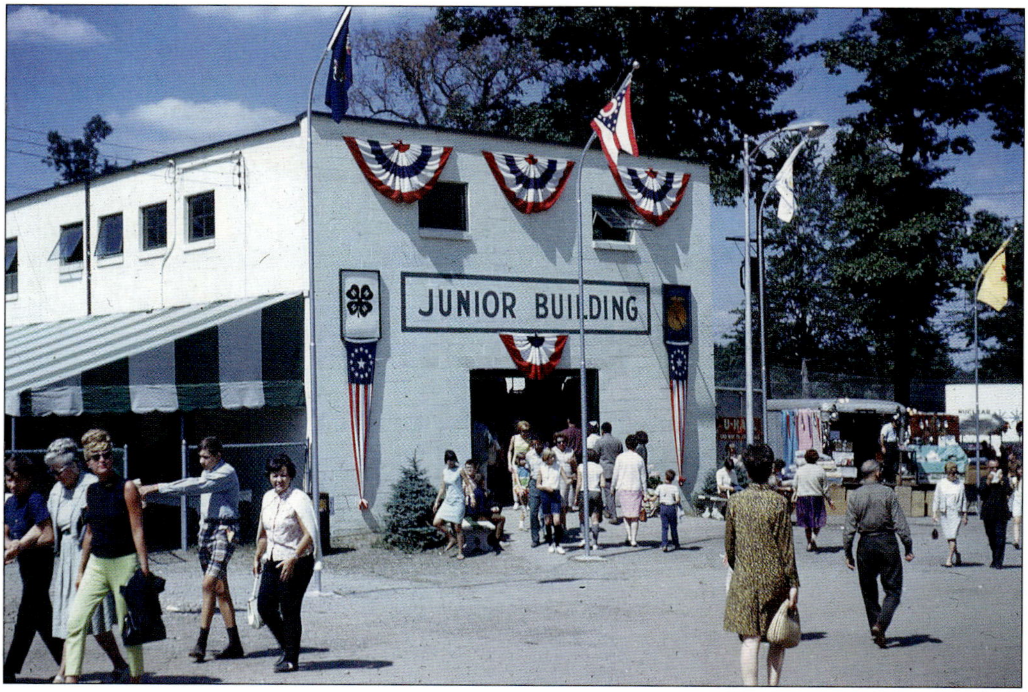

The fair opened the doors to the new Junior Building in 1959. The building on the current Avenue of Flags was erected as a showplace for 4-H clubs and their exhibits. The second floor housed a dormitory with shower and toilet facilities for 60 to 70 competitors who would stay with their exhibits during the course of the fair.

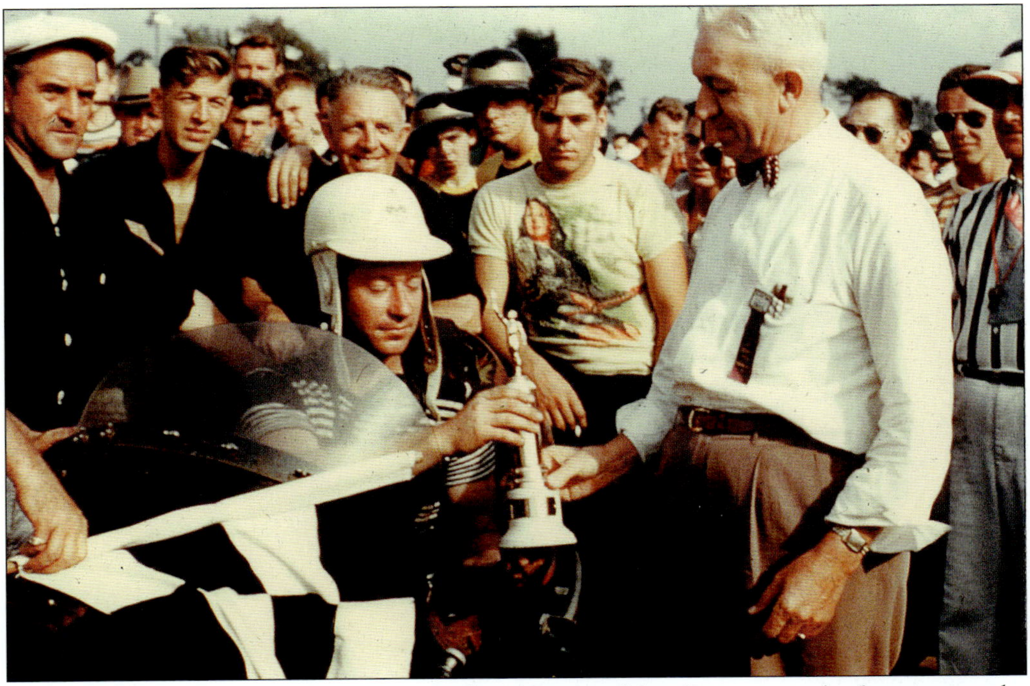

Arthur G. Fries presents Bobby Courtwright of Ramsey, New Jersey, a trophy for winning the 1956 Erie County Fair auto race. Courtwright captured the 32-lap race that was part of an eight-event auto-racing program.

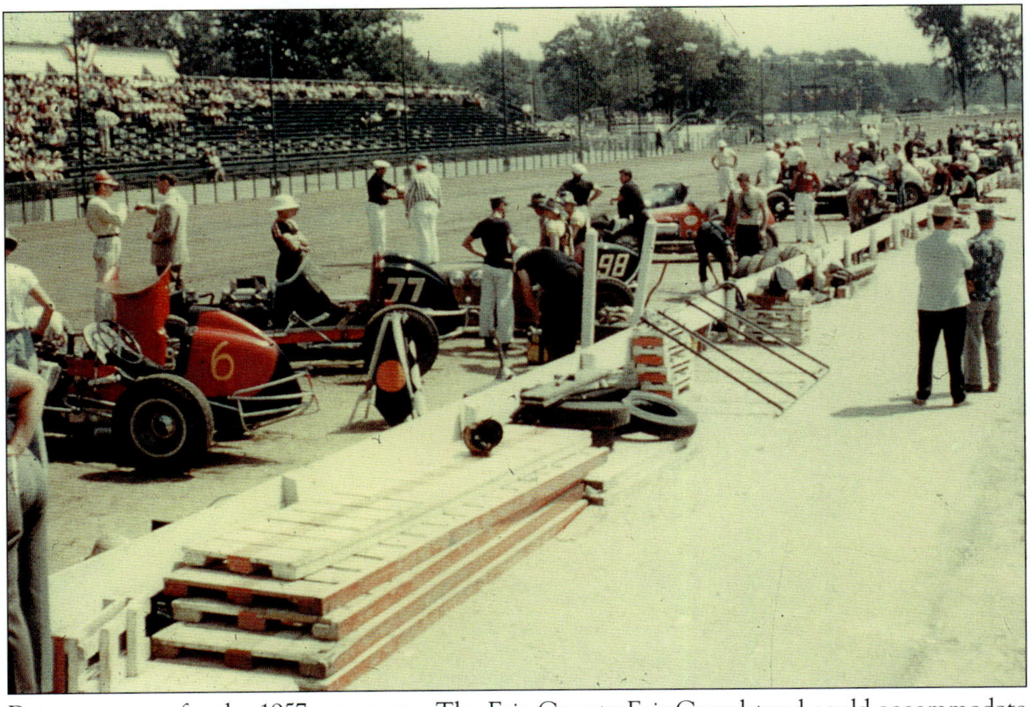

Drivers prepare for the 1957 auto races. The Erie County Fair Grandstand could accommodate over 10,000 spectators for motor events.

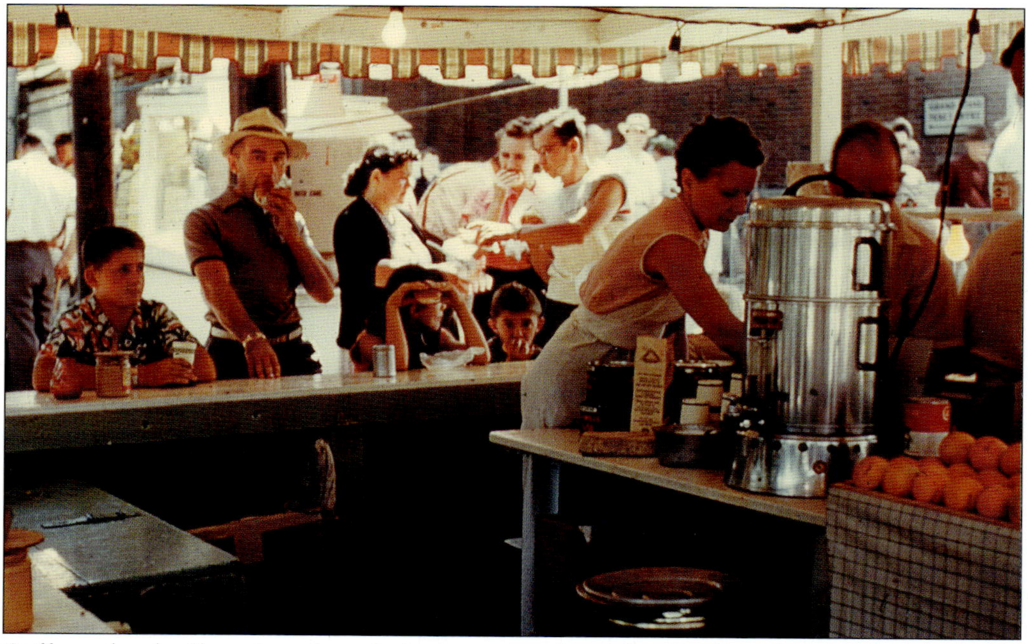

Coffee, a hard roll, and maybe a fresh orange was breakfast for these fairgoers in 1955. Most concession stands of the era, like this one pictured located behind the Grandstand, were considered "stick joints" due to their wood and canvas construction.

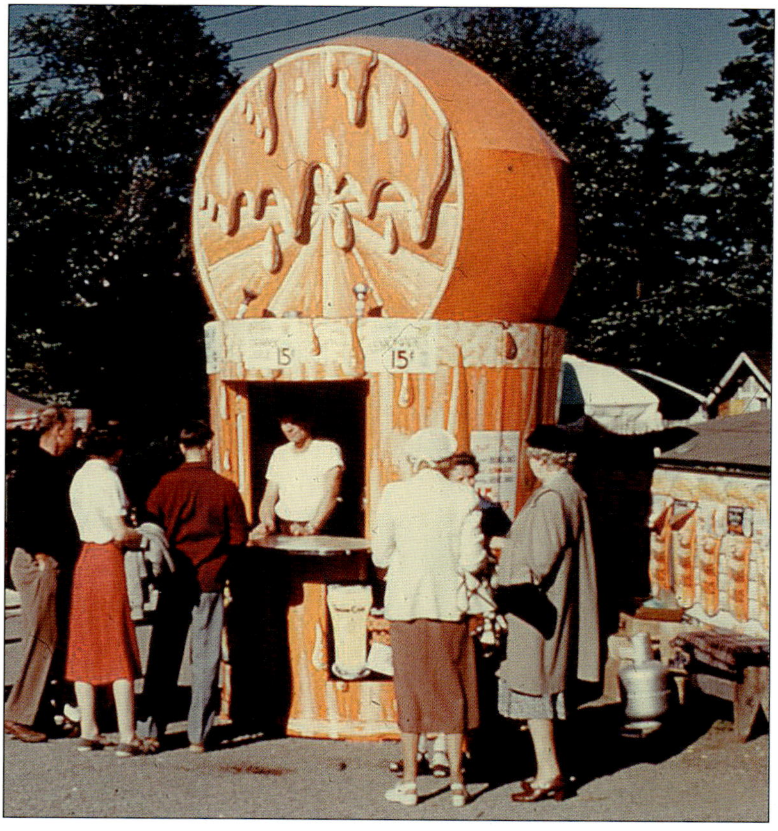

In 1956, concession vendors looked for creative ways to distinguish themselves from the growing competition. New products and colorful displays, like this stand featuring a giant slice of an orange, began to change the look of the fairgrounds.

The "fool the guesser" age and weight game has been a feature on the modern Erie County Fair midway since the turn of the 20th century. With a light joke and a scratch of a number on a pad of paper, the carnival worker tries to guess the patron's birth month within two months, age within two years, or weight within three pounds in this image from 1955.

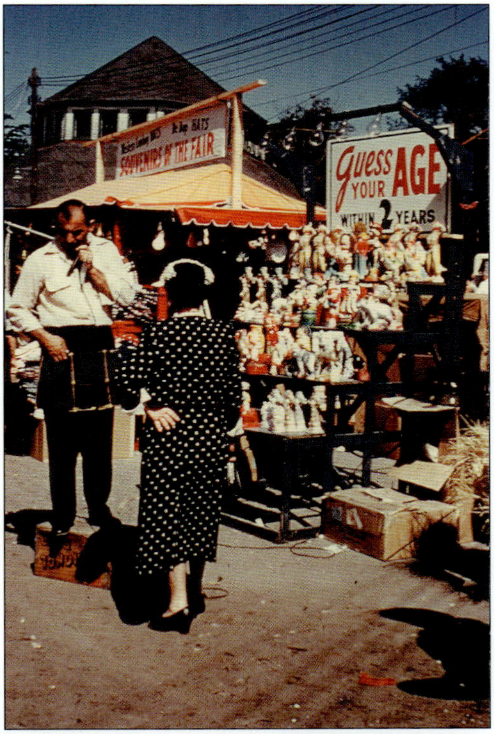

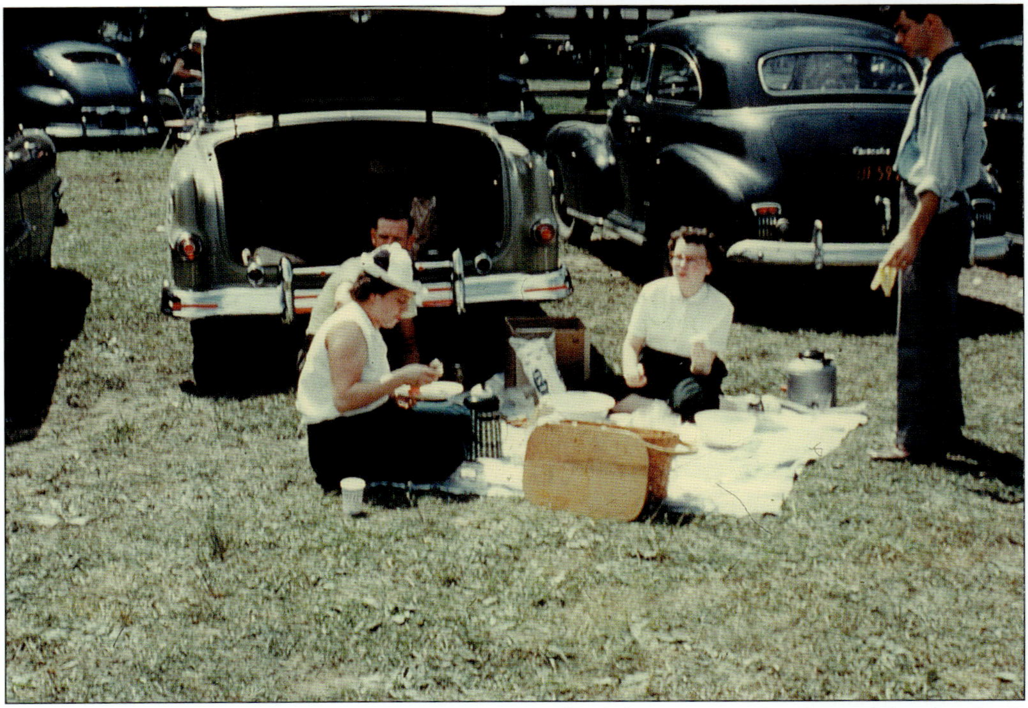

Taking time away from the midway, competition, and exhibits, many a family would retreat back to their automobile for an afternoon tailgate picnic. Although the smell of barbecue chicken and fresh pizza was tantalizing to the senses, the simple time spent together as a family eating a home-packed sandwich is a cherished memory for many.

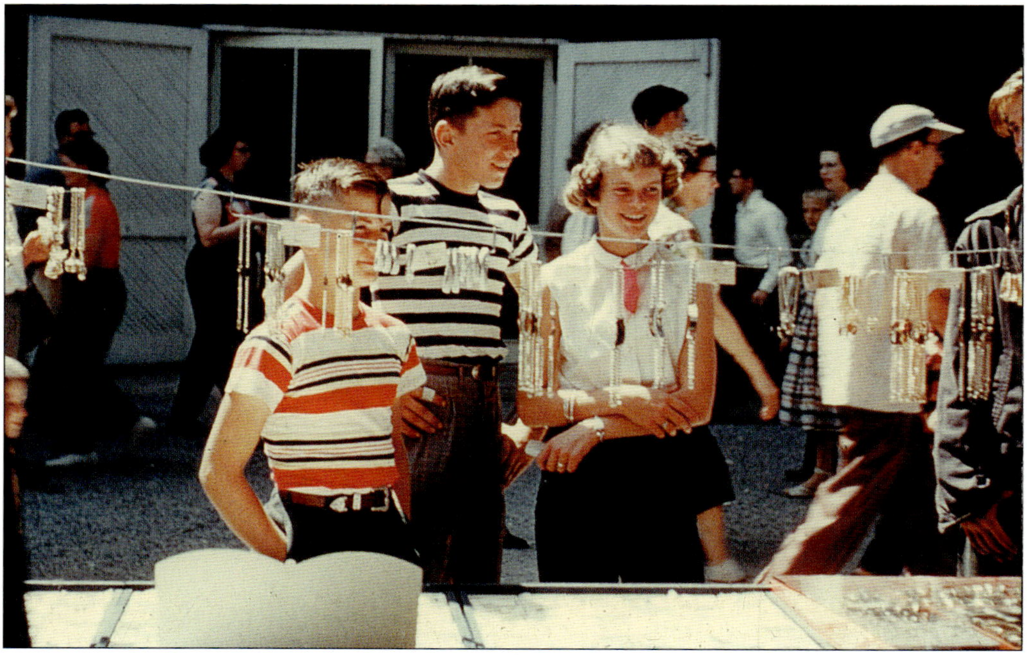

A vendor sells trinkets and treasures outside of the Bazaar Building in 1955. Bracelets, like the ones shown, were cheap keepsakes of a trip to the fair.

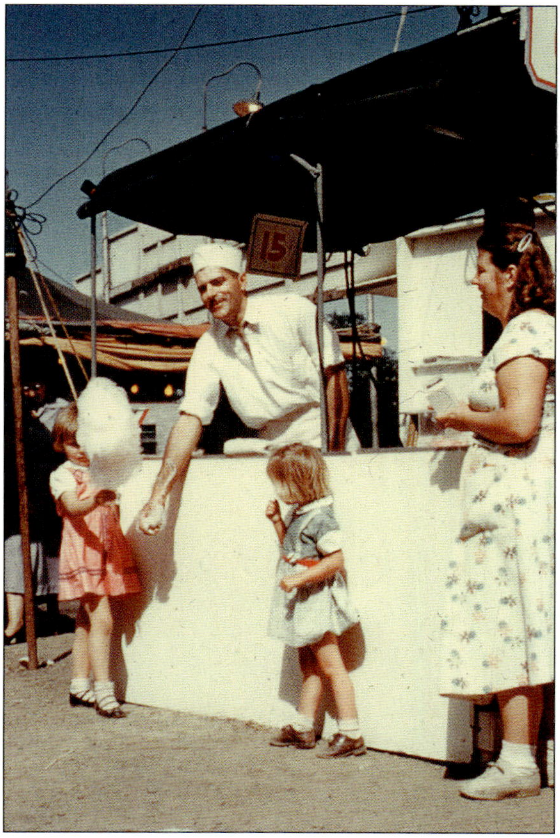

In 1958, a child-size serving of cotton candy cost 15¢. Cotton candy became a popular midway treat after being introduced during the 1904 St. Louis World's Fair. The process includes the spinning of granulated, colored sugar until it melts. The melted sugar is then spun through tiny holes where it is caught in the air and served on a stick or put into a bag.

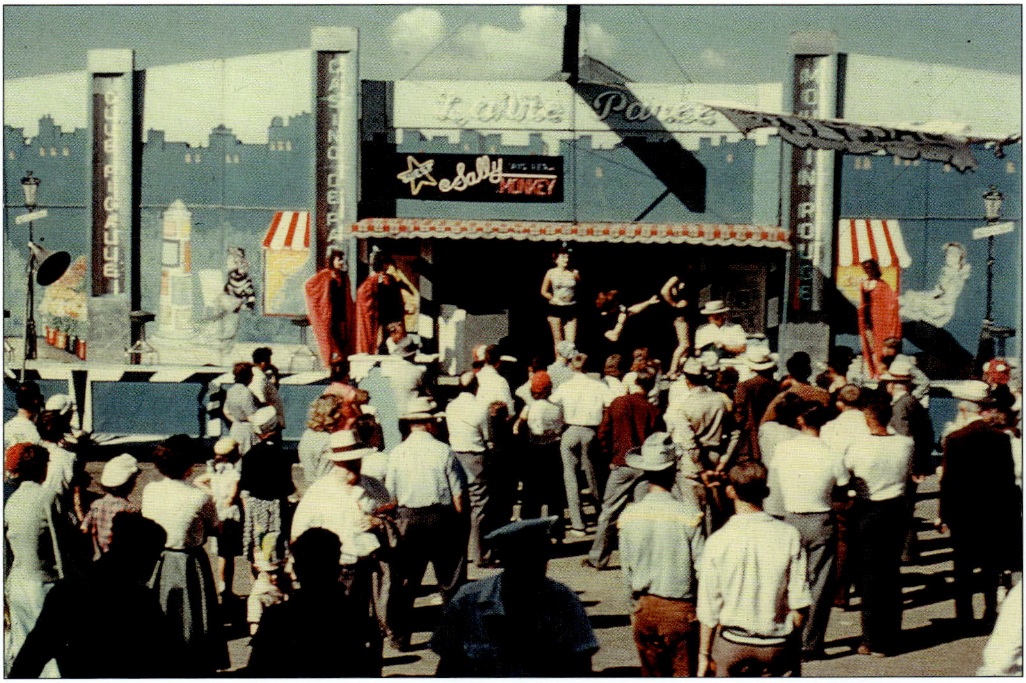

Considered one of the finest girlie shows in America at the time, the "La Vie Paree Revue," operated by Eddie Keck, was part of the James E. Strates midway lineup in 1956. As an added feature, the show also featured a performance by Sally Lane and her monkey.

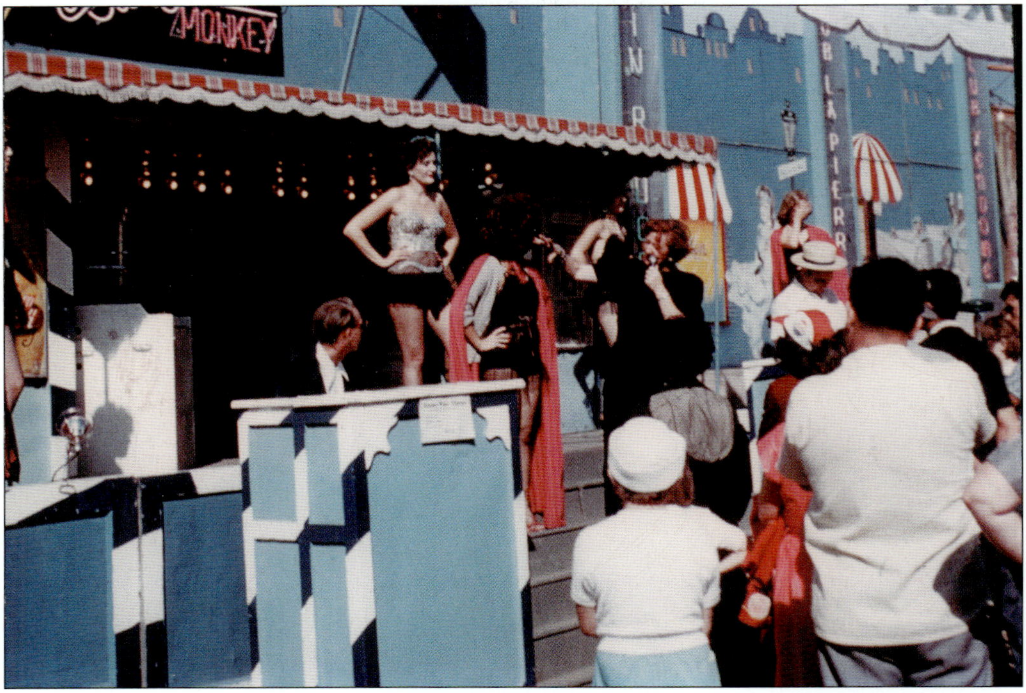

With its live organ music and the constant, flamboyant, and exaggerated ballyhoo of the announcer, young men and curious women were drawn into the midway's girlie show. The last of these shows appeared on the Strates's Erie County Fair midway until the 1980s.

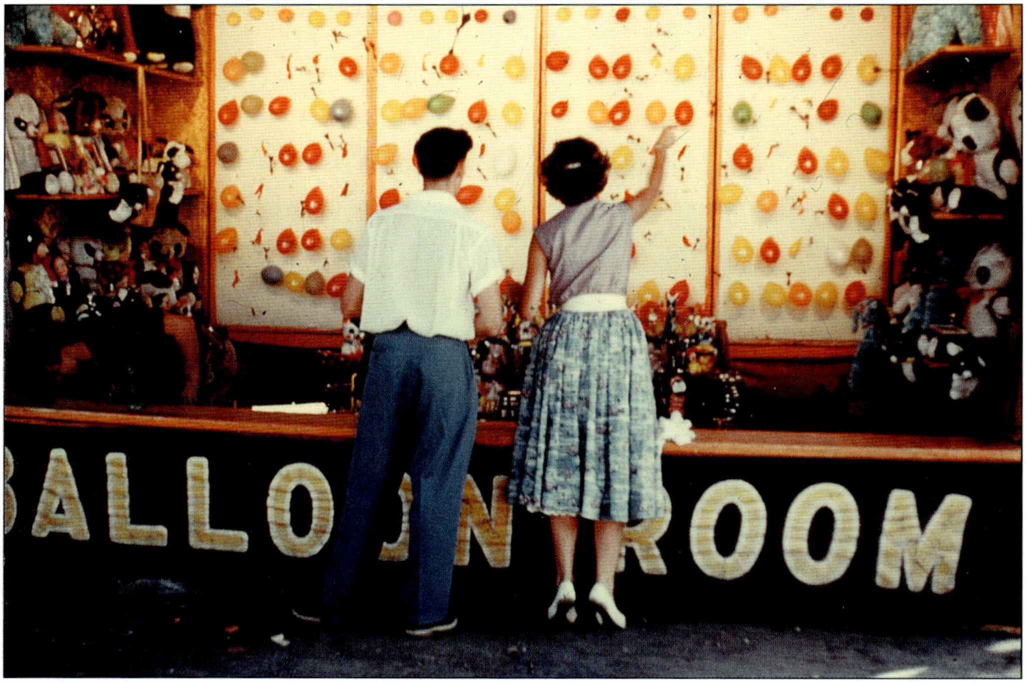

A couple on a date tries their luck at one of the fair's balloon dart throw midway games in 1958. An old carny trick for keeping the house ahead was the use of dull or light darts or to just inflate the balloons to 30 percent of their full air capacity.

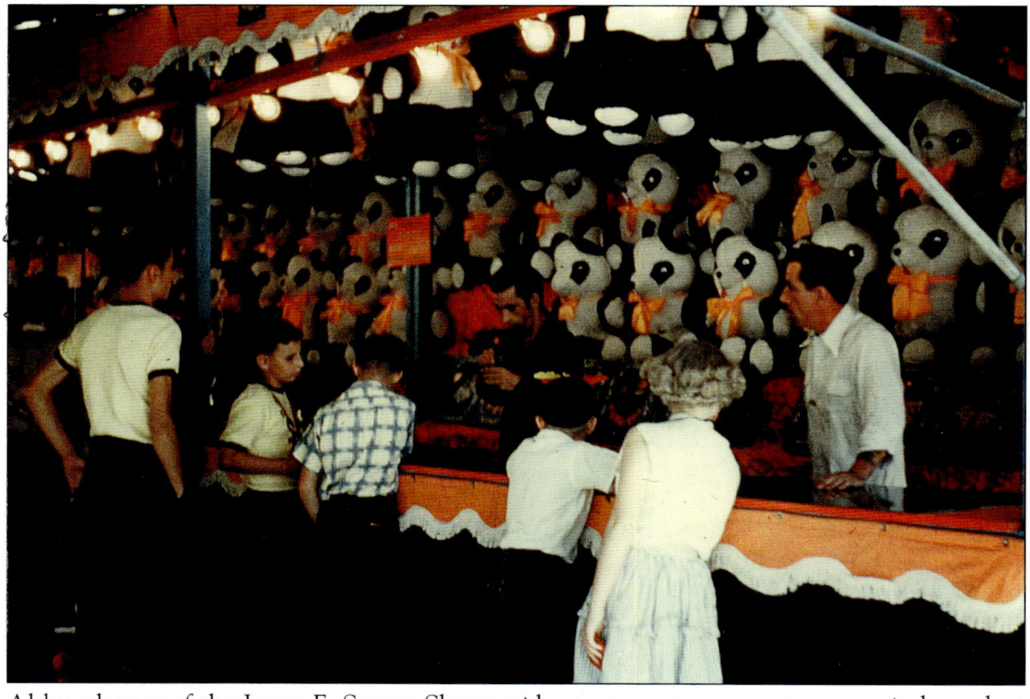

Although part of the James E. Strates Shows midway, many game operators were independent contractors that would travel their own fair routes. This practice continues in the modern era of amusements and fairs.

A rare poster is from the very first rock-and-roll show hosted by the Erie County Fair in 1956. Clean-cut Pat Boone was used as the headline act for a show featuring future Rock and Roll Hall of Fame inductees Carl Perkins, Gene Vincent, Bill Haley, rockabilly legend Johnny Burnette, and the "Queen of Rock 'n' Roll," Lillian Briggs.

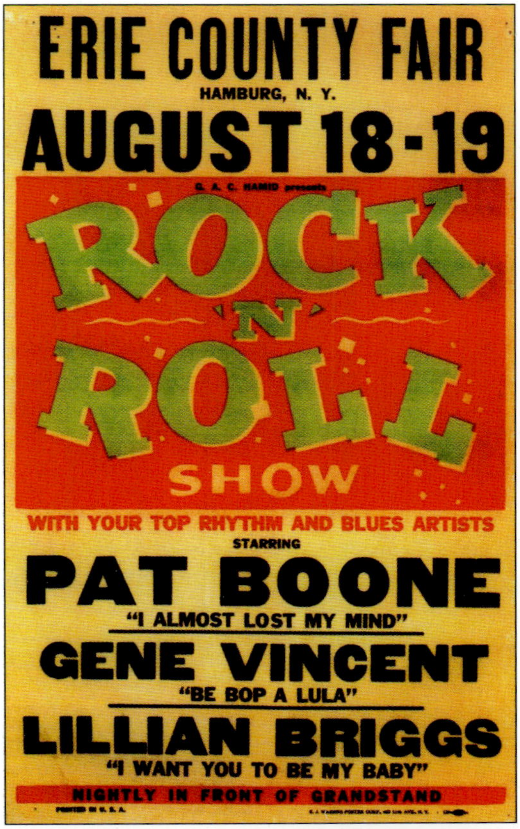

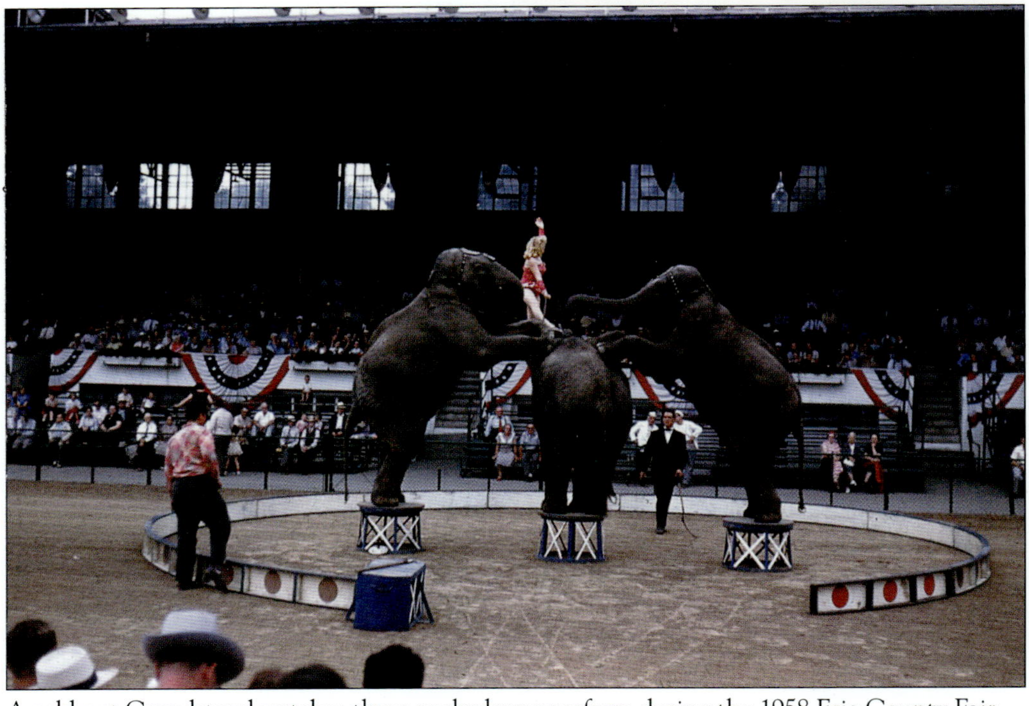

A sold-out Grandstand watches three pachyderms perform during the 1958 Erie County Fair.

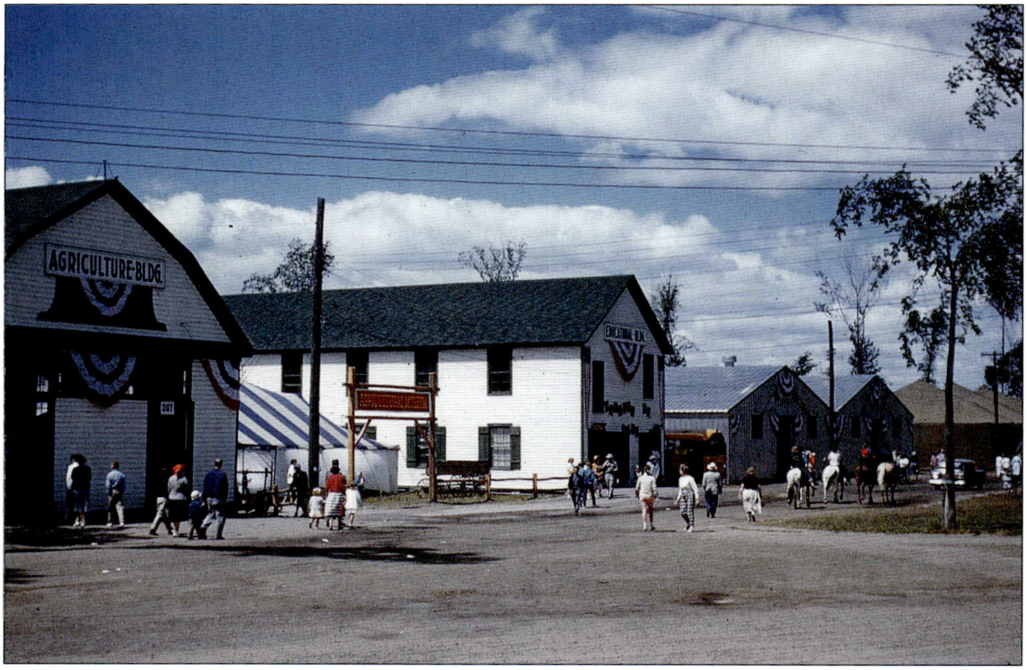

Originally located near the track, the Agriculture and Education Buildings were relocated to Bandstand Park, now known as Slade Park, in the late 1950s. These buildings would once again be moved in the 1960s to become the Historical and Mount Vernon Buildings.

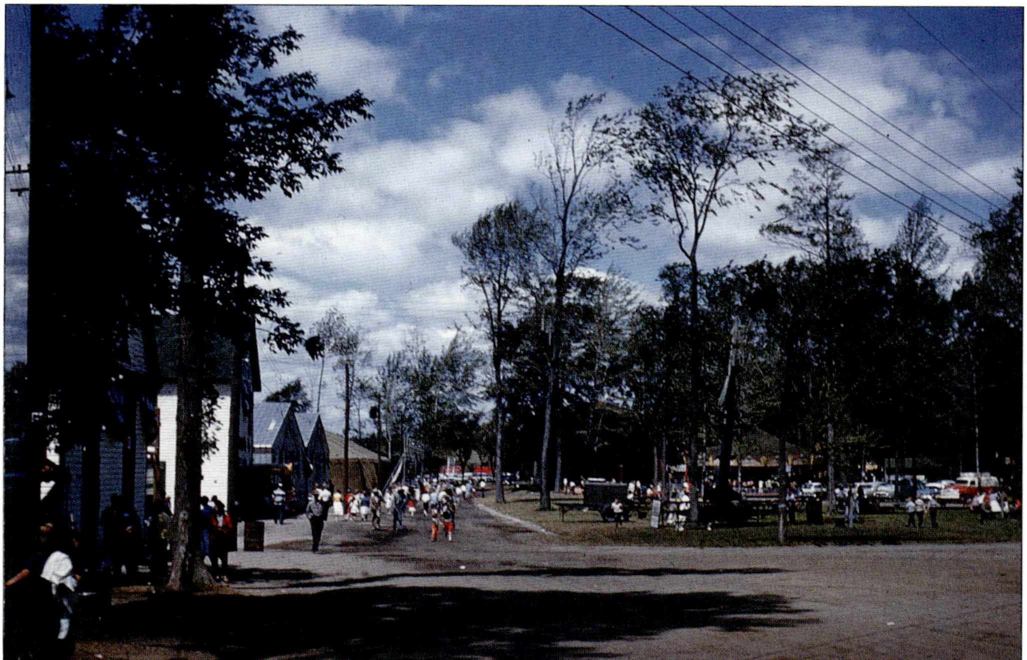

A sign of the Cold War, a US Army Nike missile is on display in this 1959 view of Bandstand Park. Hamburg was home to Nike Missile Base BU-52, which was part of a defensive plan to protect the city of Buffalo as well as the important nearby steel and iron mills. Also seen at the center of the park is a Western New York–manufactured Herschell carousel.

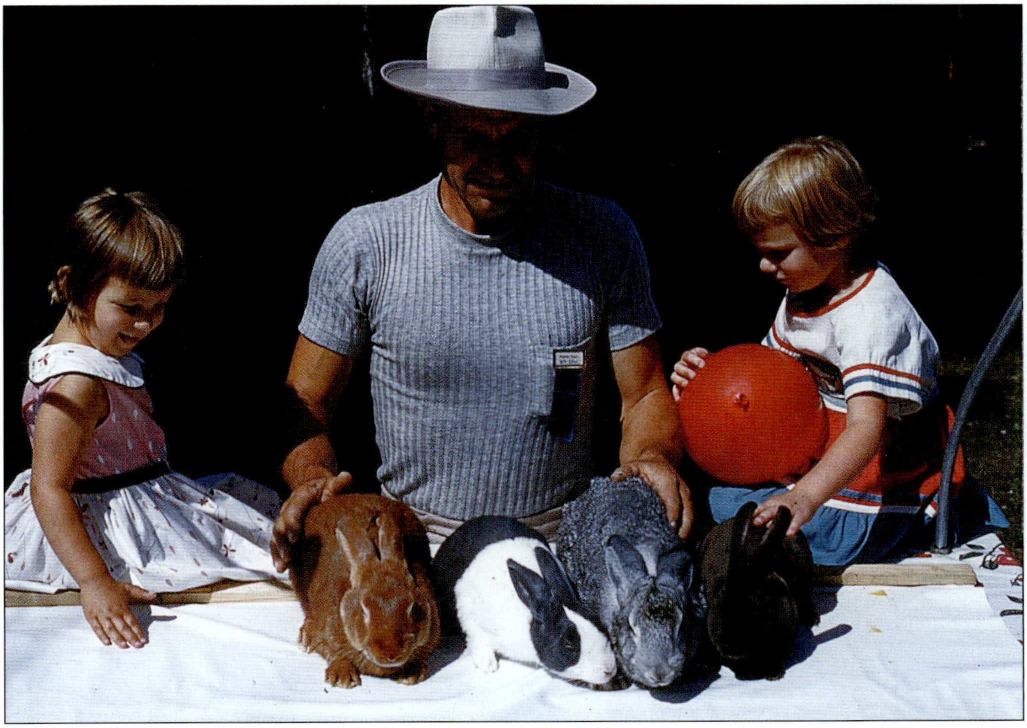

Windwood Farms of Boston won awards for best display and best breed during the 1958 rabbit competition. A total of $447 was paid out in rabbit premiums that year.

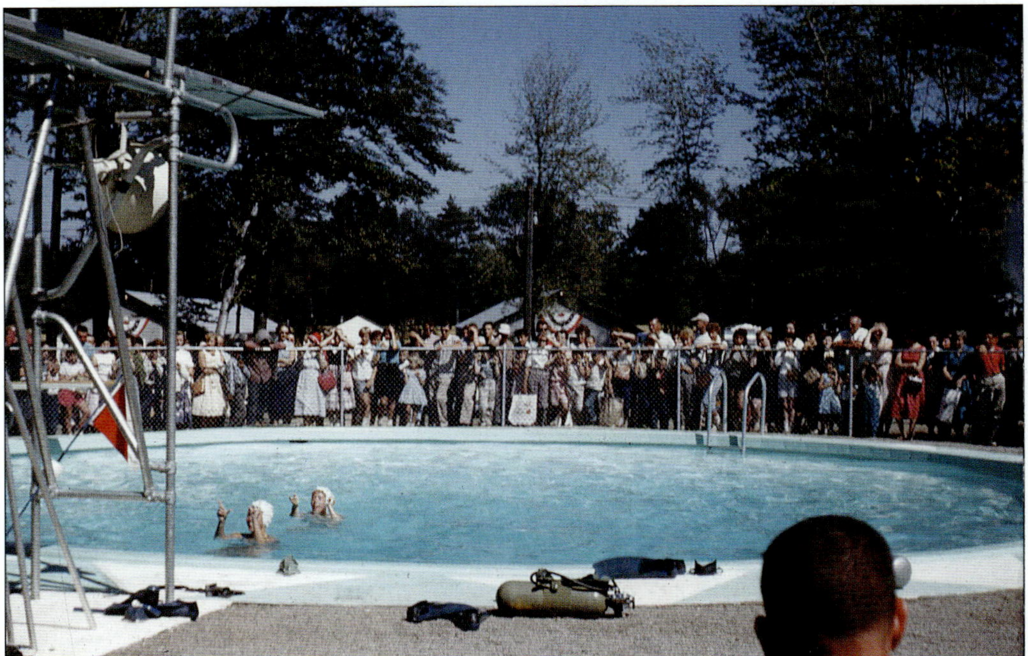

In 1958, the Lancaster Silo and Block Company donated a 40-foot-diameter and 11-foot-deep Amateur Athletic Union–sanctioned diving pool. Located near the Conservation Building, the pool featured synchronized swimming, diving, and skin-diving demonstrations.

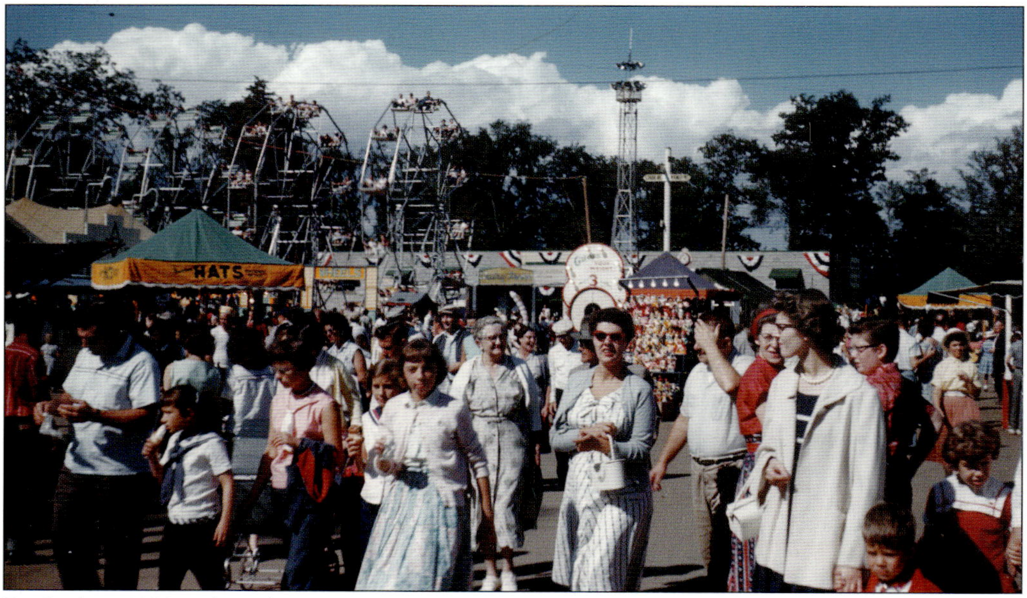

By the late 1950s, when this picture was taken, the Erie County Agricultural Society was able to move its financial status from the deep red to the solid black. It was the first time since the turn of the century that the group's annual account was soundly budgeted. Society treasurer George G. Sipprell reported that the group was well on its way to a financial spot that would "insure the Erie County Fair forever."

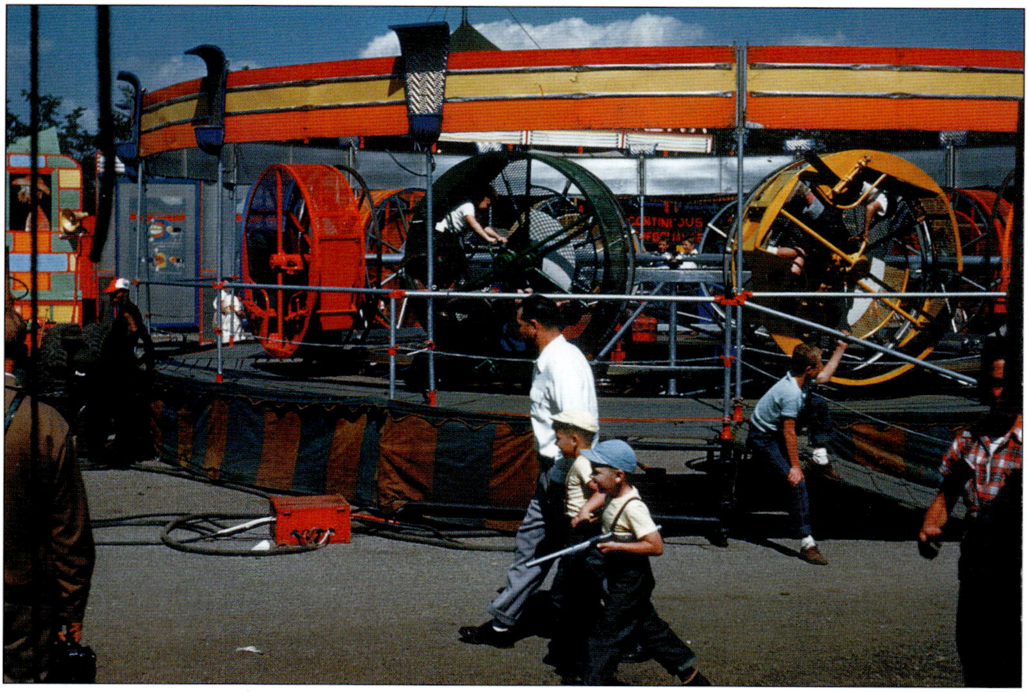

In 1956, the Strates Shows midway included the Rok 'n' Rol. The ride was designed in 1942 by Allan Hershel Manufacturing Co. and commonly known as "the Herschell Looper." This design featured a rider-activated pedal that could be pressed by the riders' feet, engaging a clutch to flip the tub.

Two

The 1960s

Superiecountyfairious!

"Superiecountyfairious," the theme of the 1965 Erie County Fair, was a big word for a big fair, with attendance reaching a record 364,187 fairgoers. By the midpoint of the decade, with ever-increasing attendance, the Erie County Fair began to take on the look and feel of a major state fair. Organizers were greatly influenced by the 1964–1965 New York World's Fair and Montreal's Expo 67. They bolstered the fair's offerings by adding corporate and international exhibits as well as the adoption of a master plan for modernization and beautification of the fairgrounds. Structures and improvements added included the Industrial Building (1960), Education Building (1961) Agriculture Grange Building (1964) Mount Vernon Building (built 1888; moved and rebuilt 1964), Indian Village (1965), Historical Building (moved and rebuilt 1965), Avenue of Flags (1966), addition to Conservation Building (1967) and the Community Outdoor Theater (1969). The decade also saw the establishment of the "Fantastic Fanfaironade" parade in 1965.

In 1963, the fair celebrated its 123rd anniversary, but a change in fair numbering would have the following fair being named the 125th celebration. In preparation for its 1964 exposition, the fair added two "lost" fairs to its official numbering system. Historical research spearheaded by Barbara Wicks of Hamburg and board member George Sipprell fully documents the region's pioneer agricultural fairs held at Buffalo in 1820 and 1821. This added two fairs to the cumulative count maintained by the Erie County Agricultural Society, which had dated the fairs from 1841. Hence, the 1964 fair would be the society's 125th venture. Looking for an acceptable term to define 125 years, the fair turned to Rev. Louis Mesko, professor of history at the Calasancius Preparatory School who, using traditional Latin, coined the term "quatro-sequennial."

To reflected the broadened scoop of the fair's entertainment and exhibit offerings, the word *exposition* was added to its official name in 1965. By the end of the 1960s, the Erie County Fair and Exposition had grown into one of the largest events of its kind in the United States.

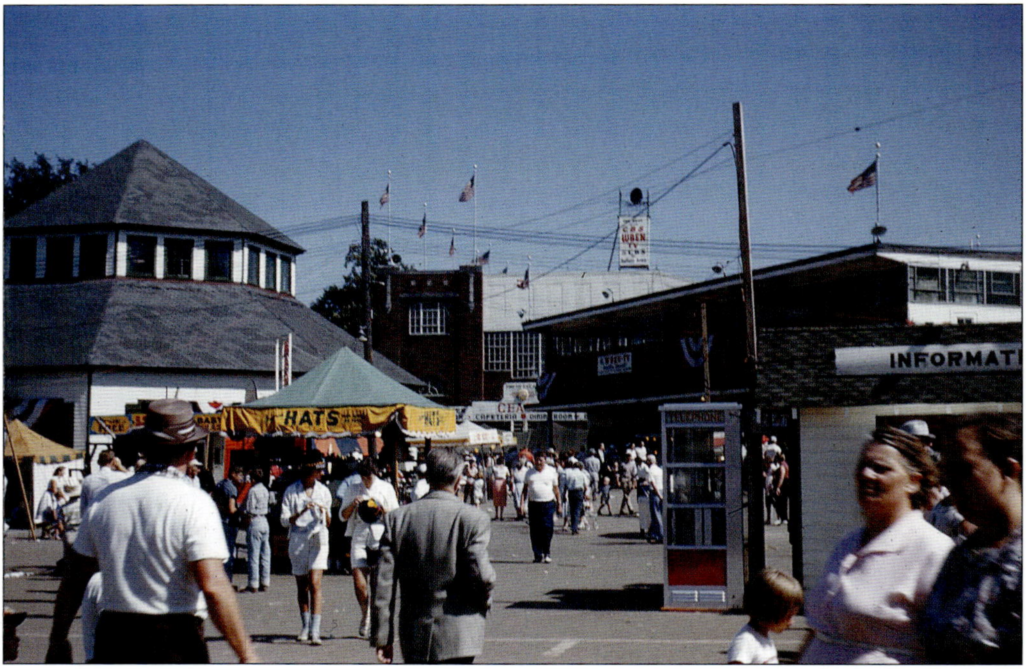

In this image from the early 1960s, the fair's 1885 Octogon Building is seen, located at the top of the midway. Built for the cost of $2,037.50 to house exhibits of the Women's Department, the historic structure served as the Health Building when this picture was taken.

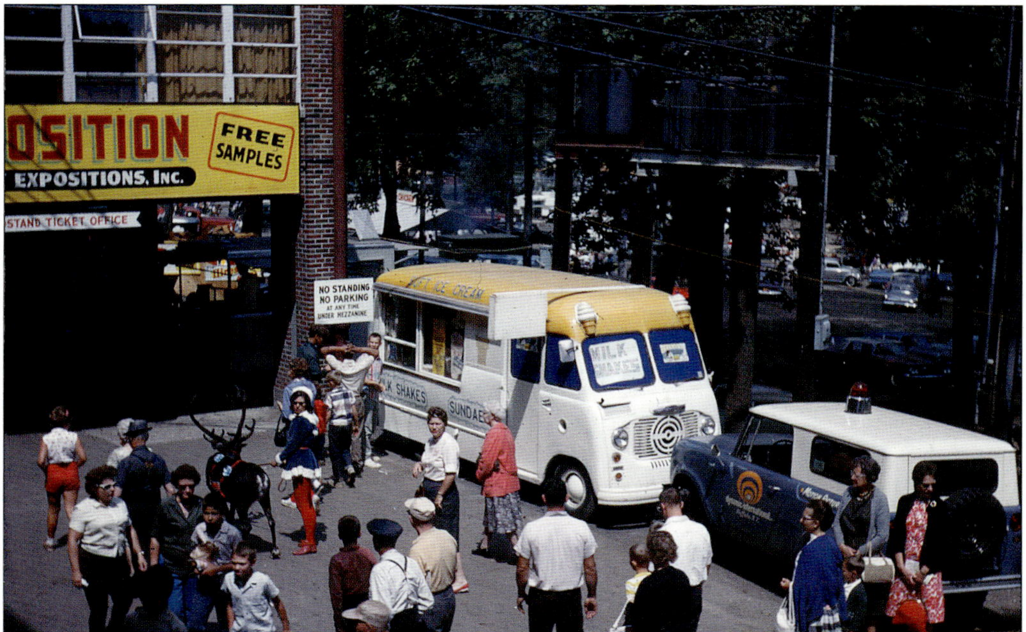

The increase of nonagricultural exhibits and vendors resulted in the fair being able to attract bigger audiences from across Western New York and Southern Ontario. In 1963, the lower Grandstand featured a food expo with over 75 vendors. A hit with visitors, it was looked upon negatively by vendors whose profits suffered when fairgoers filled up on free samples.

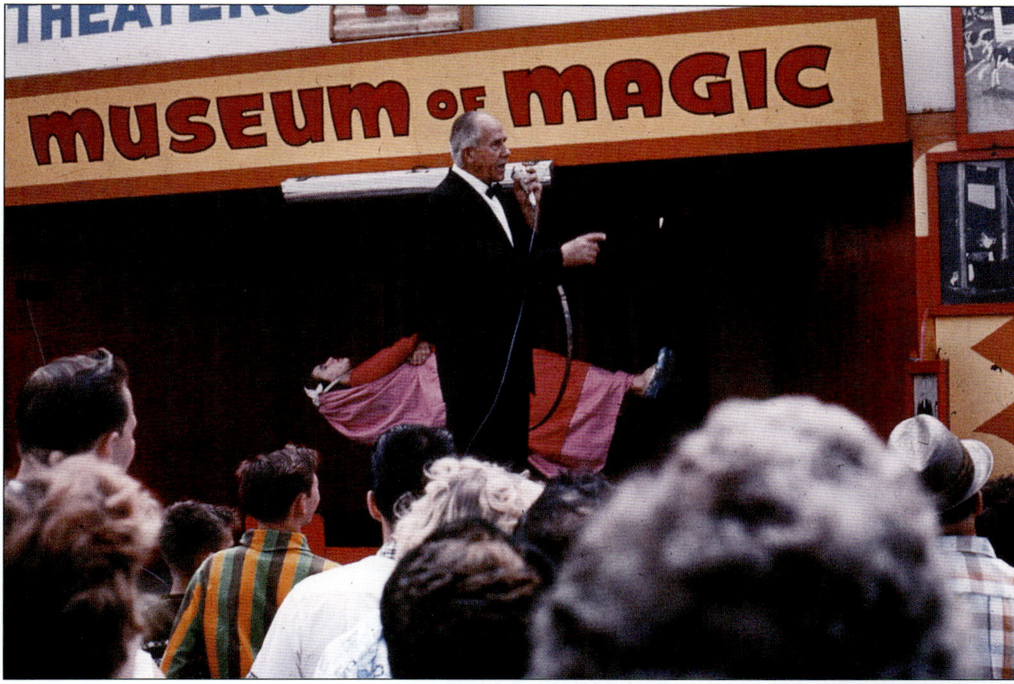

Emcee-magician the Great Noel Lester was a fixture on the midway in the early 1960s. With his circus ballyhoo, he gathers fairgoers to enter the Museum of Magic on the Strates Shows midway in 1962. Lester was known for his buzz saw illusion in which he used his wife, Phyllis, as the victim.

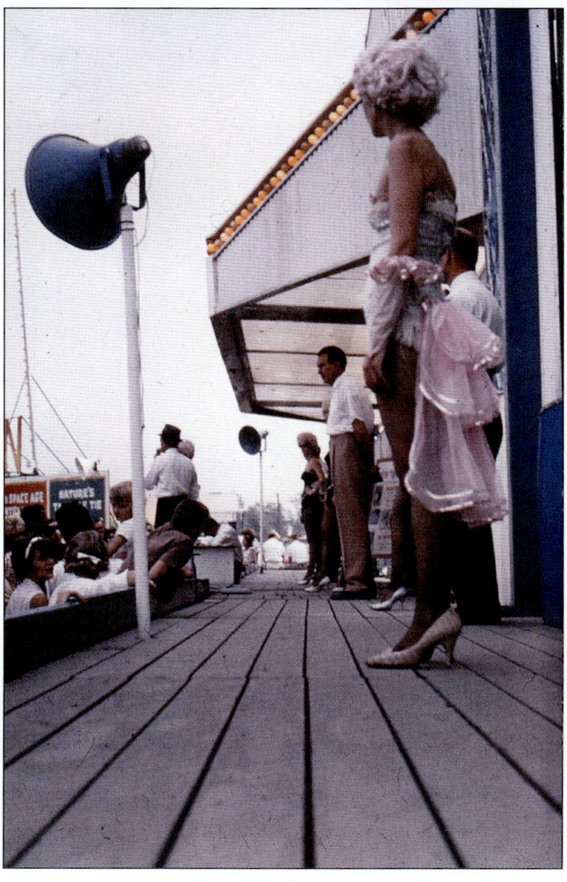

"When you have good attractions, you are bound to do business. The business is going to have to reach out and invest in worthwhile show," said James E. Strates. At one time, the Strates Shows included up to four girlie shows at the fair.

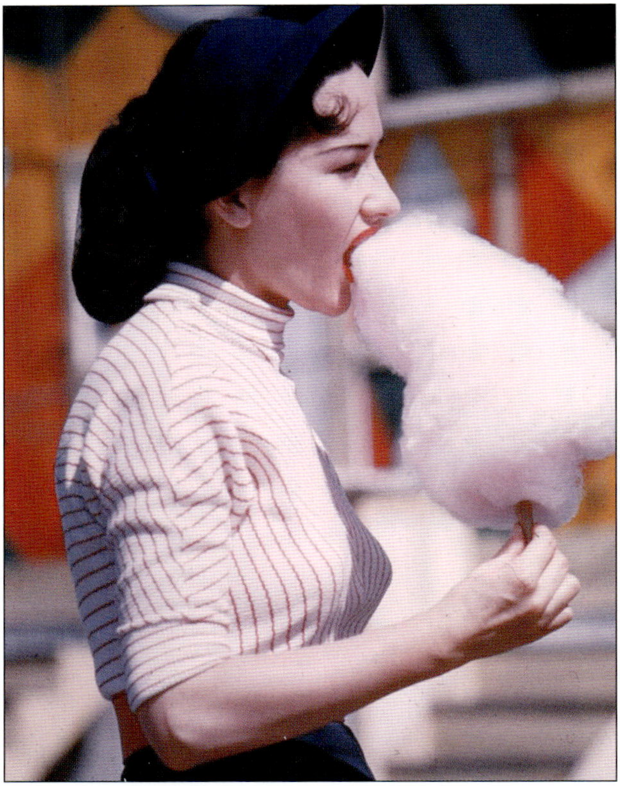

Teenagers of postwar America, like this girl pictured in 1961, had more leisure time and economic power than previous generations their age. Fair management realized the potential of this market and targeted advertising directly to them through the use of Top 40 radio stations, like WKBW-AM, and on public transportation.

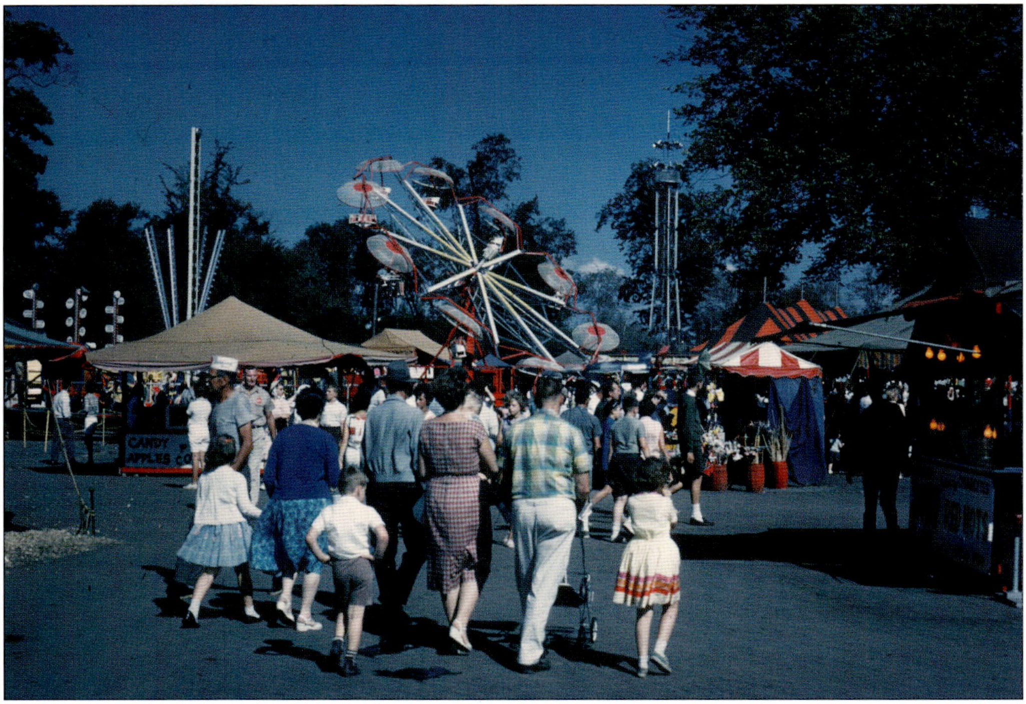

The Paratrooper ride (at center) first appeared on the Strates Shows midway around 1960 and was part of the midway until 1968. It was replaced by a newer model with solid parachutes in 1969.

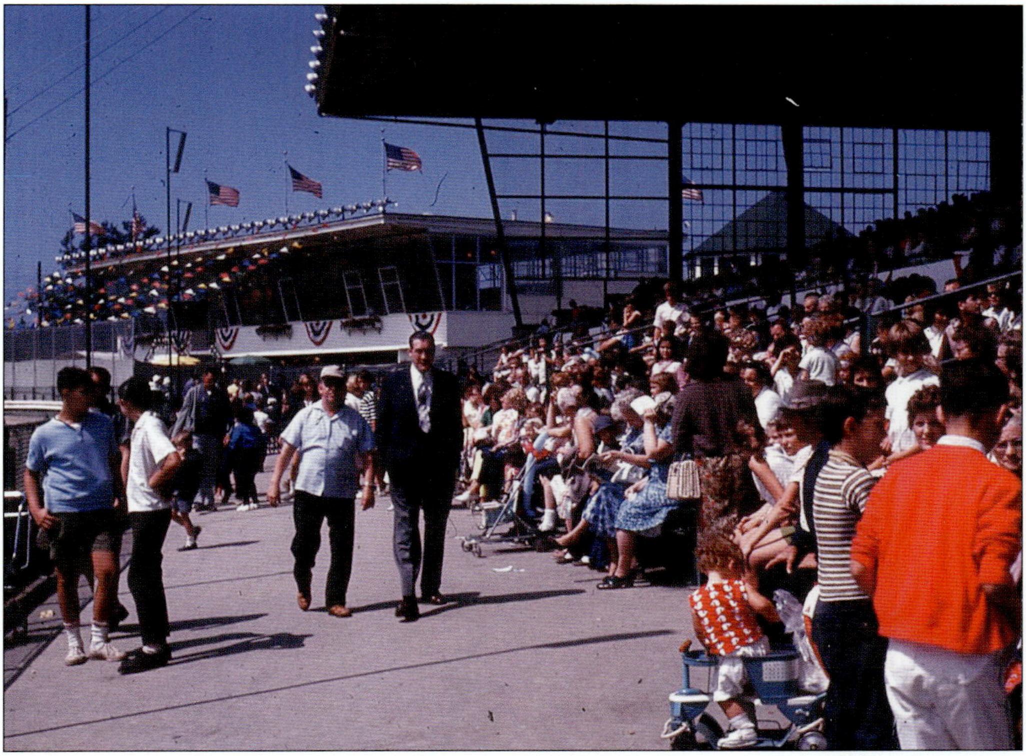

Fair officials walk past a large crowd gathered in the Grandstand for a 1962 performance of the Air Force Band.

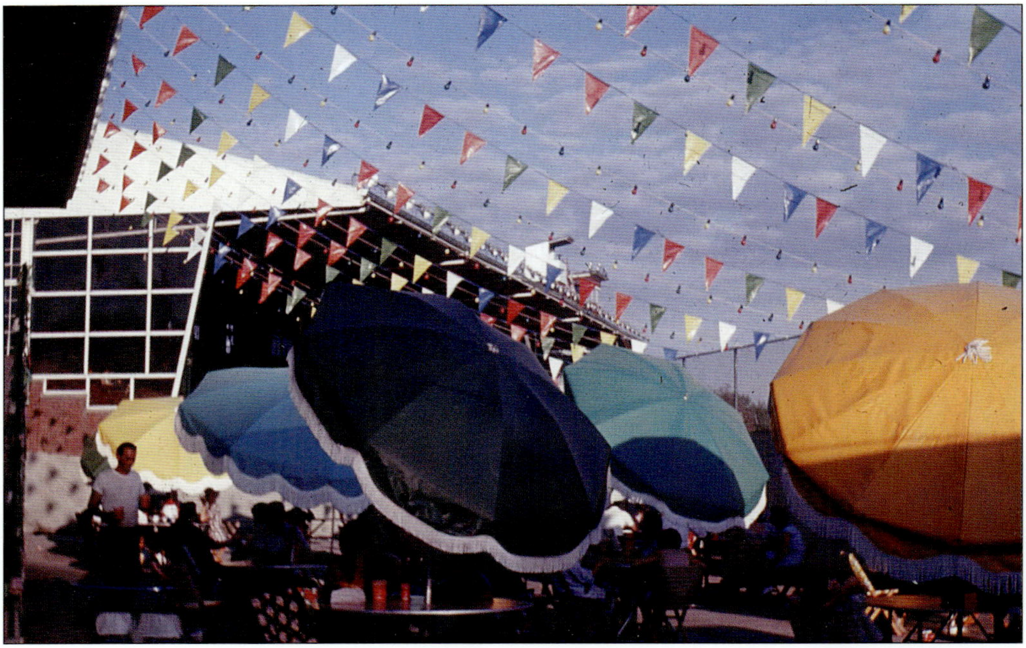

Cease Commissary provided meal service inside the Club House Restaurant as well as outside dining at the Grandstand track's northwest turn. White linens and glove-wearing servers greeted guests inside, while patrons outdoors could drink a cocktail under brightly colored patio umbrellas.

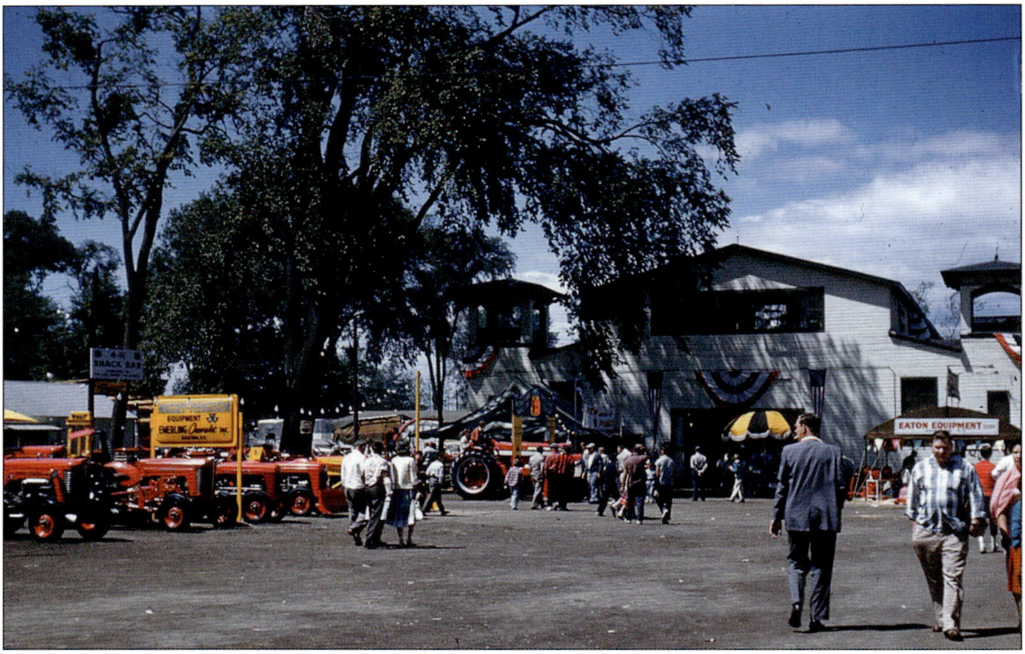

A 1961 equipment display near the Bazaar Building featured Massey Ferguson tractors from Emerling in Boston, a display from the International Harvester Dealers of Western New York, and smaller consumer-grade implements from Hamburg's Eaton Equipment Corporation. Originally built in 1904, the Bazaar Building ranks as one of the oldest remaining structures on the Erie County Fairgrounds.

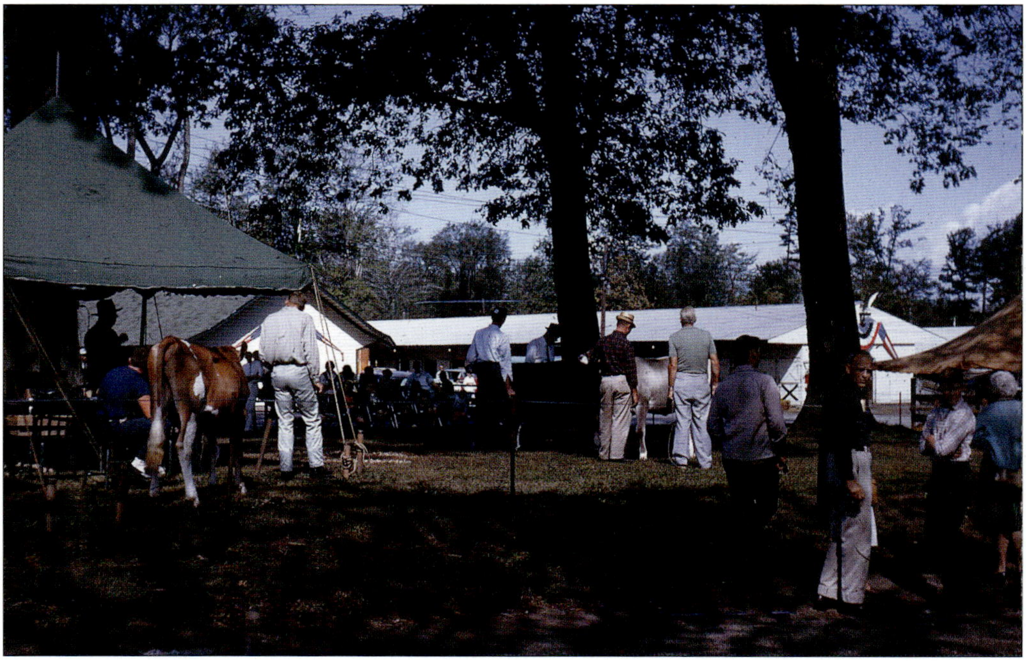

A fawn-and-white Guernsey cow waits to be judged near the Cattle Barn in 1962. The Cattle Barn, later known as Barn 4, was constructed in 1901 and taken down to accommodate the Agriculture Discovery Center in 2013.

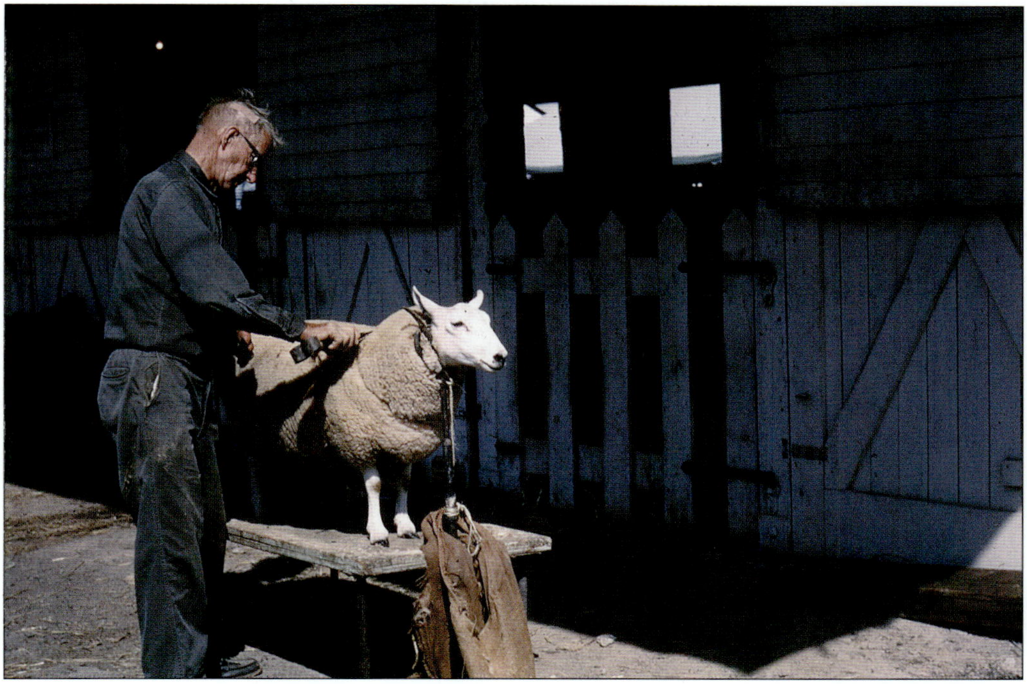

The raising and grooming of sheep takes considerable dedication. On a hot August fair day in 1962, this sheep must feel relief as its thick, woolly coat is sheared off prior to showing.

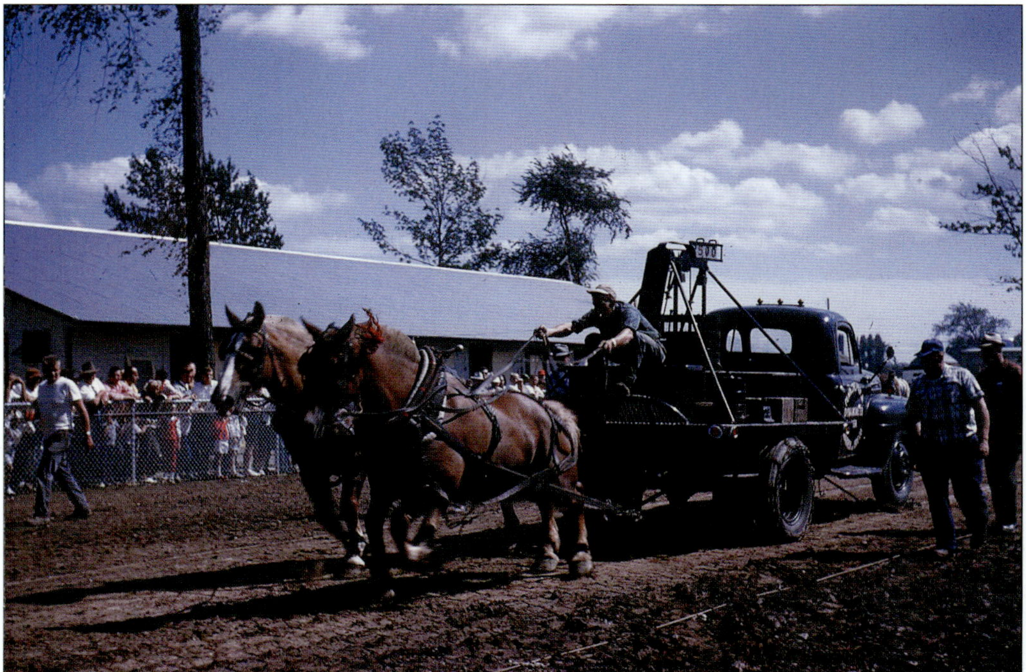

The origins of horse pulling can be found in the simple act of challenging fellow teamsters to determine the strongest horse. In the early days of competition, horses were hooked to heavy logs or canvas bags filled with rocks. Breeds like Percherons and Belgians are most commonly used in competition.

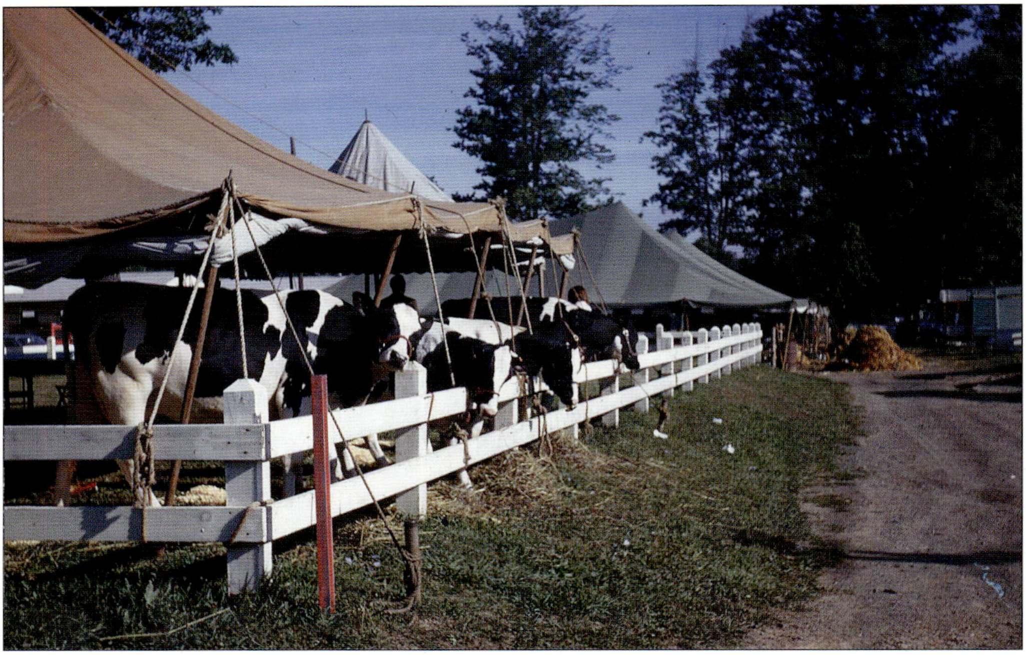

Each year, a series of tents was erected along the McKinley Parkway side of the fairgrounds to house the growing number of cattle for arriving for show. In many ways, these temporary accommodations were more comfortable on summer days than older barns, which lacked proper ventilation.

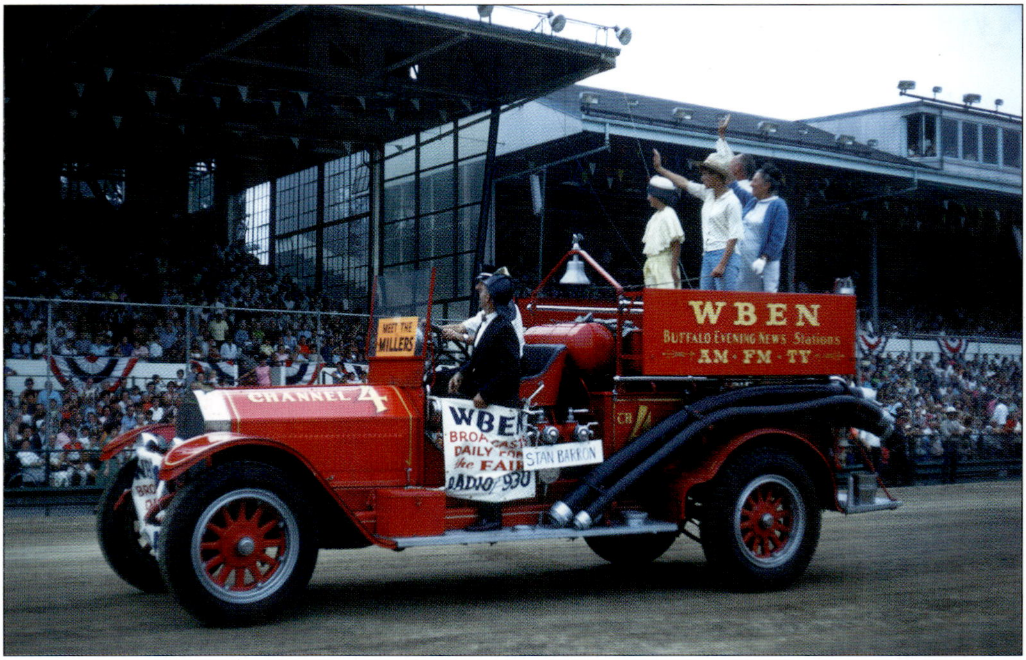

The tradition of the annual fair parade, named the "Fantastic Fanfaironade," began in 1965. The two-hour parade, featuring 25 marching bands, originated at Lake and Main Streets in the village of Hamburg and continued past thousands of people seated inside the fair's Grandstand. In 1967, Channel 4's Bill and Mildred Miller (right) along with WBEN radio's Stan Baron (left) ride past the Grandstand on an antique fire truck.

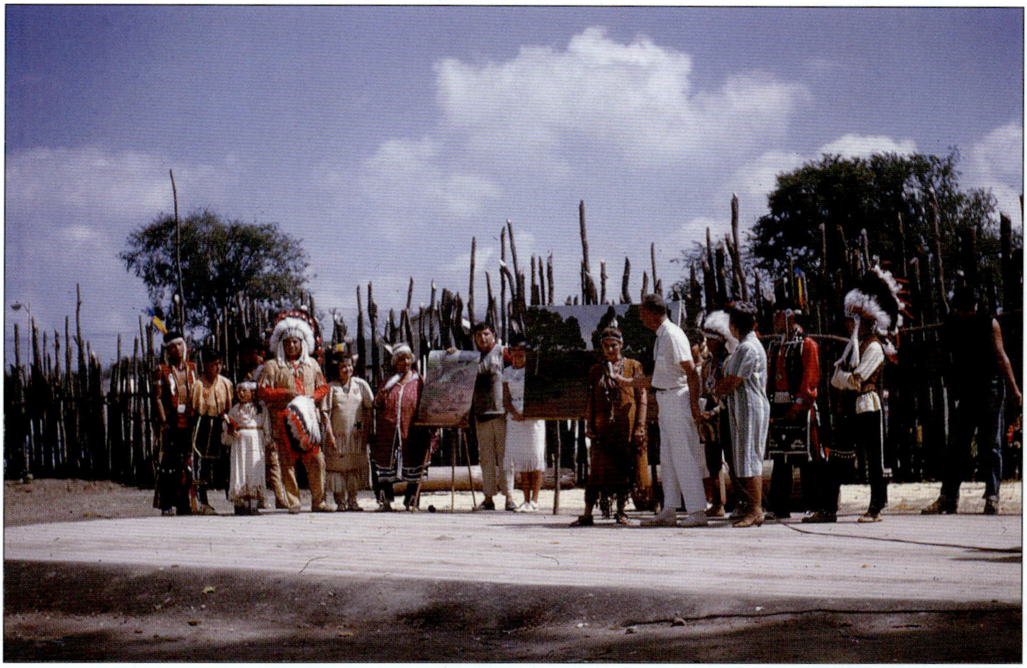

WBEN-TV's Bill and Mildred Miller interview native dancers inside the Indian Village on their daily telecast from the fair. The Millers hosted a television show on Channel 4 from 1950 to 1970 and began broadcasting from the fair in 1955. At the time, the stations were owned and operated by the Buffalo Evening News company.

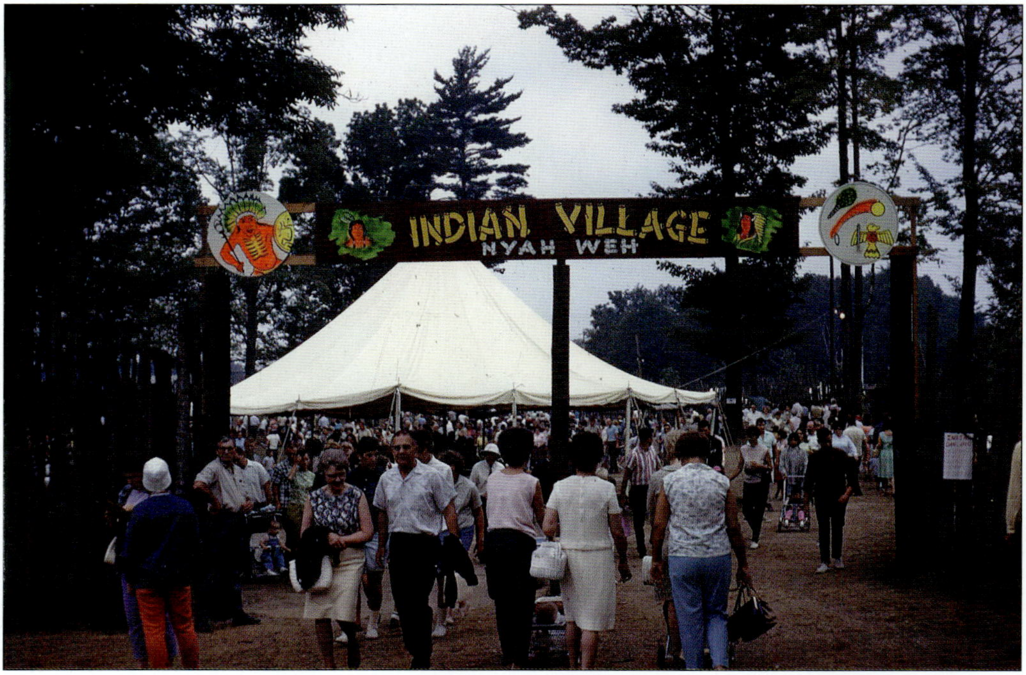

The Nyah-Weh Indian Village was dedicated on August 22, 1965. When it opened, it featured an authentic longhouse and stockade fence that were designed by local Native American craftsmen.

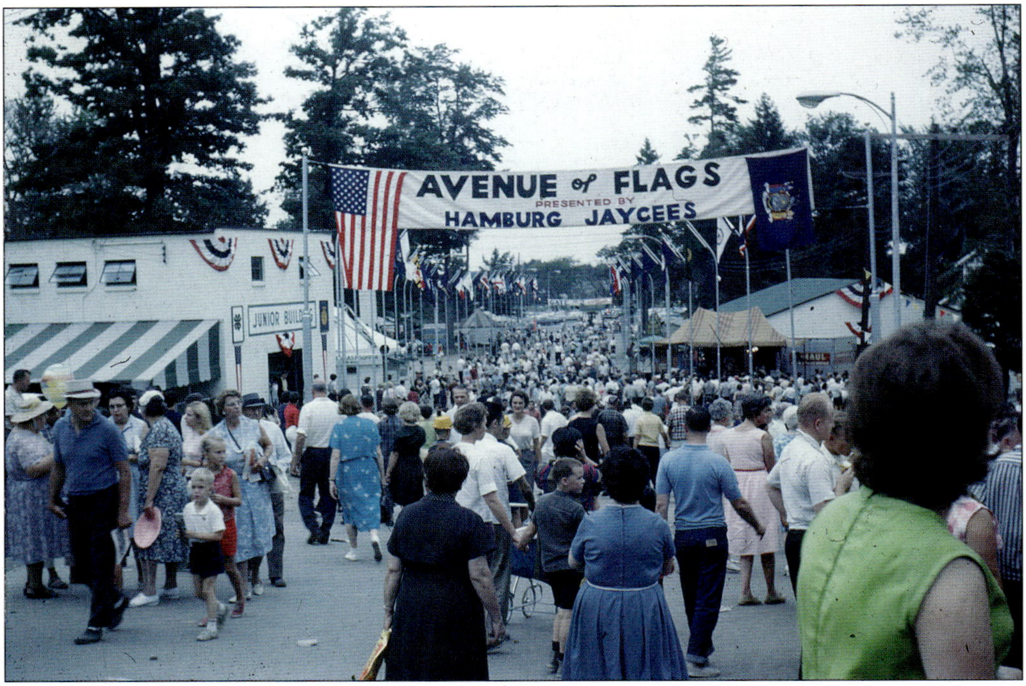

In 1966, the Erie County Fair dedicated the Avenue of Flags. The display was presented by the Hamburg Junior Chamber of Commerce and featured flags from all 50 US states. In 1976, during the celebration of the American bicentennial, state flags were replaced by US flags—a tradition that continued until the mid-2000s.

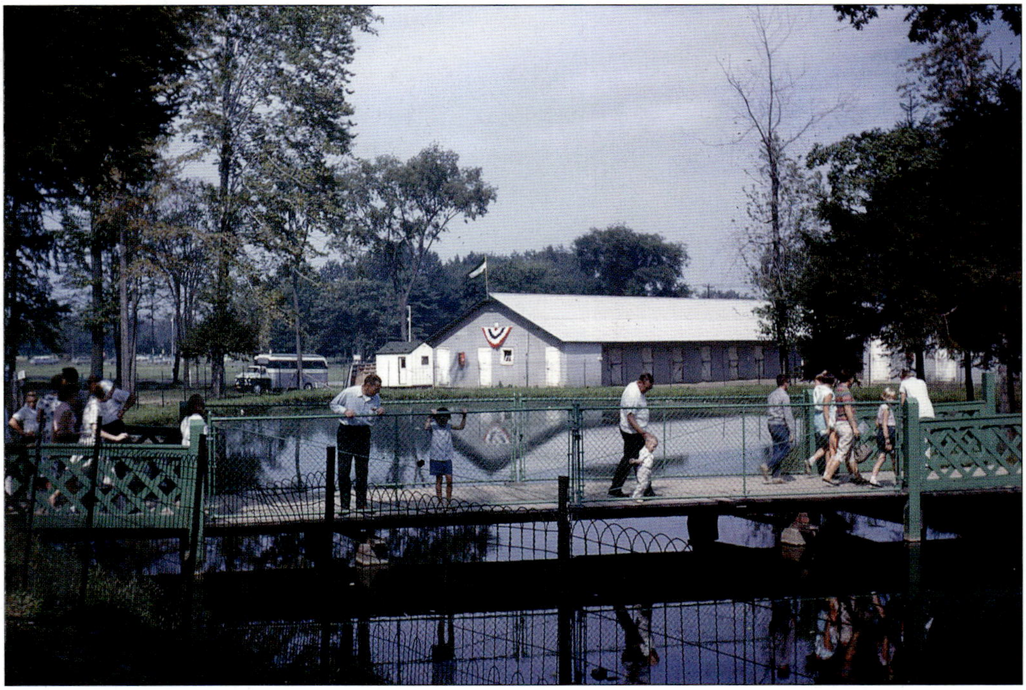

This is a 1965 view of the fair's fishing and duck pond that was once located behind the Conservation Building. The bridge was the site of the annual Erie County Fair casting competition.

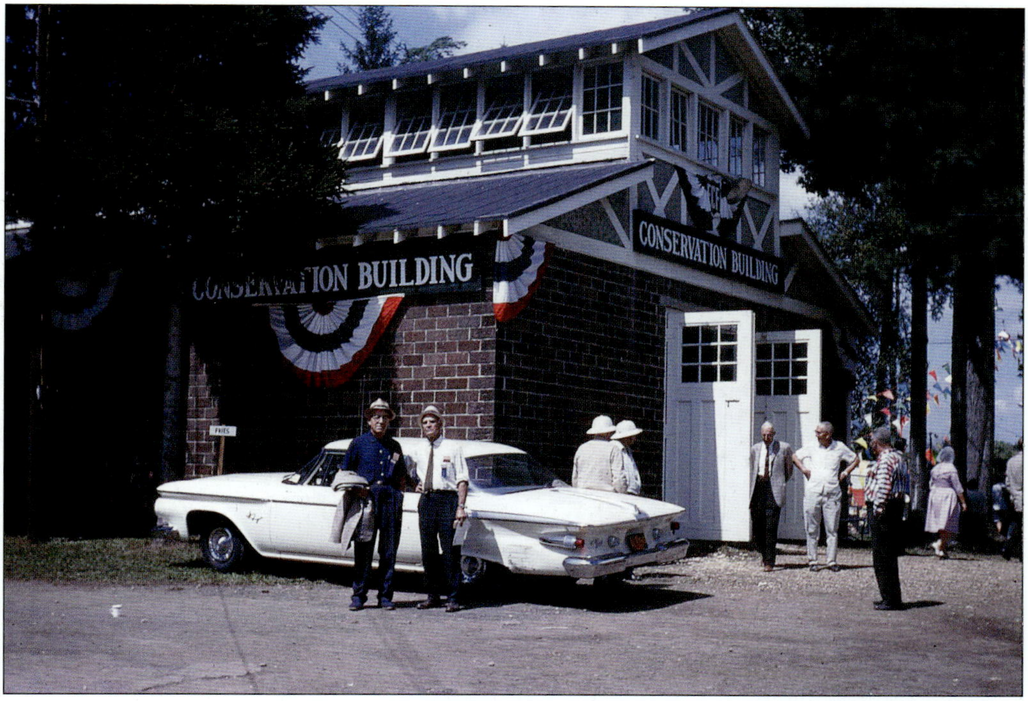

Constructed in 1922, the Conservation Building has had a primary mission to "protect and perpetuate conservation of our national resources and wildlife as endowed by the Creator."

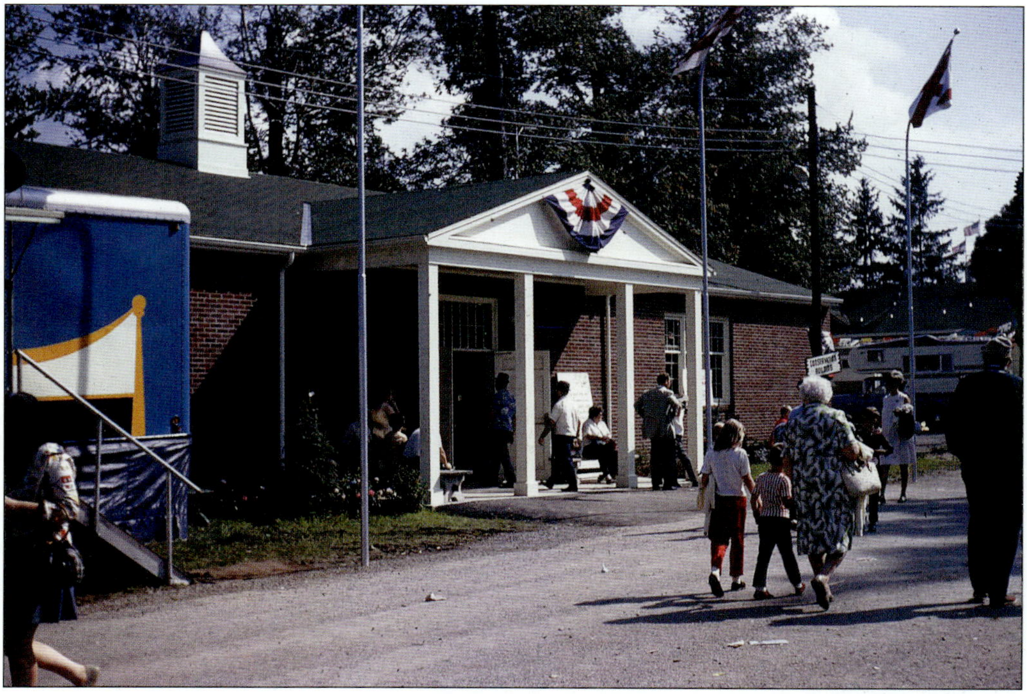

The Conservation Building received an addition in 1966 that extended its front door to the Avenue of Flags. The space allowed for an increase in exhibits geared for hunters, fishermen, and outdoor enthusiasts.

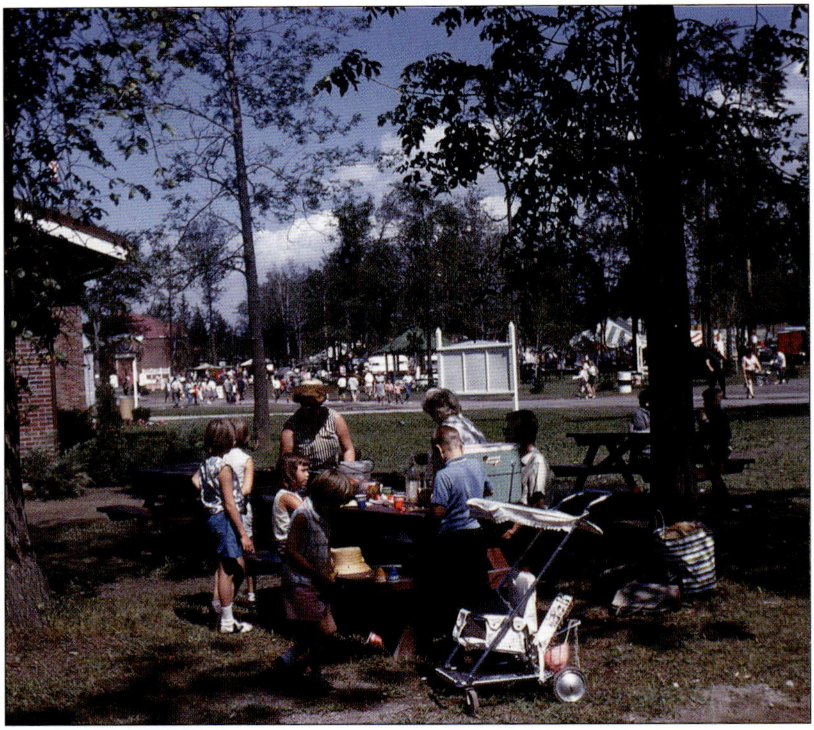

A family gathers for a picnic at Slade Park near the Agriculture Grange Building in 1964. While the midway generally does not open until 11:00 a.m., many families have arrived on the grounds when gates opened at 9:00 a.m. to stake out a picnic location. Some families have set up shop at the same location for decades.

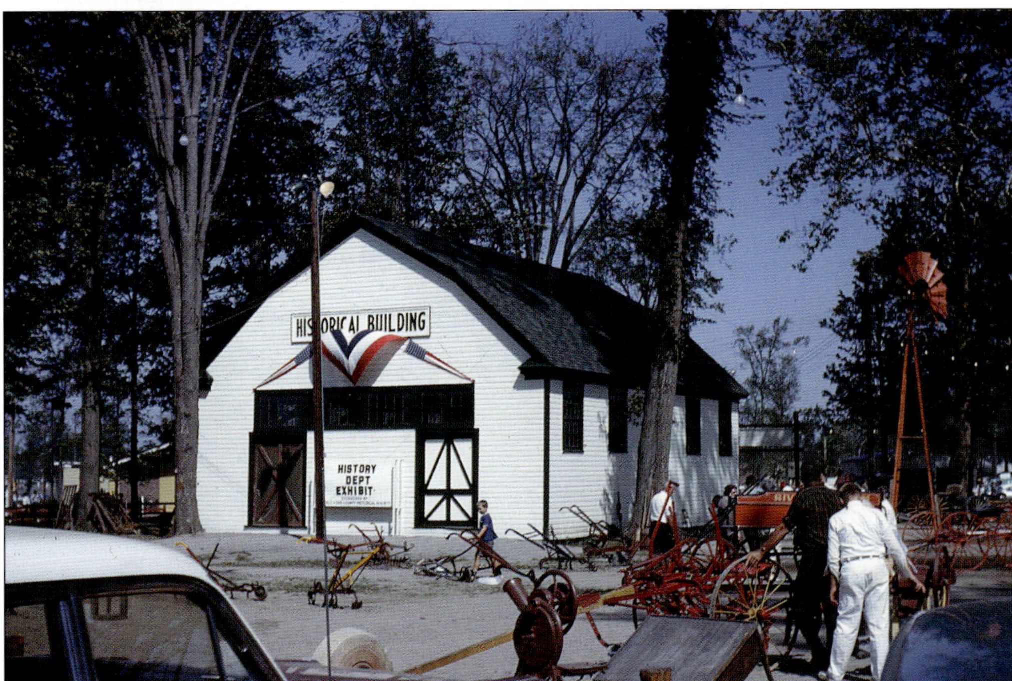

When the threat of destruction shook the foundation of the old Agriculture Grange Building, the then treasurer of the fair, George G. Supprell, saw to it that the structure was instead moved and renovated. Since 1965, the building has housed exhibits from a variety of Western New York historical societies. An expansion was added to the back of the building in 1971.

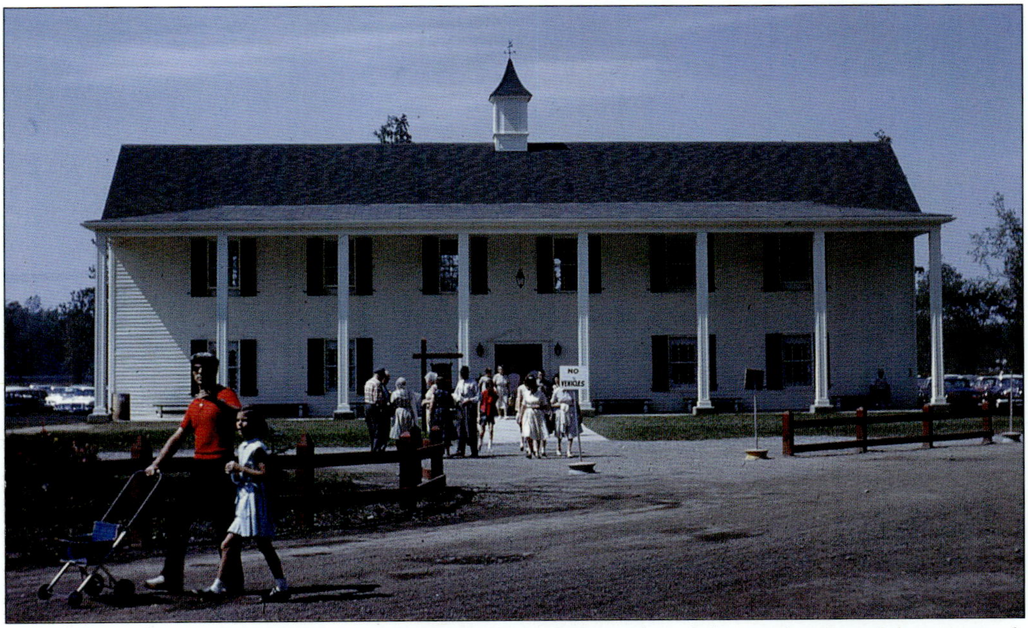

The Mount Vernon Building, originally erected in 1888, was located near the rear of the racetrack and was the fair's Floral Hall. In later years, it would be called the Educational Building and also serve as the Erie County Parks and Recreation Building. In 1964, the building was moved to its current location in Slade Park and remodeled to resemble the home of George Washington on the Potomac River.

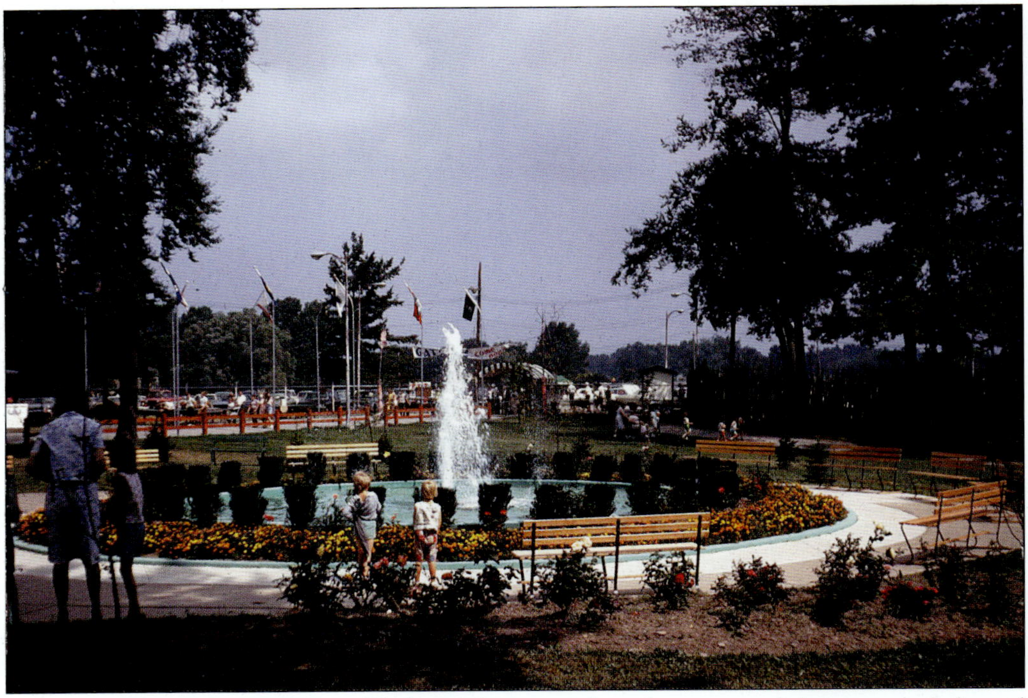

In 1969, the fair's beauty pool was filled in and converted to a fountain, and the area was dedicated as park honoring longtime Conservation Building superintendent Arthur G. Fries.

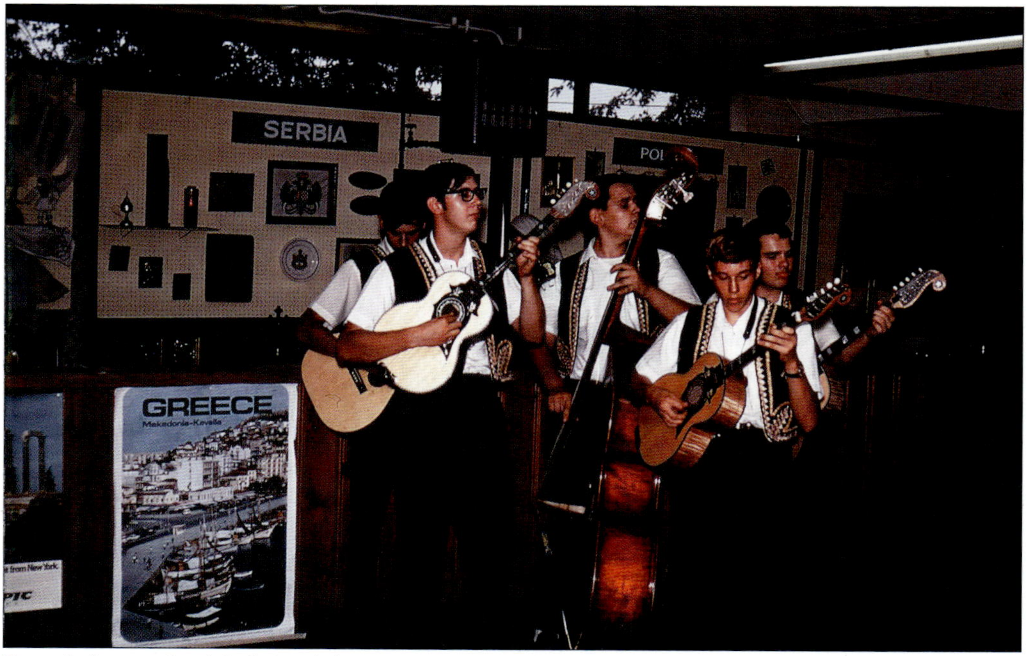

From left to right, Mark Medakovic, George Medakovic, Don Milosevic, Ray Ranic, and Ron Conrad perform traditional Serbian folk music. The display was part of the fair's 1969 International Exposition. Located in the Grandstand mezzanine, the "world tour" featured ethnic crafts, music, and demonstrations from 50 countries.

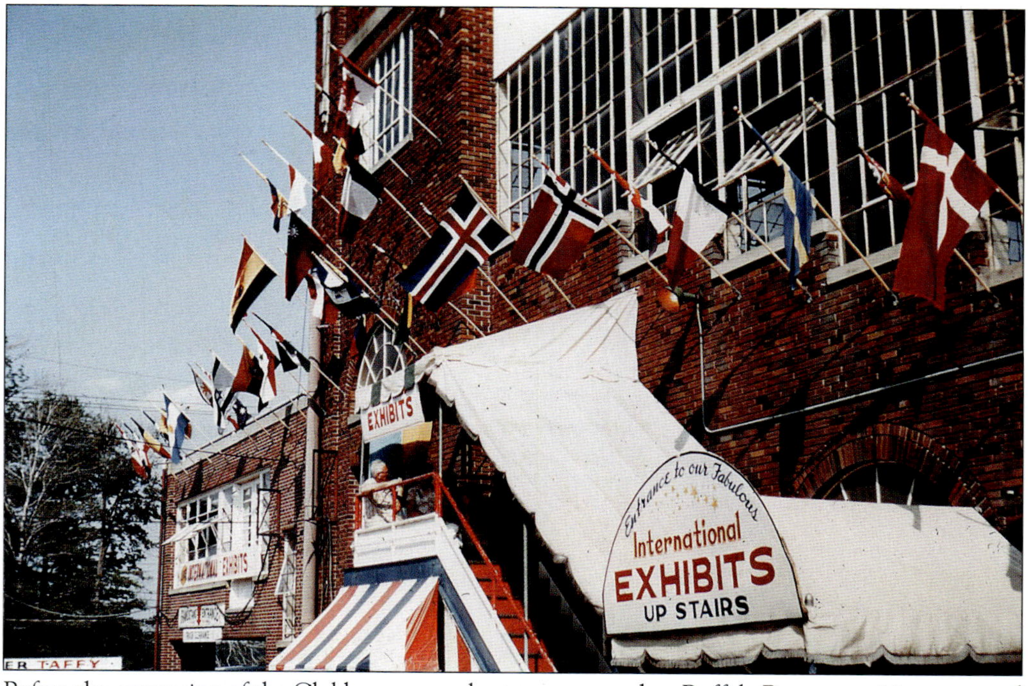

Before the expansion of the Clubhouse complex to accommodate Buffalo Raceway, visitors entered the fair's international exhibits under a colorful display of flags on the side of the Grandstand.

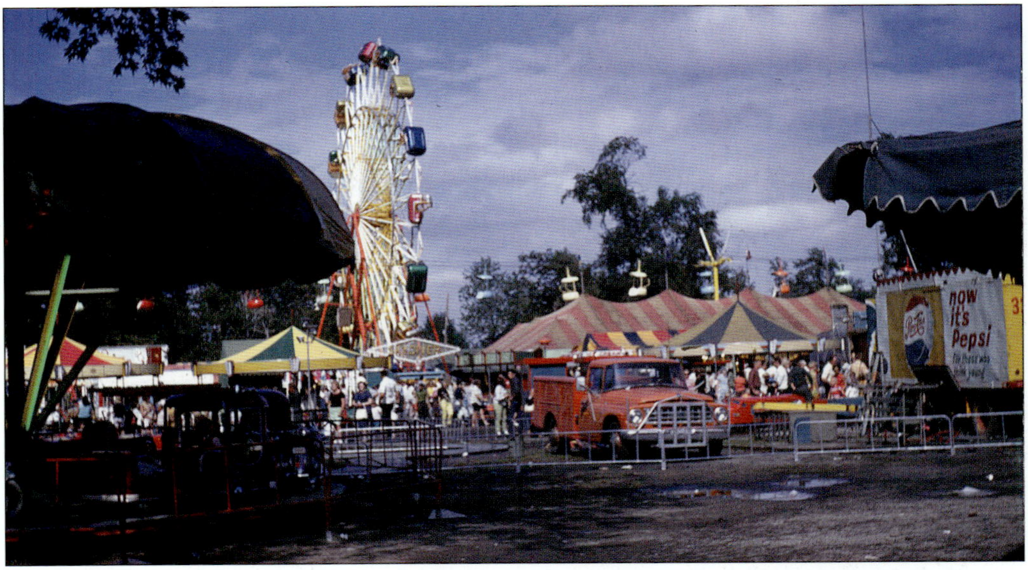

Following the sudden death of James E. Strates on October 11, 1959, his son E. James Strates led the family business to great success during the decade of the 1960s. When this picture was taken in 1967, thirty-seven-year-old Strates was quoted as saying, "You know, you never really realize the wisdom of your parents until they're no longer with you."

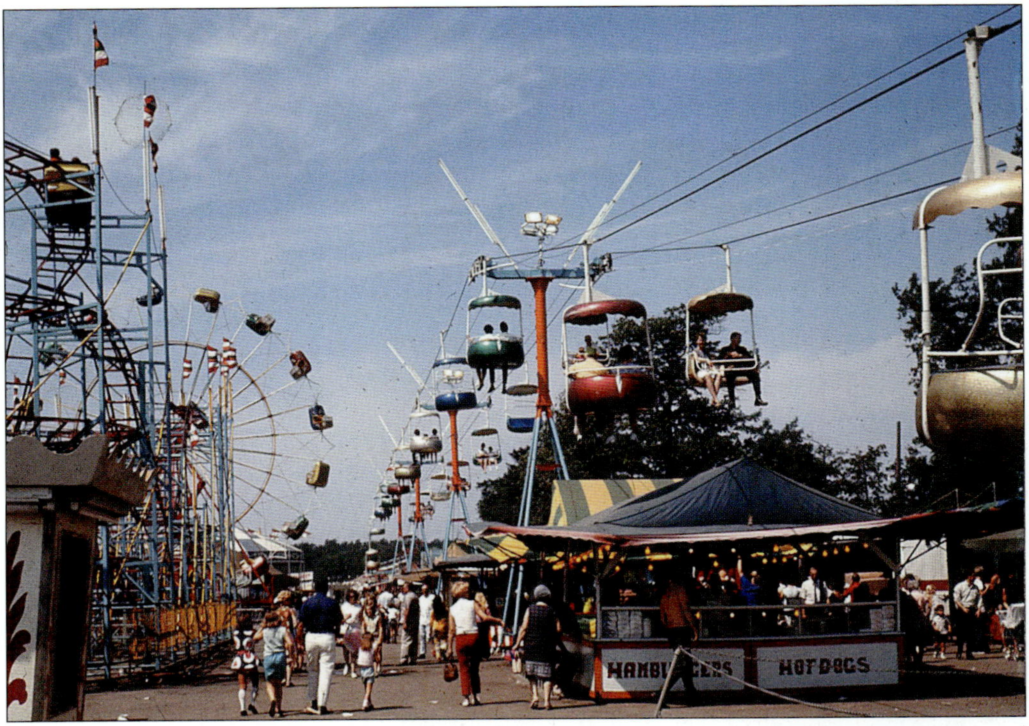

The Strates Shows' formula for success was simple: create a bigger, better, more attractive, and safer product year after year. By the mid-1960s, with over 100 rides and attraction, the Strates Shows was one of the biggest touring carnivals in the world. The Sky Ride was a new feature in 1965 and played the Erie County Fair every year through 2001—except for 1997, when it was being refurbished.

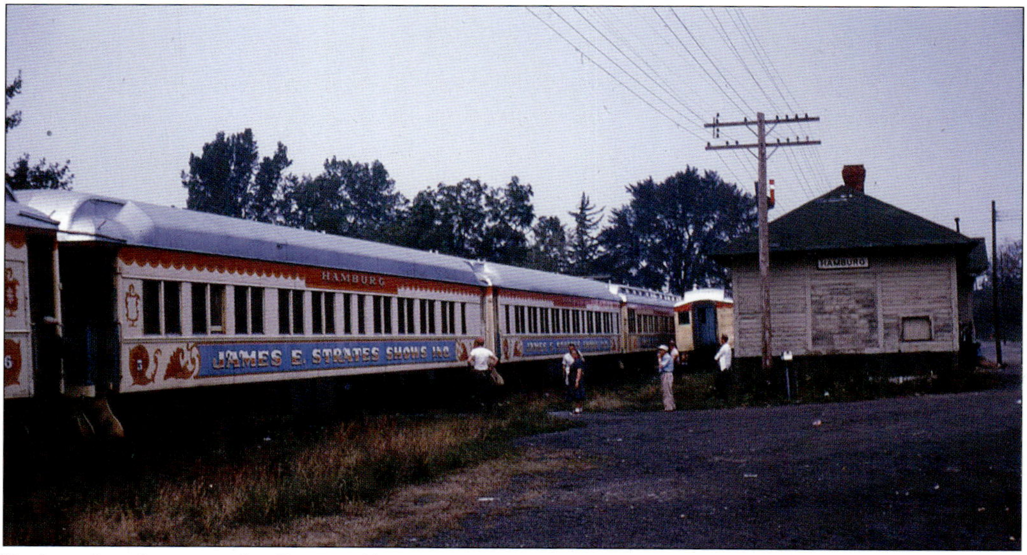

Each railroad car on the Strates Shows' train was named for a city or town at which the show played. In 1964, the *Hamburg* car passes the Erie Railroad Depot in Hamburg, New York, as it arrives for the start of another fair.

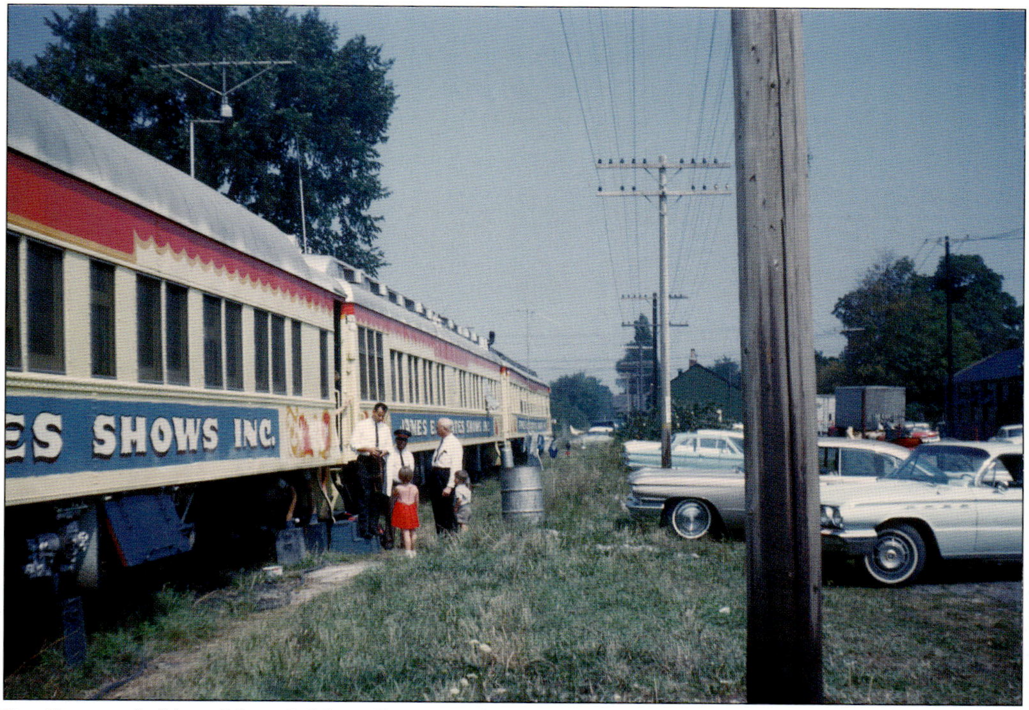

Jim Strates (left) and his children Susan and James E. are joined by Erie County Fair manager William Mullaney (right) outside of the States Shows' train parked along Scott Street in 1964. Behind the group is a States Shows' porter known as "Juice."

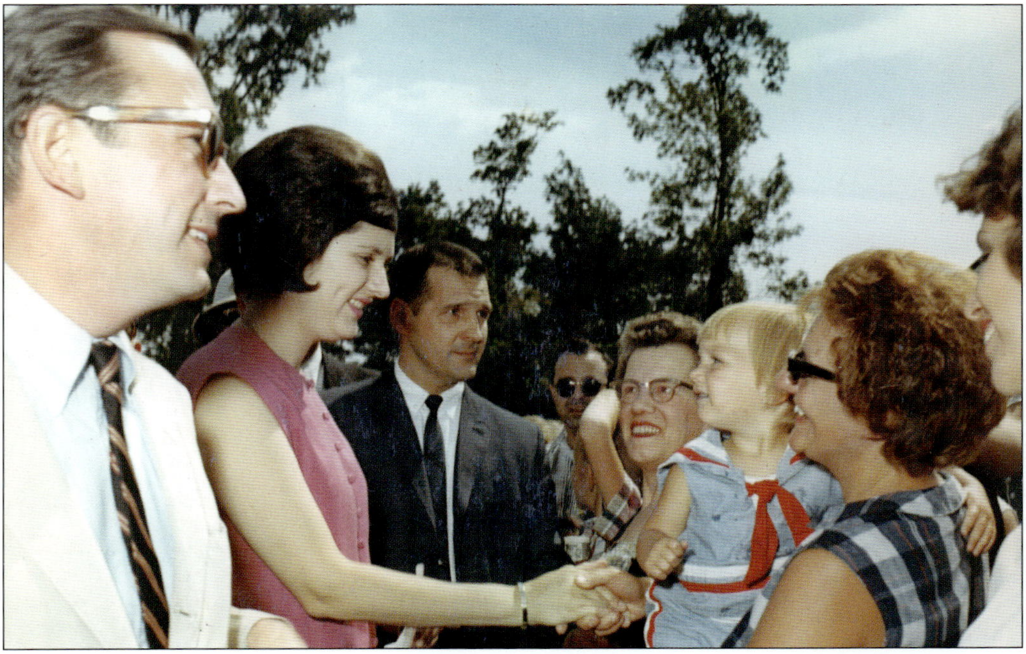

Twenty-one-year-old Lynda Bird Johnson (second from left), the daughter of then president Lyndon B. Johnson, is greeted by fairgoers on August 23, 1965. Her visit to the Erie County Fair coincided with the formal dedication of the fair's Historical Building.

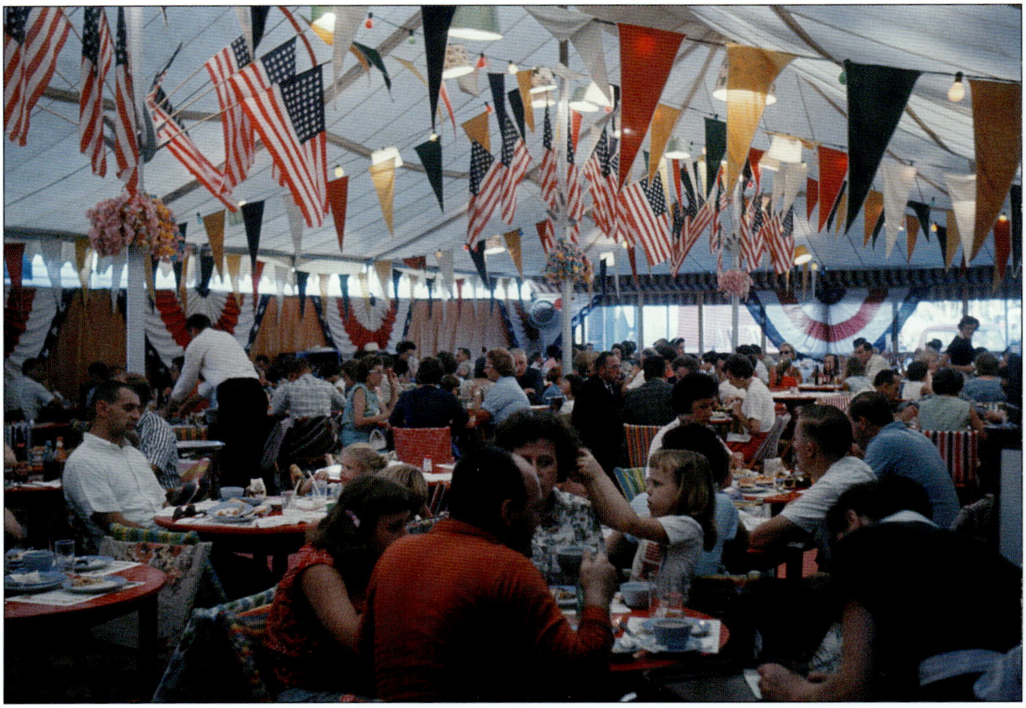

Concessionaire Lou Horschel operated his dining tent on the Erie County Fairgrounds from 1919 to 1969. In addition to the fair, Horschel at one time managed concessions at major Buffalo venues like Broadway Auditorium, Memorial Auditorium, and Civic Stadium.

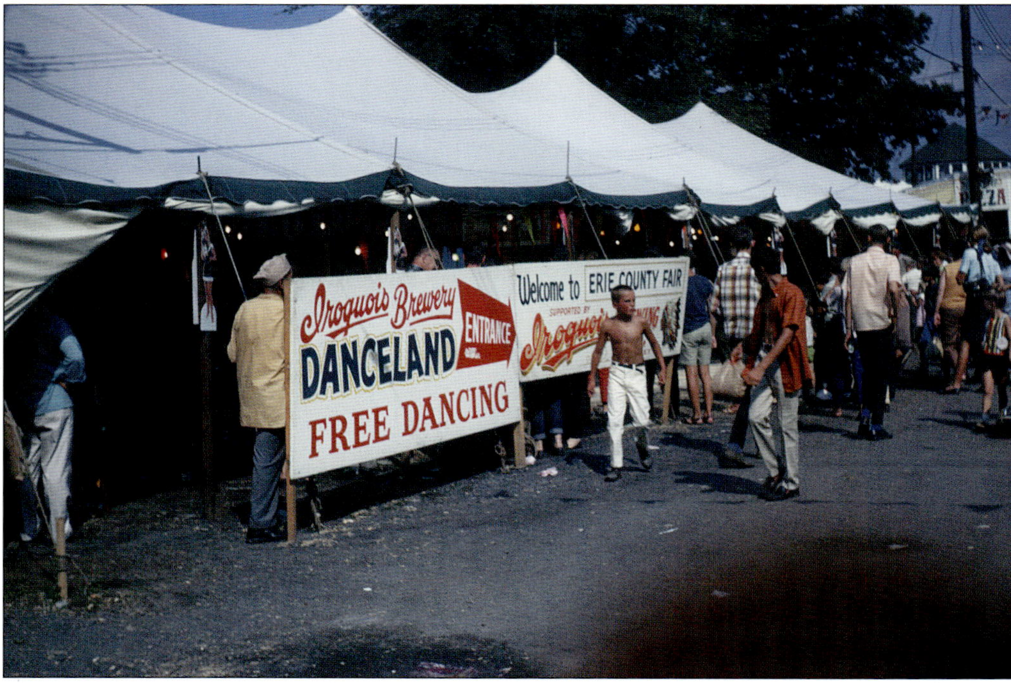

Housed in an enormous tent, the Iroquois Brewery Danceland featured nonstop square, polka, and ballroom dancing plus visits by the Iroquois Brewery Indian princess. Facing increased competition from national brands, Iroquois, Buffalo's largest major local brewer, shut its doors in 1971.

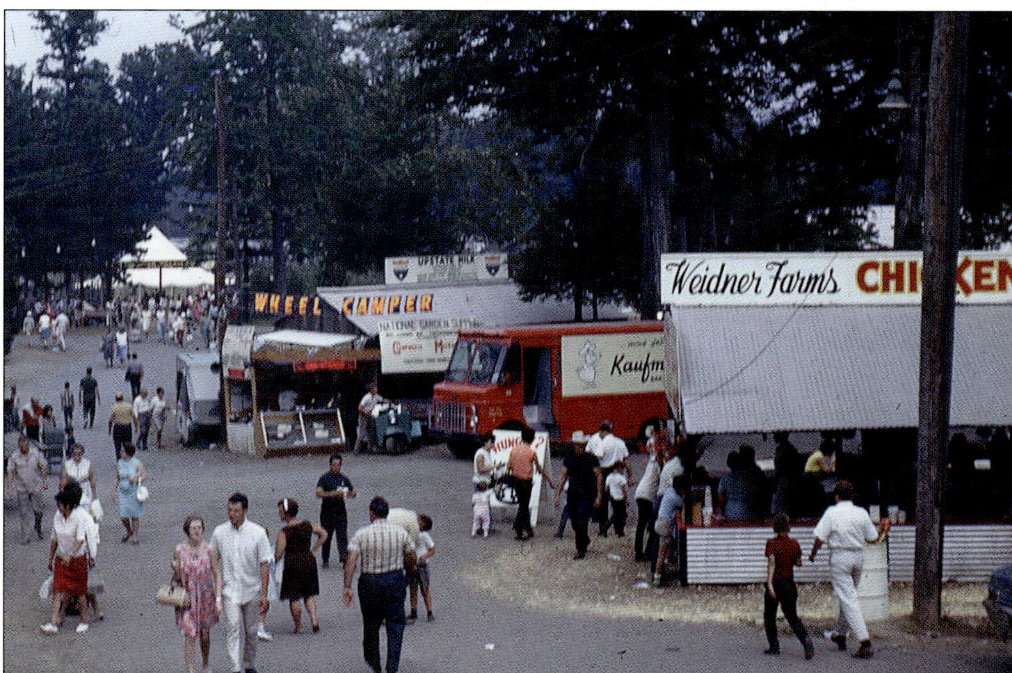

In this view looking down from the Grandstand in 1967, one can see Weidner's Farms barbecue chicken and the Upstate Milk dairy bar. In the 2000s, state-of-the-art cattle and horse barns were constructed to complete a complex of agricultural buildings in this area.

Three

THE 1970s

LARGEST COUNTY FAIR IN THE USA

The Erie County Fair began the decade by shattering all previously held attendance records. A total of 600,960 visitors walked through the gates in 1970. William Mullaney, fair secretary stated, "The formula to success was simply to present a program that people cannot turn on their TV sets to see."

At the annual convention of the International Association of Fairs and Expositions in 1970, the *Buffalo Evening News* reported, "California may be ahead of New York in population, but those concerned with the quality of life, rather than quantity can give the Empire State a new first. The Erie County Fair now is rated the biggest county fair in the country, passing the Los Angeles County Fair in Pomona, California, the leader for many years."

The following year, in 1971, the fair board proudly proclaimed its position as the "Largest County Fair in the U.S.A." in all of its advertising. That year, the fair celebrated the sesquicentennial of Erie County, which was founded in 1821, with a large addition to the Historical Building.

In early 1971, the New York State Urban Development Corporation considered the fairgrounds as the site of a proposed 80,000-seat stadium to host the NFL's Buffalo Bills. The 15-acre facility would have been located near South Park Avenue. The society rejected the proposal and stated, "We have a solemn obligation to the preserve the continued growth of the Great Erie County Fair as an essential part of our regional and American heritage." Shortly after, the focus switched to a site three miles north of the fairgrounds. It would be at this location that the Bills would play their first game at the new Rich Stadium in 1973.

The 137th edition of the Erie County Fair in 1976 commemorated America's bicentennial in true red, white, and blue fashion. The Avenue of Flags replaced the display of state flags with a glorious sea of Old Glory. A stainless steel time capsule was buried near the Historical Building. The capsule, containing histories, letters, papers, book and memorabilia from the 20th century, is to be opened during the 2076 fair.

Improvements to the grounds took place with the construction of a new pedestrian promenade named 42nd Street in 1978 and the addition of two geodesic domes purchased from NASA in 1979.

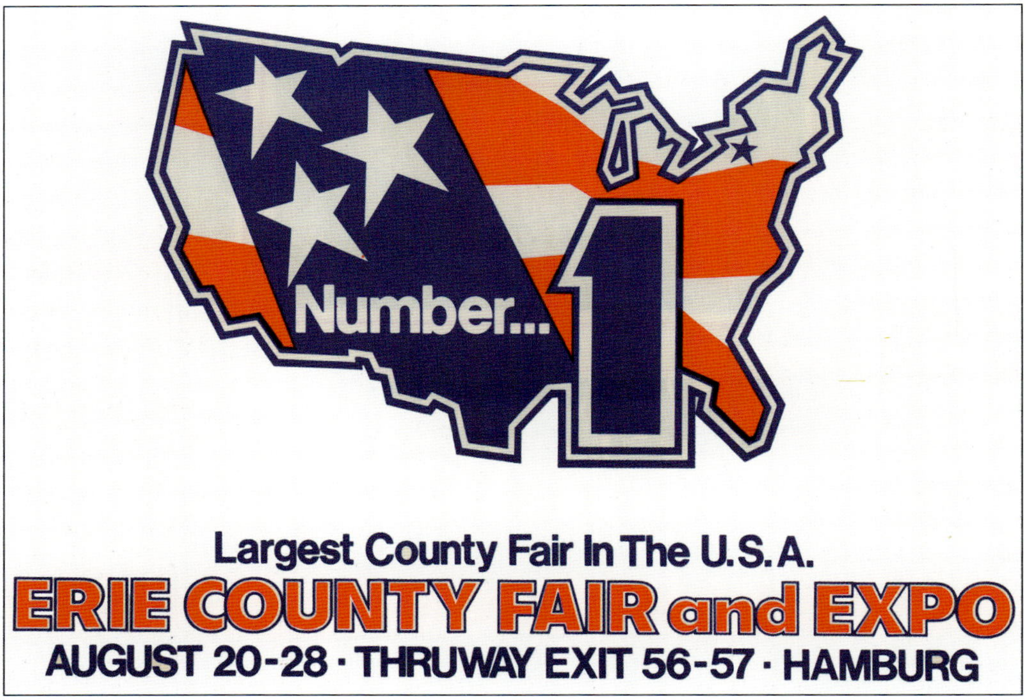

After the close of the 1970 fair, the International Association of Fair and Expositions bestowed the honor of naming the Erie County Fair the largest county fair in the United States. The ranking was based on annual attendance for the nine-day fair.

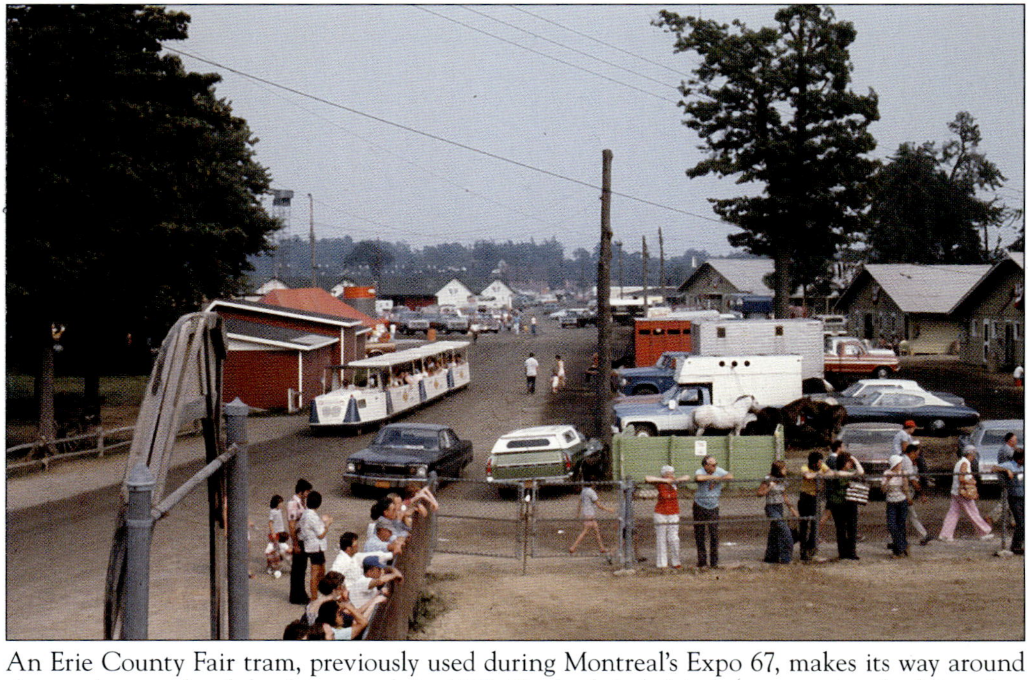

An Erie County Fair tram, previously used during Montreal's Expo 67, makes its way around the southeast side of the fairgrounds in 1975. To the left, behind the tram, is a building that once housed historical farm equipment, vintage carriages, and a blacksmith shop as part of the Historical Building's displays.

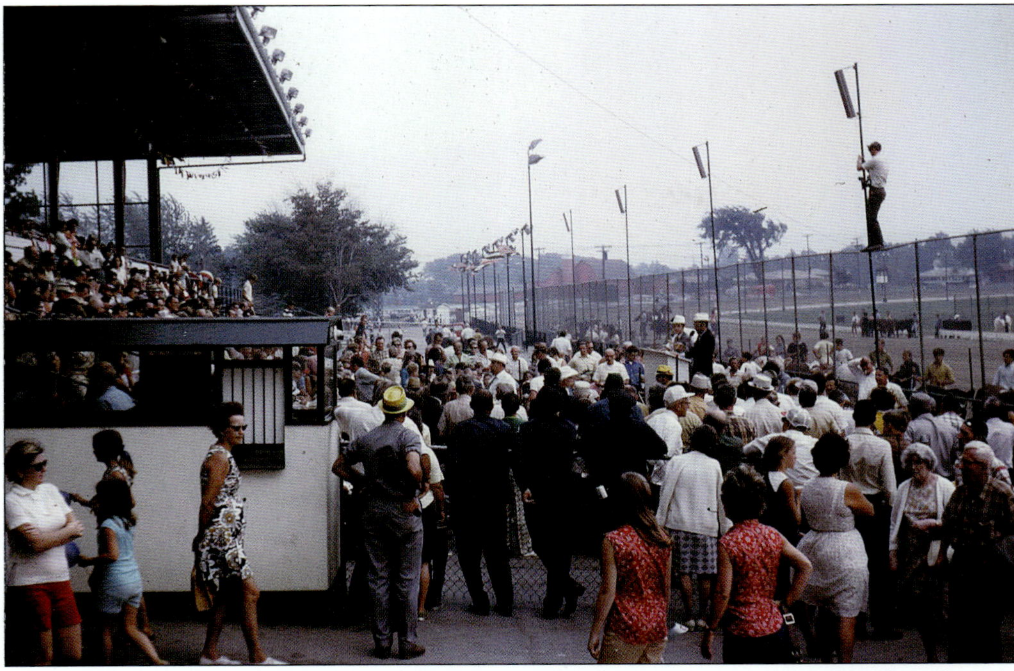

On August 29, 1970, a large crowd gathers as Harris Wilcox and his son Craig conduct the Baby Beef Auction in front of the Grandstand. Important life lessons are experienced through the raising, showing, and selling of animals by children. The fair environment fosters a spirit of responsibility, strong work ethics, and the setting of goals.

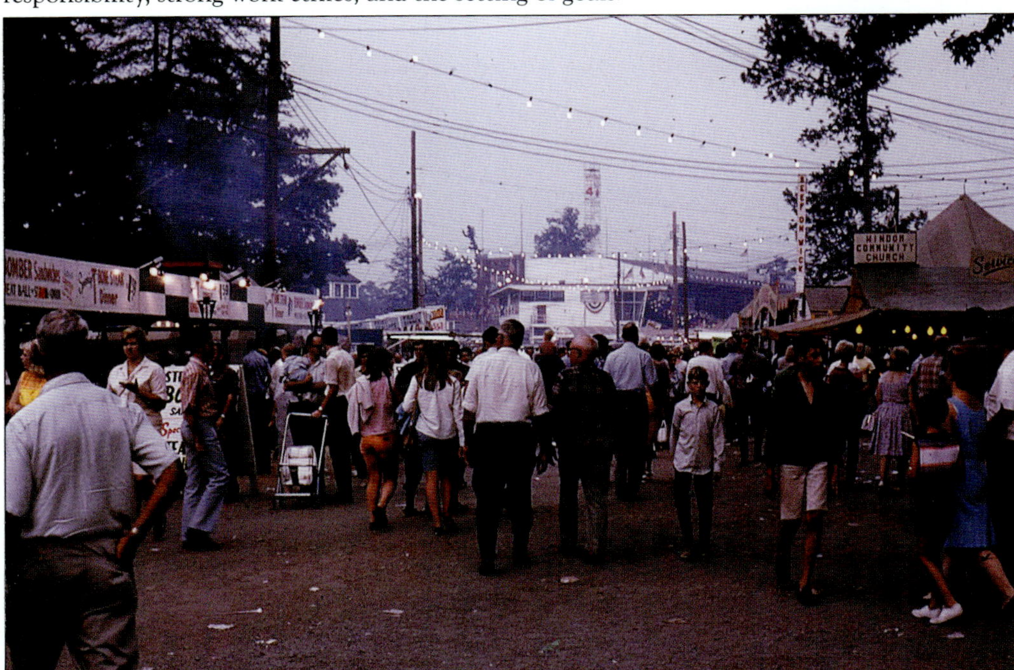

During its recording-breaking year in 1970, fairgoers decide on what food to sample along "Food Alley." Various styles of pizza, beef on weck, Polish and Italian sausage, bomber sandwiches, and fried delights tantalize the senses.

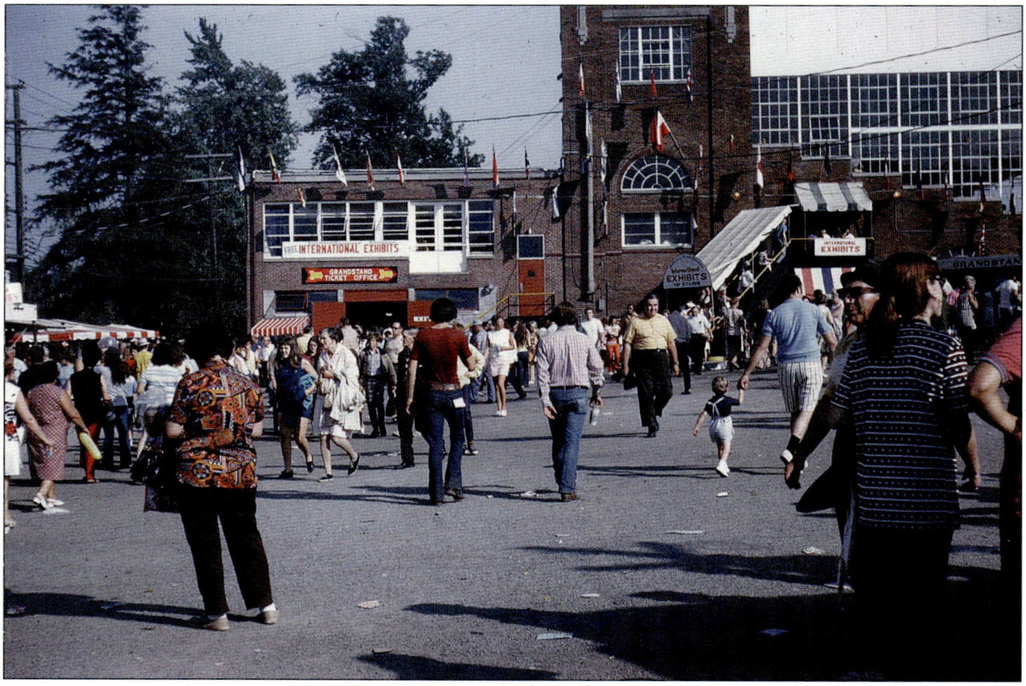

Before the expansion of the Grandstand and Clubhouse, the area behind at the top of the midway was designated as Central Square and served as a key crossroads on the fairgrounds.

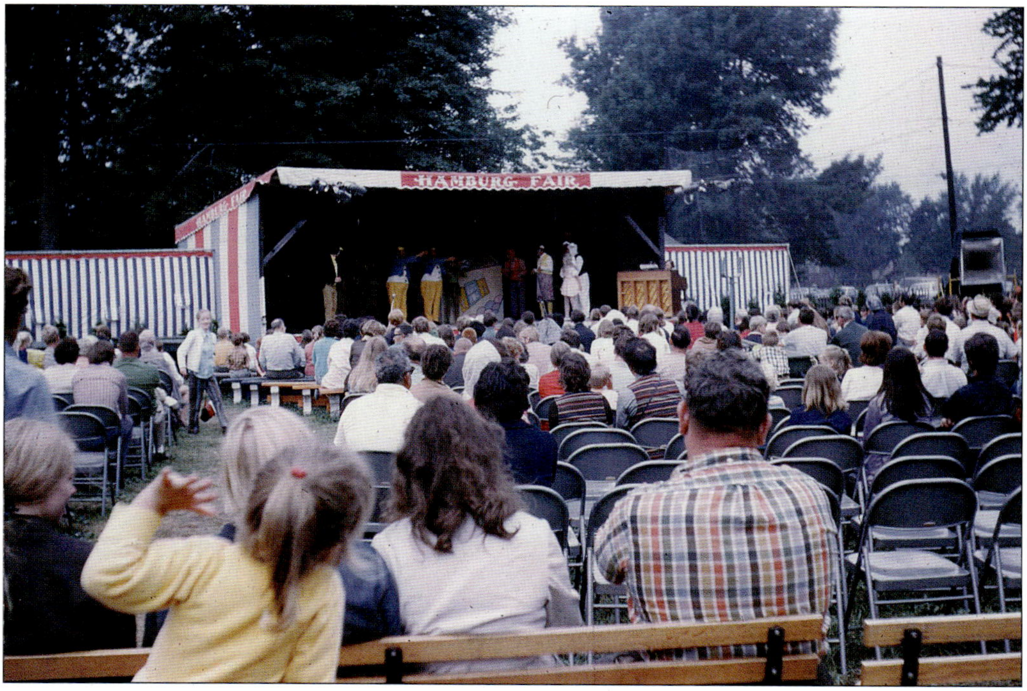

A performance of *Alice in Wonderland* is staged at the Outdoor Theater in 1971. Originally meant to spotlight local theater groups, offerings on the stage were gradually expanded to include musical performers, competitions, and live media broadcasts.

During the fall of 1971, the Octagon Building was moved from its original 1885 location near the racetrack at the top of the midway to a new location on the Avenue of Flags. The move was necessary because of expansion of the Grandstand and Clubhouse.

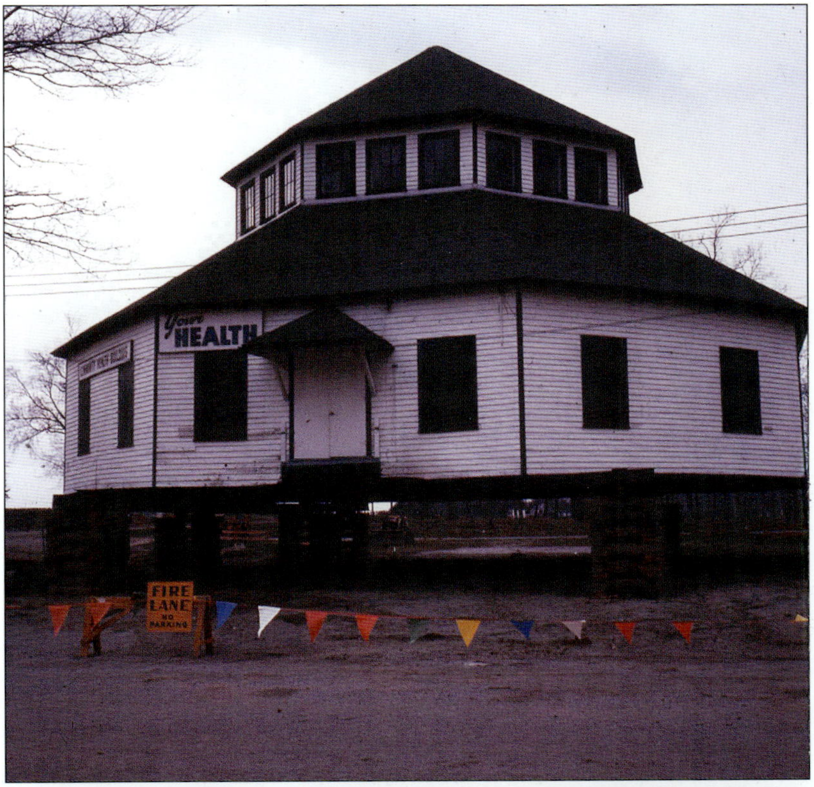

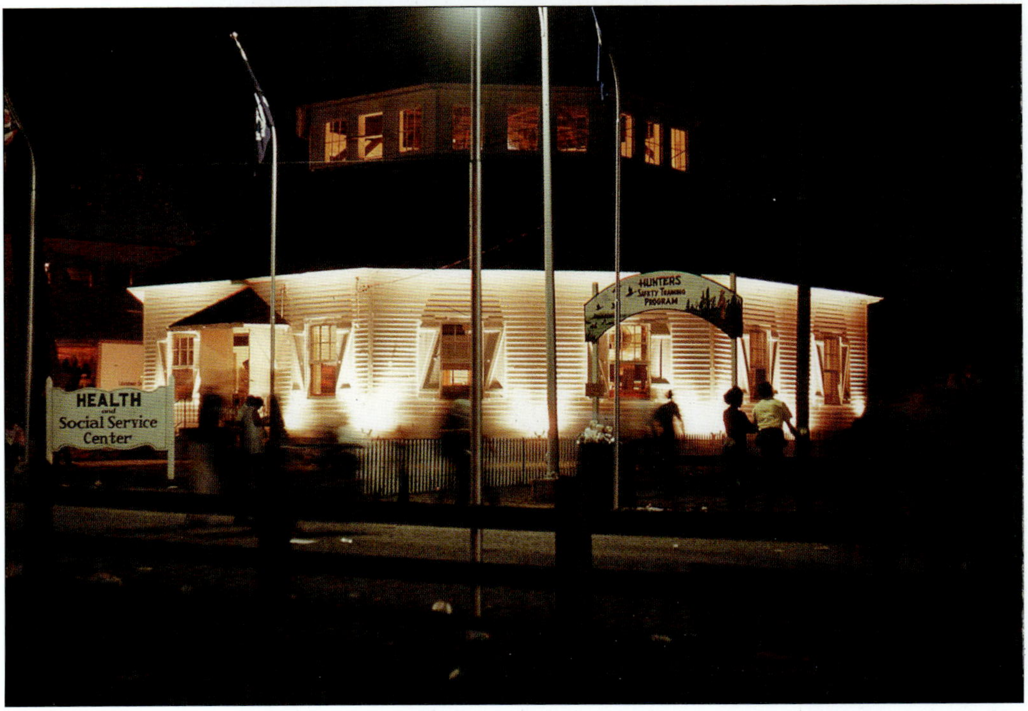

In its new location, the Octagon Building shines at night during the 1972 fair. In 2016, the building was designated as the fair's Heritage and History Center.

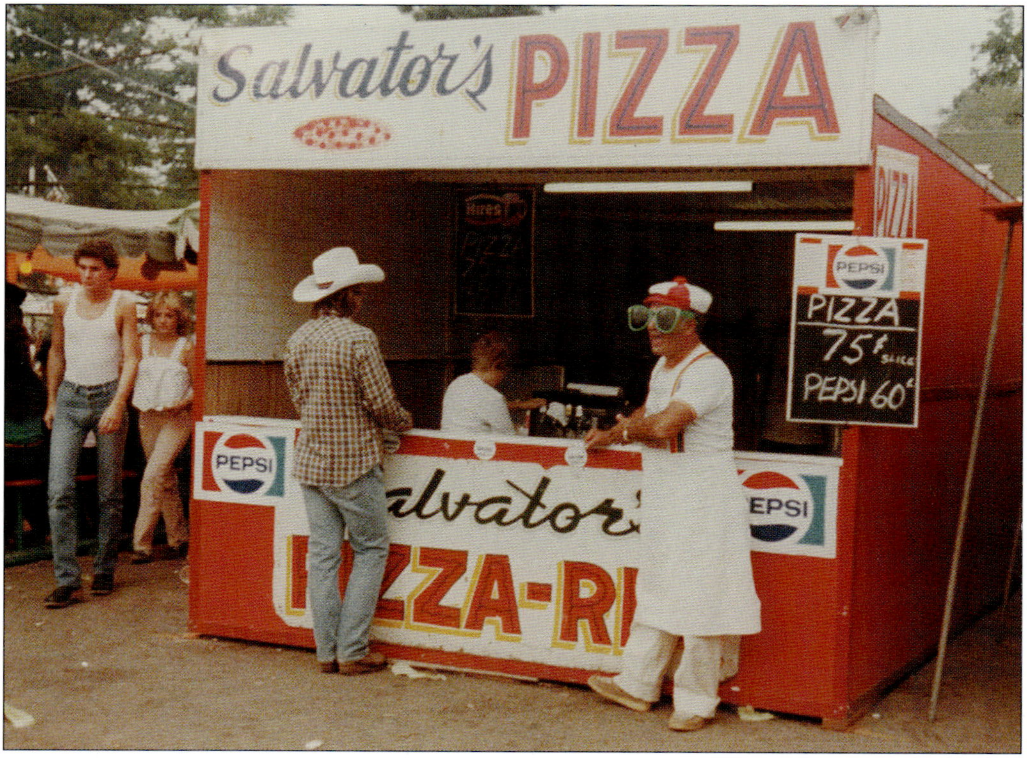

Sal Butera's pizza concession is pictured here in 1972. In 1956, Salvatore and his wife, Philomena, ran one of the first concession stands to introduce pizza to the Erie County Fair.

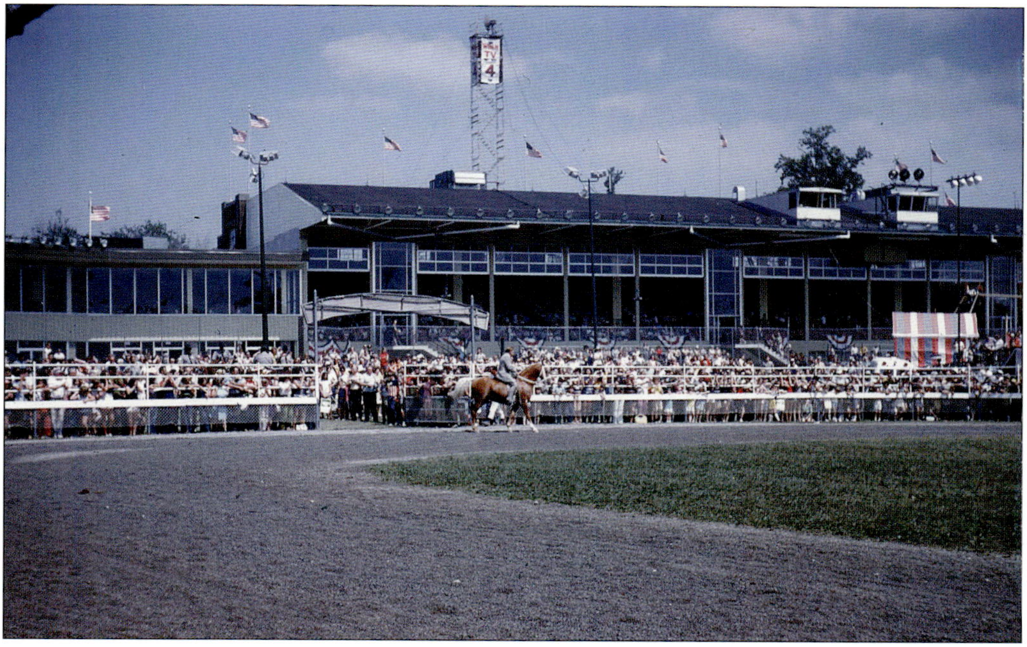

A veteran of radio, television, and the Broadway stage, Arthur Godfrey parades his famed palomino stallion Goldie during the 1972 fair. Godfrey returned to the Erie County Fair in 1974 to act as the fair's goodwill ambassador.

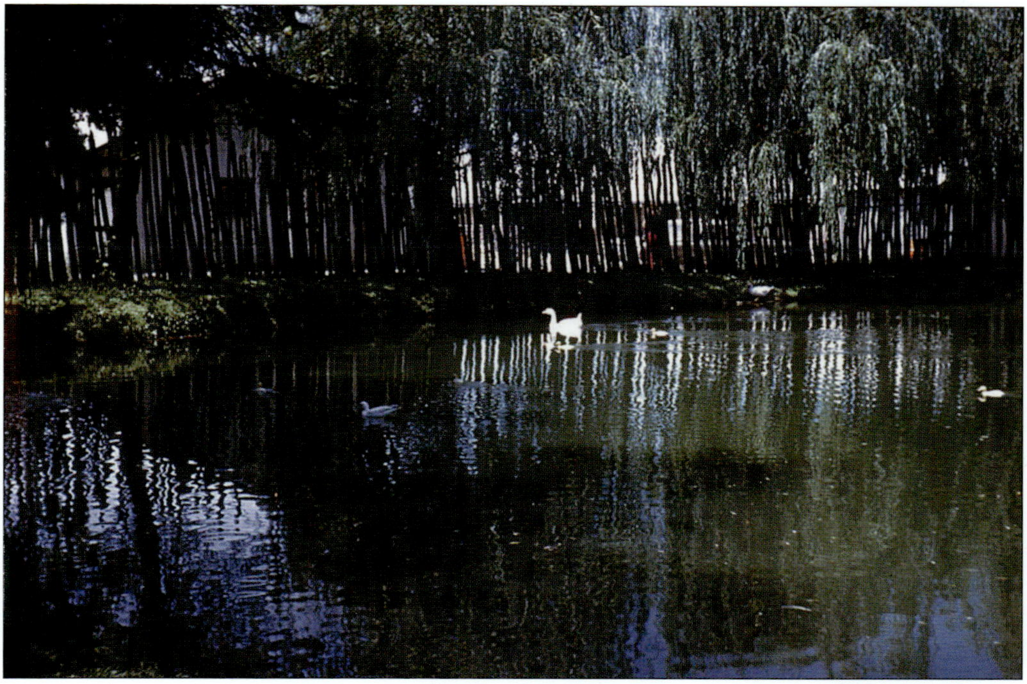

Once used primarily for fire protection, a large, spring-fed pond occupied a location near the Indian Village and behind the Conservation Building. Known as the Lake of the Weeping Willows, the pond featured fishing contests, canoe rides, and a collection of prized waterfowl.

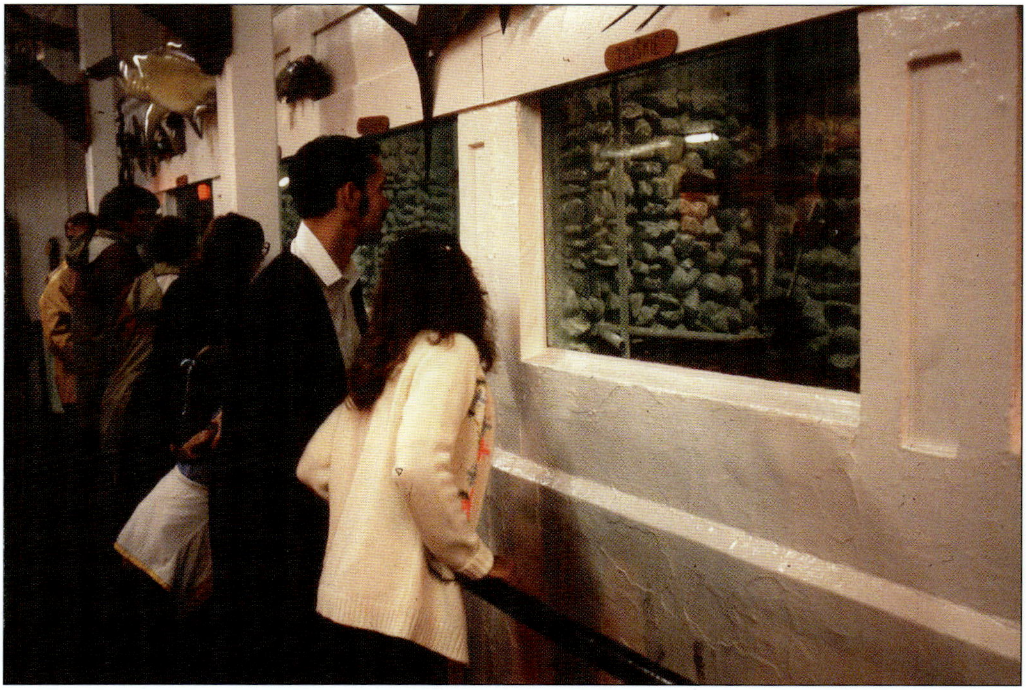

Freshwater fish captured in nearby streams, rivers, and lakes are on display in the Conservation Building's aquariums. Originally constructed in the 1920s, the tanks were rebuilt for the 176th fair in 2015.

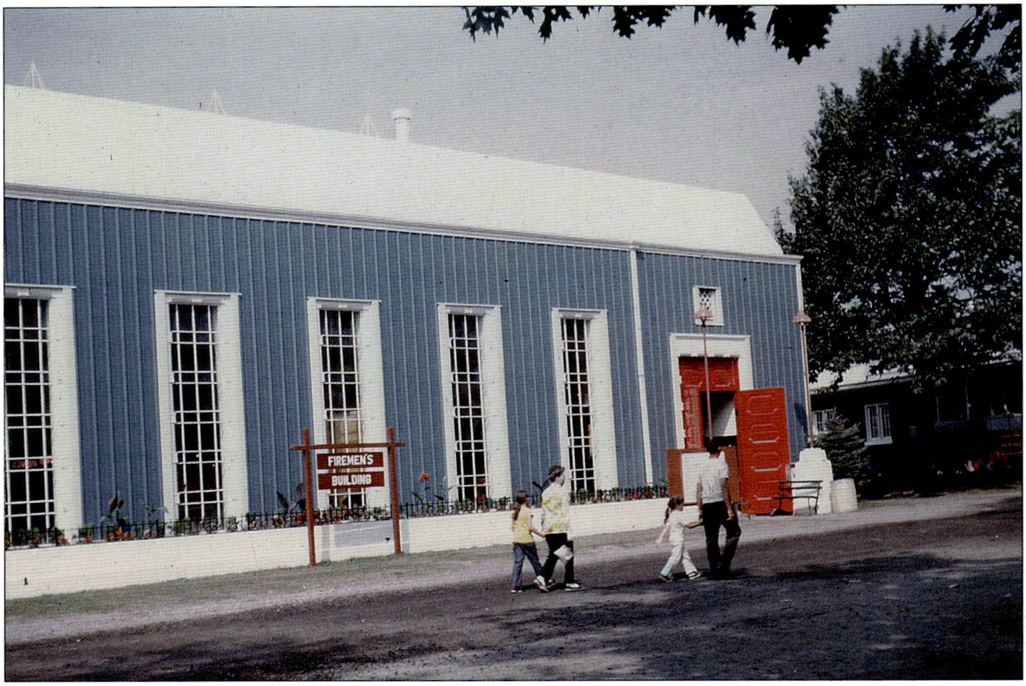

The Firemen's Building received a covering of blue aluminum siding in the 1970s as drainage issues led to the deterioration of outside masonry. The temporary fix lasted almost 30 years until the building was renovated in 2011.

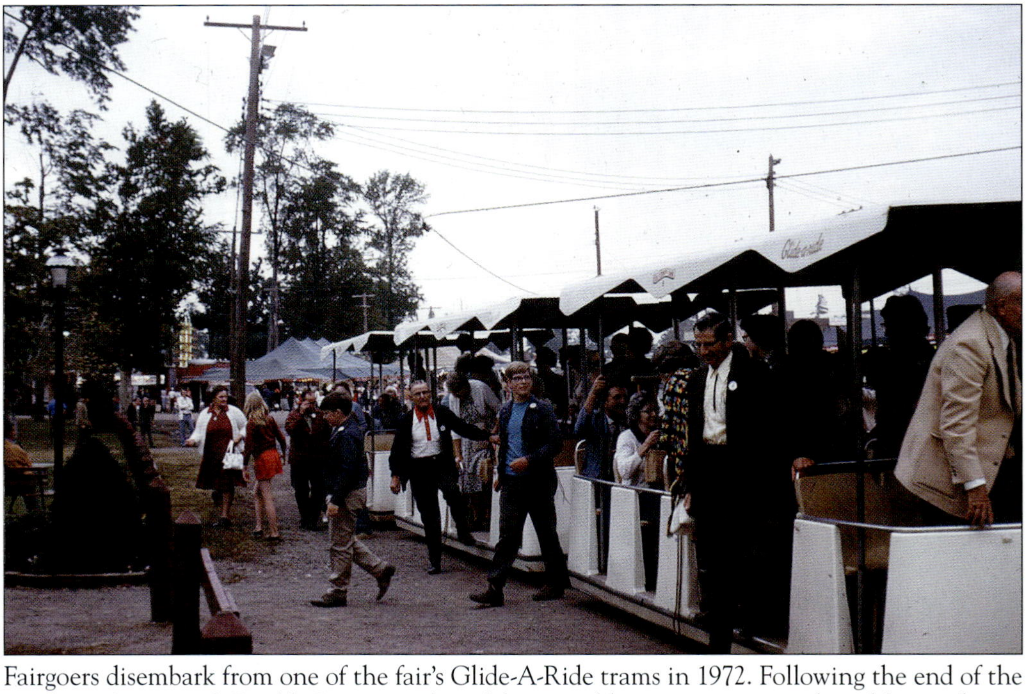

Fairgoers disembark from one of the fair's Glide-A-Ride trams in 1972. Following the end of the 1964–1965 New York World's Fair, a number of these trackless trams were purchased for use during the Erie County Fair. With over 275 acres of fairgrounds to cover, these sightseeing trains were a popular way to travel around the fairgrounds.

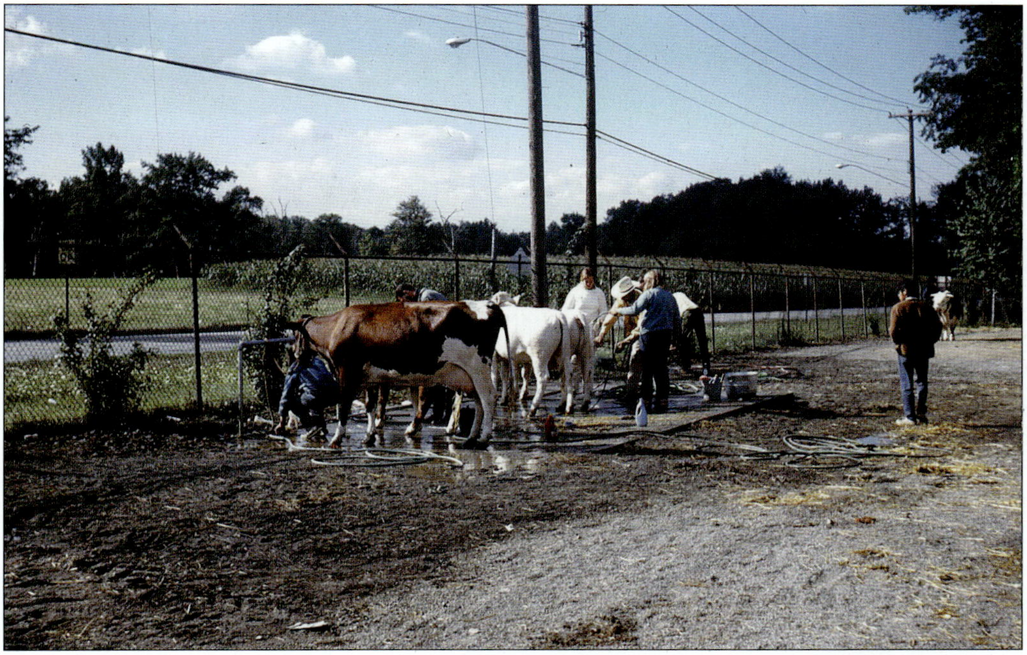

Cattle get hosed down at a primitive wash facility located along the McKinley Parkway side of the fairgrounds. Animal comfort and amenities for animal owners and competitors became a priority for the agricultural society in the 1970s as new barns were constructed and old structures renovated.

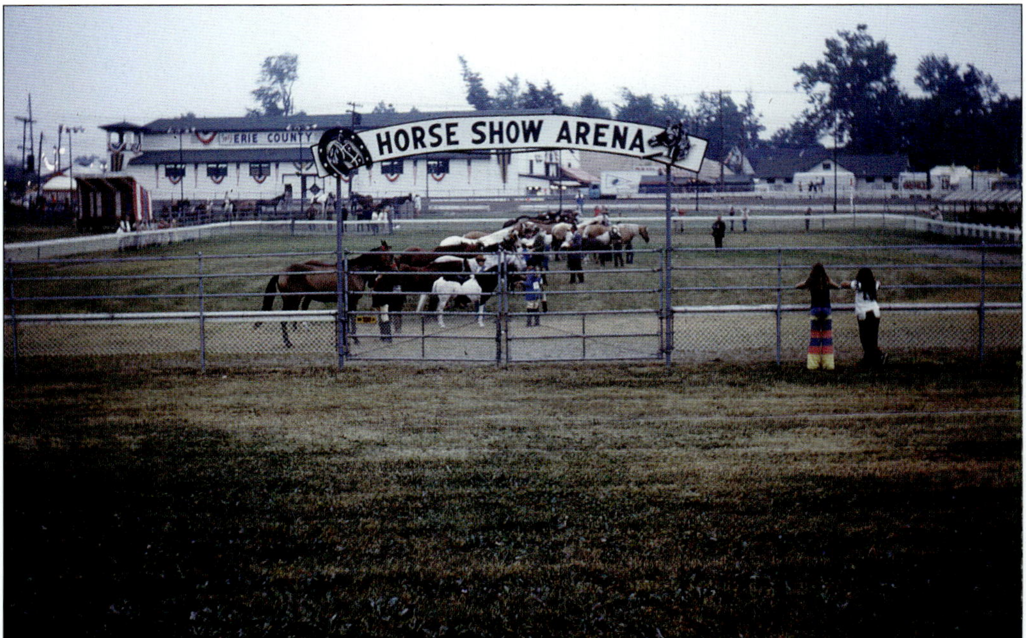

The Horse Show Arena was located in the infield during 1971 and featured over 2,500 equines from all over the United States and Canada. Competition divisions included Pinto, Palomino, Amateur Owner Working Hunter, Junior Working Hunter, Children Hunters, Palomino Youth Activity, Arabian, and Half Arabian classes.

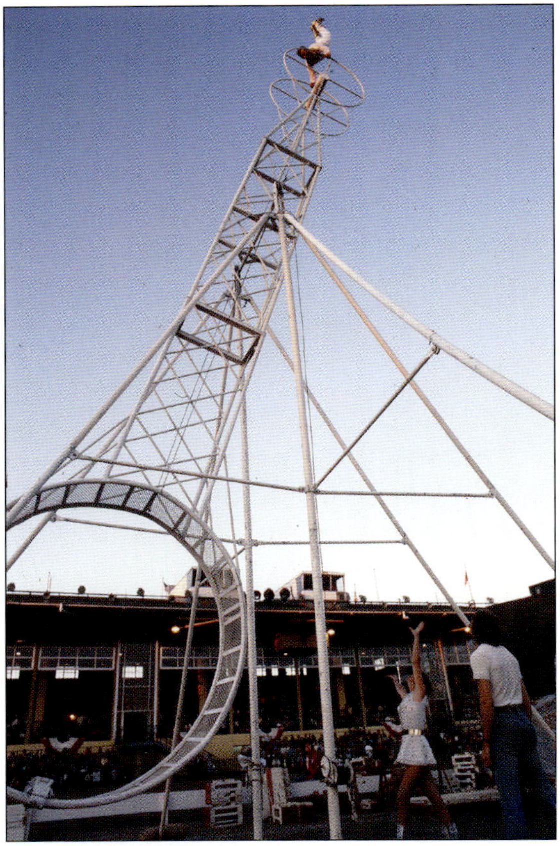

Known in the circus industry as the Wheel of Death or the Space Wheel, this rotating apparatus was part of a 1978 circus performance at the Grandstand. The act required synchronized acrobatic and balancing skills.

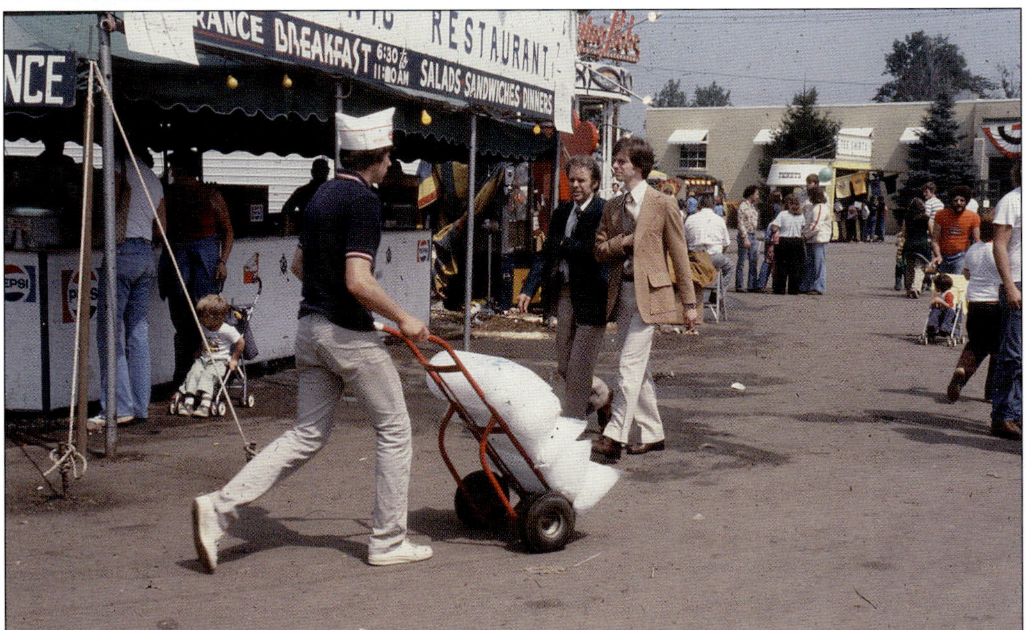

A concessions worker races past the Masonic Restaurant with a delivery of ice in 1978. The Masons began serving food at the fair in the 1920s and operated a concession until 2004.

Originally a rural event among farmers, tractor pulling rose in popularity during the 1970s. A wild and woolly form of competition, it featured the mechanical strength of supercharged engines fed by high-octane fuels and built by talented mechanics. The fair's pull attracted world champion pullers from all over the United States.

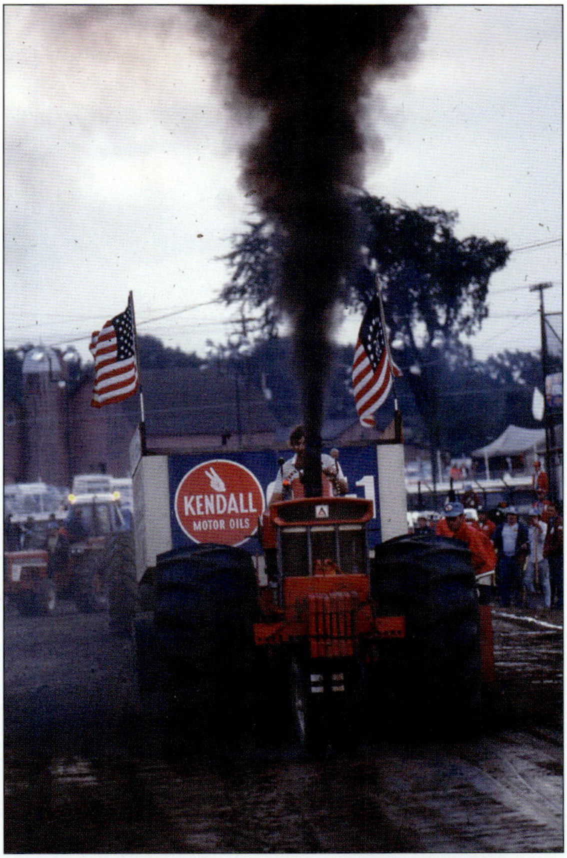

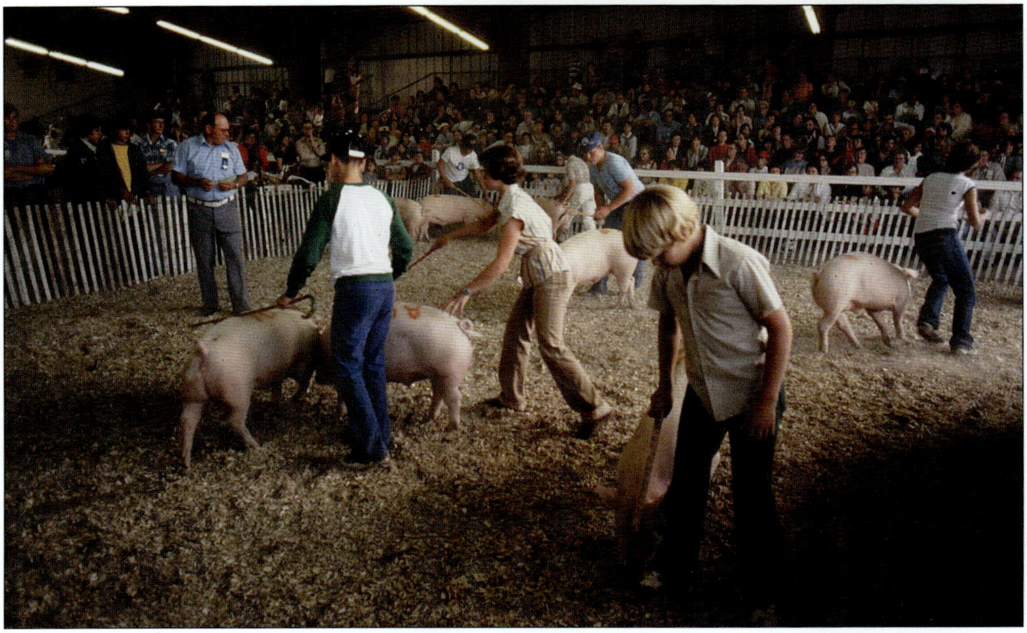

Competitors within 4-H work their pigs during a 1977 competition. A new Livestock Exhibition Building for shows and judging was constructed in 1976.

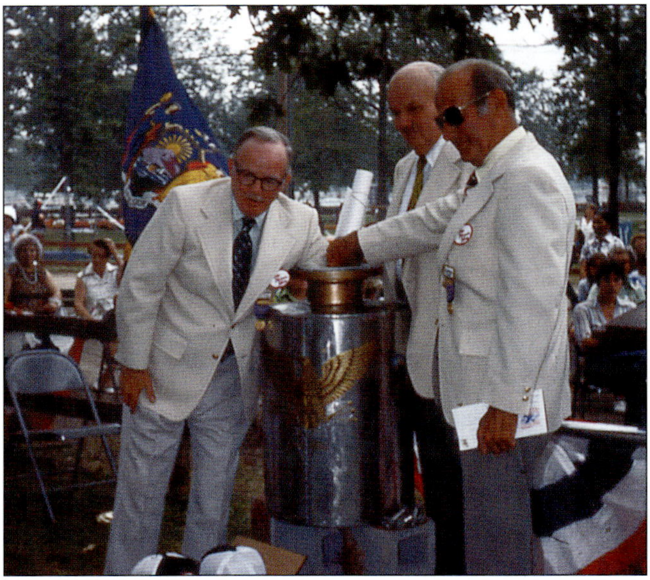

The nation's bicentennial was commemorated by the burial of a time capsule to be opened in the year 2076. Located on the lawn of the fair's Historical Building, the capsule included a $500 US Savings Bond. When buried, it was estimated that the bond would be worth $66,000 in 2076. A letter accompanying the bond recommends that the proceeds be used for agricultural scholarships and grounds improvements. In addition to the bond, the time capsule contains copies of 1976 newspapers, fair premium books, coins from 1876, and other fair memorabilia.

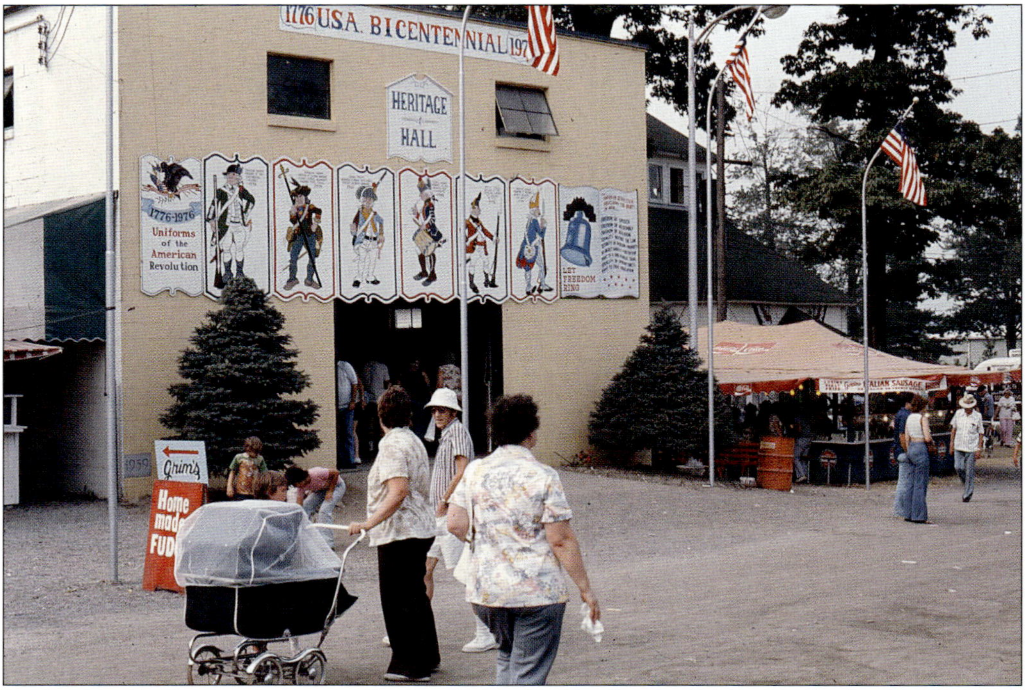

During the 1976 American bicentennial, the former Junior Building on the Avenue of Flags was transformed into Heritage Hall. The building was dedicated to the history of the Erie County Fair and included exhibits on harness racing at Buffalo Raceway and Western New York agriculture.

The Avenue of Flags made its fair debut in 1966. The display was presented by the Hamburg Junior Chamber of Commerce and featured flags from all 50 US states. In 1976, state flags were replaced by a sea of US flags.

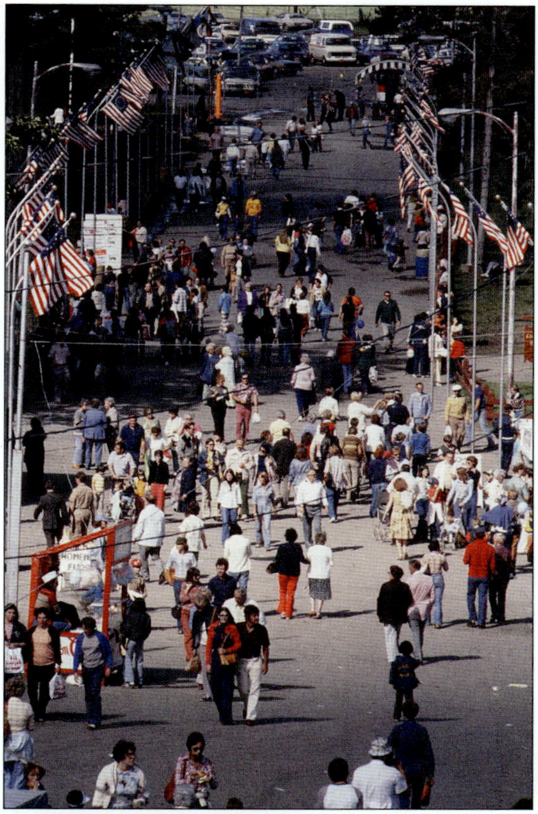

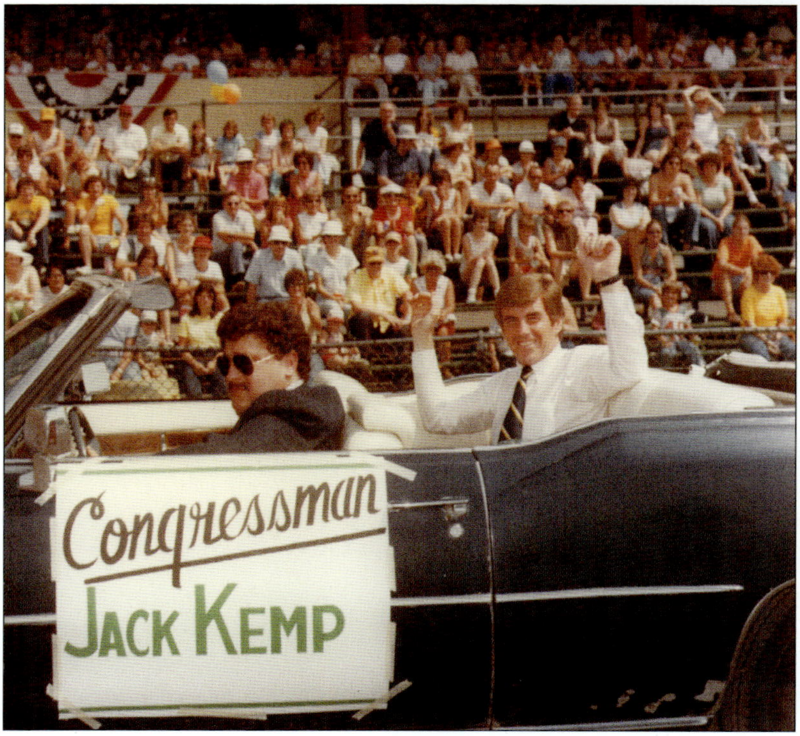

Former Buffalo Bills quarterback Jack Kemp, then a US congressman, appeared in the 1978 Erie County Fair Parade in front of the Grandstand. In 1996, Kemp made an unsuccessful run for vice president on the Republican ticket with Sen. Bob Dole.

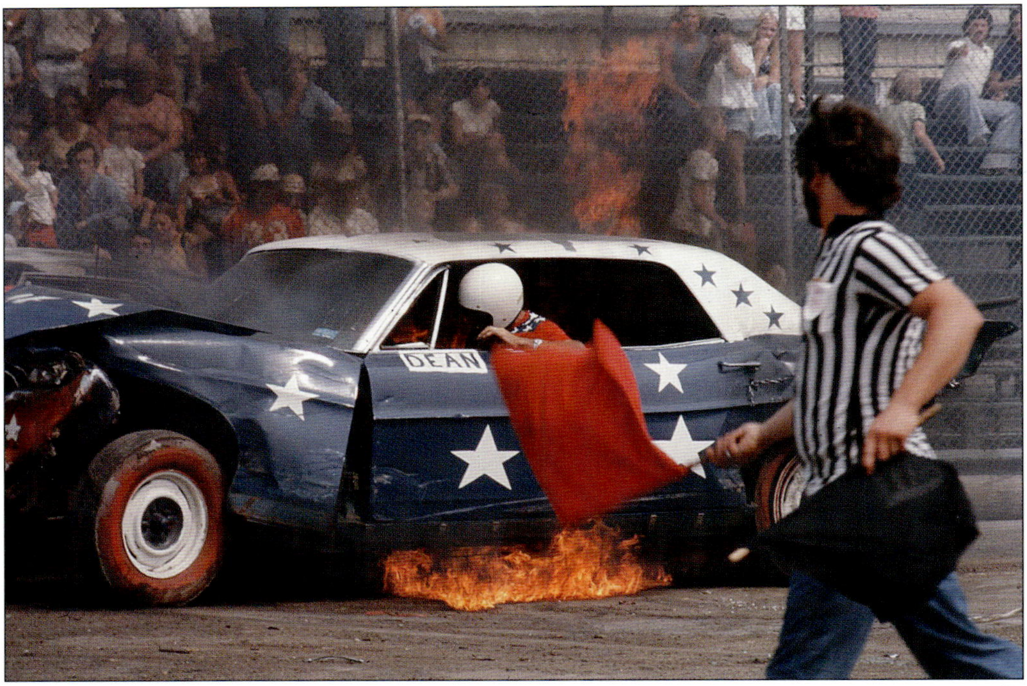

A demolition derby judge throws down the red flag as flames begin to fill the interior of a patriotically painted demo car. Over 200 automobiles were entered during the 1976 competition.

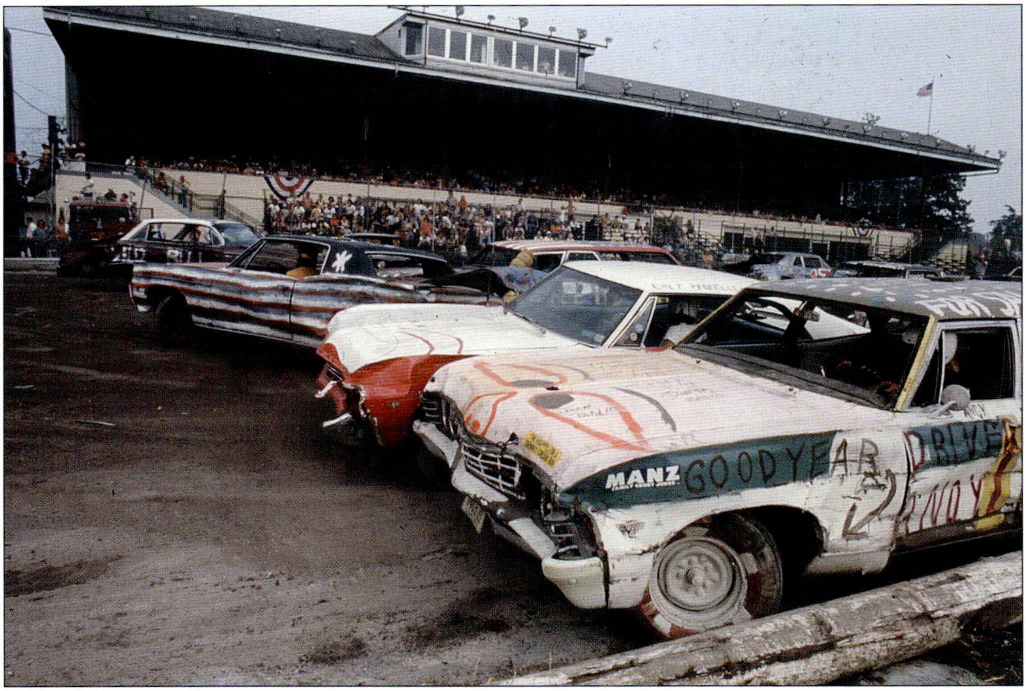

While some men race to win, others crash to win. A full slate of competitors participated in the 1977 demolition derby produced by Lou Heller Promotions.

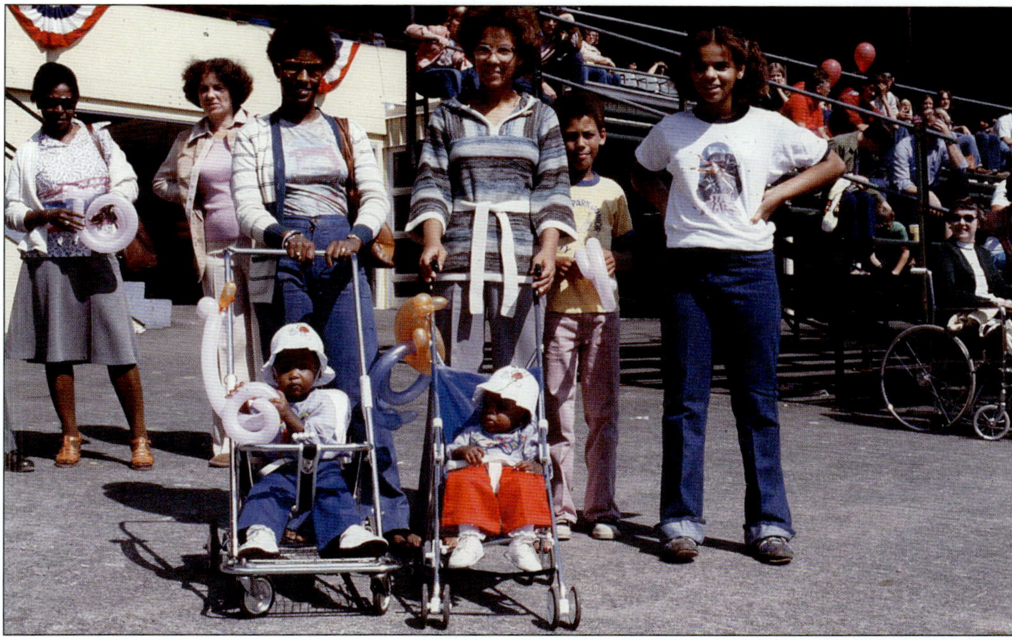

During its eight-day run in 1977, the Erie County Fair welcomed 501,797 people through its gates. They experienced the abundance of sights and sounds that could be enjoyed every hour.

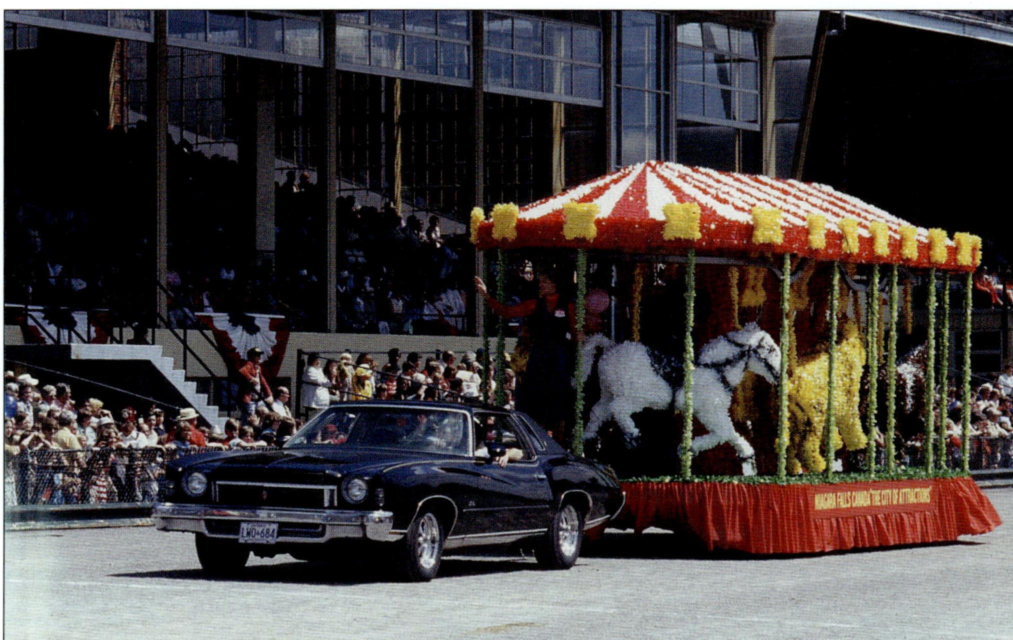

The 1977 Fantastic Funfaironade Parade featured a long line of marching organizations and floats, including one from Niagara Falls, Ontario, carrying Miss Dominion of Canada and O's Gold Fantastic Forty Horse Hitch.

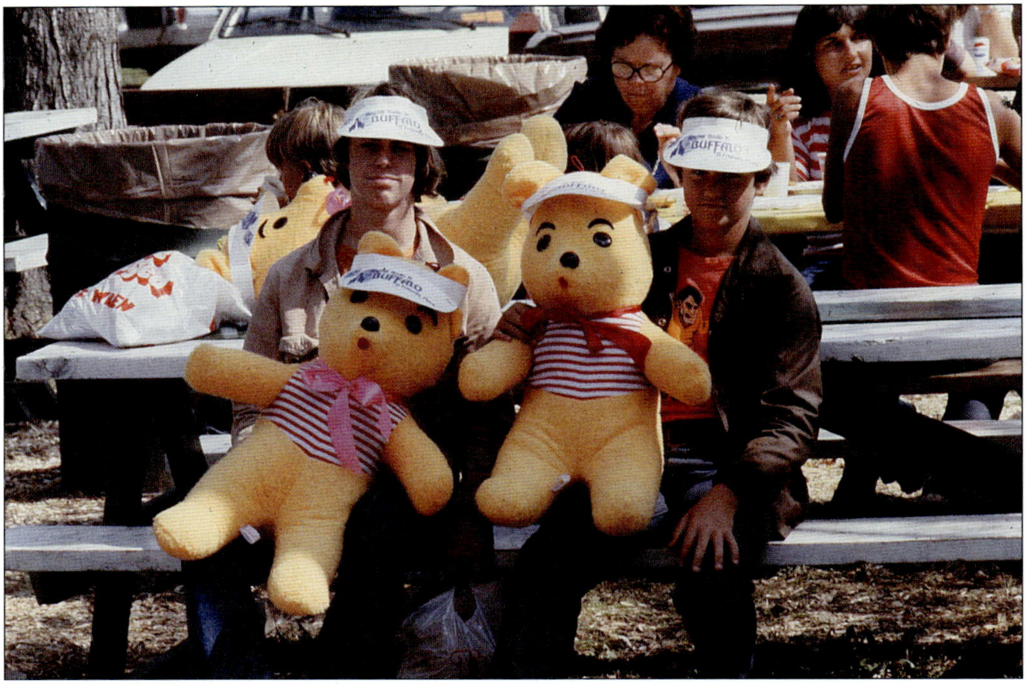

Two young men take a break after winning matching teddy bears on the midway in 1978. Games of chance and skill appearing at the fair included the ladder climb, milk bottle ringtoss, shooting gallery, and the Ping-Pong ball and fishbowl toss.

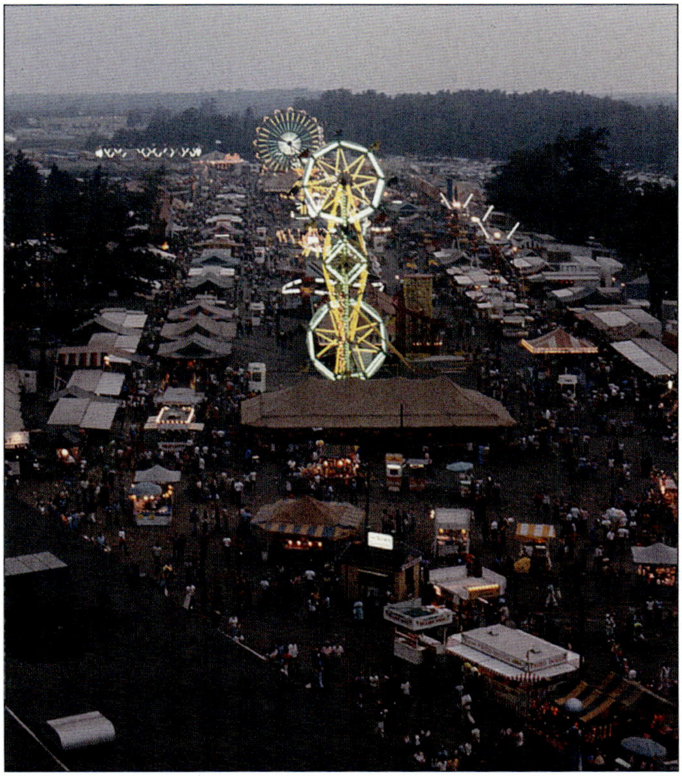

Blaring music, streaking neon, sideshows, rides, pitch games, and all the excitement of the midway are on display at the Strates Shows midway in 1976.

Four

The 1980s

Welcome to Fairadise!

After three decades of intense growth in both attendance and infrastructure, the Erie County Fair faced ever-increasing competition from modern amusement parks, pro-sports franchises, and festival-sized concerts. To counteract challenges, fair manager Paul C. Laing focused efforts on core themes of agriculture, traditions, and excitement and encouraged strong youth participation in the fair.

Made up of approximately 40 talented Western New York students, the Spirt of Youth debuted in 1981. The youth troupe consisted of a 10-piece band, singers, and dancers who not only preformed each day of the fair, but also traveled and performed at high-profile summer events to promote the fair. The year 1981 also marked the arrival of mascot Farley McFair the Fair Bear. The Erie County Fair Marching Band, consisting of 100 students from area high schools, made its debut at the 1982 fair.

In 1982, the Erie County Fair experimented with a new all-inclusive pricing policy based on a $7 super ticket. The "One Price to Fairadise" program included gate entry, free midway rides, and shows, as well as admission to Grandstand events based on a first-come-first-served basis. The program was quickly abandoned the following year after the fair experienced a five percent decrease in attendance.

Improvements to agricultural facilities during the 1980s included the construction of the J.C. Newton Horse Barn in 1980. That same year, the society purchased flagpoles from the Lake Placid Winter Olympic games. The poles were placed in the infield as part of a new Veterans Memorial that was dedicated in 1981.

The fair's Grandstand entertainment offering found its niche with a yearly slate of top country music performers. During the decade, the talent roster featured such legends as Charley Pride, Crystal Gayle, Mickey Gilley, Mel Tillis, Jerry Reed, the Statler Brothers, the Charlie Daniels Band, Boxcar Willie, Lee Greenwood, the Oak Ridge Boys, Willie Nelson, Loretta Lynn, Conway Twitty, George Jones, and Randy Travis.

As the decade came to a close in 1989, the Erie County Fair celebrated its 150th anniversary with the theme "America's County Fair." The society commemorated the sesquicentennial anniversary with the construction of a new gate at the South Park Avenue entrance with bricks paid for by supporters.

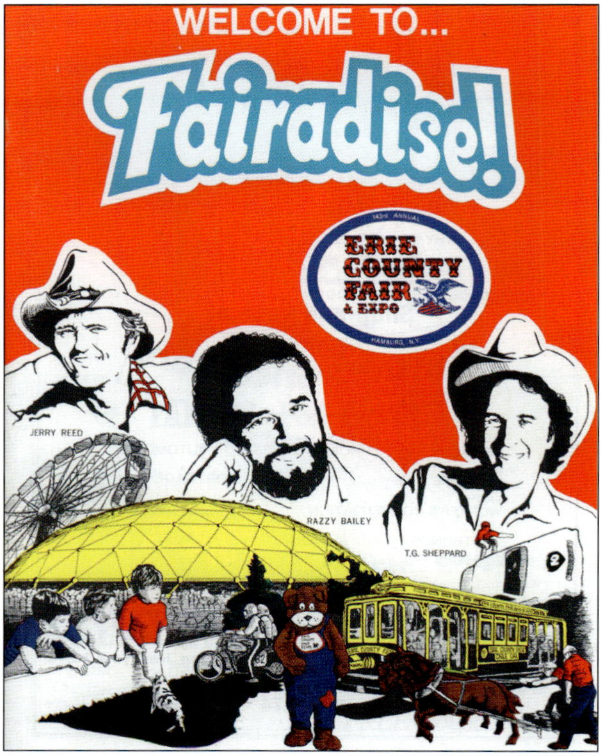

The 143rd Erie County Fair in 1982 featured this fair's first and only "super ticket." For just $7, the ticket to "Fairadise" included unlimited Strates Shows midway rides, all Grandstand shows—including concerts by T.G. Sheppard, Jerry Reed, and Razzy Bailey—and motor events.

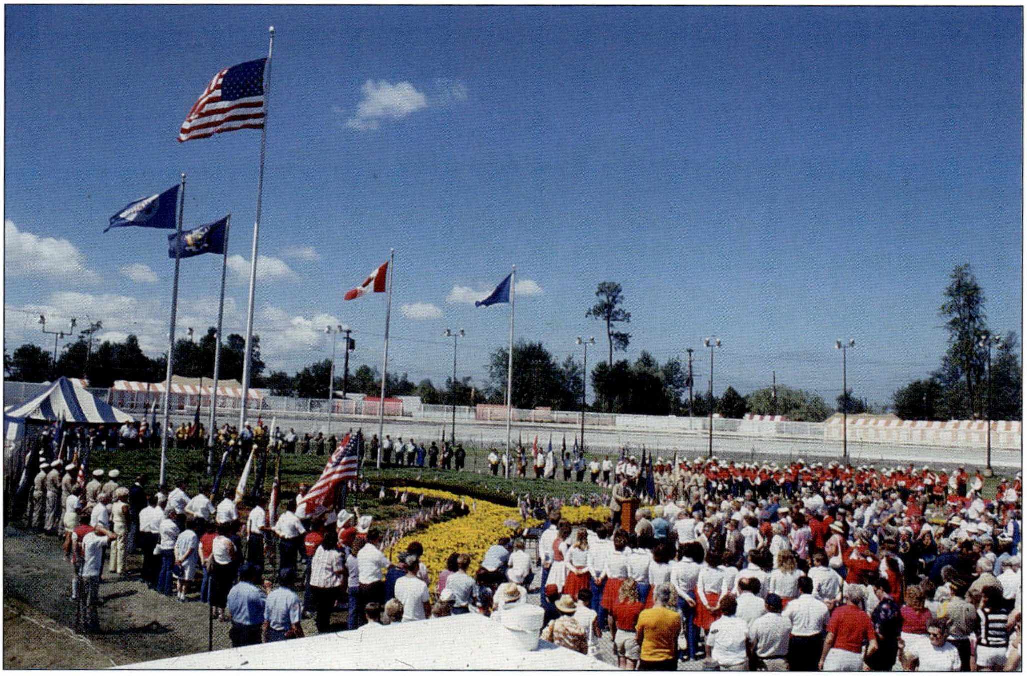

Following the closing ceremonies of the 1980 Winter Olympic Games in Lake Placid, New York, the Erie County Fair purchased a number of surplus flagpoles to use at a newly designated veterans memorial. The Veterans Memorial Park, located on the infield, became the center for the fair's annual Veterans Day memorial services.

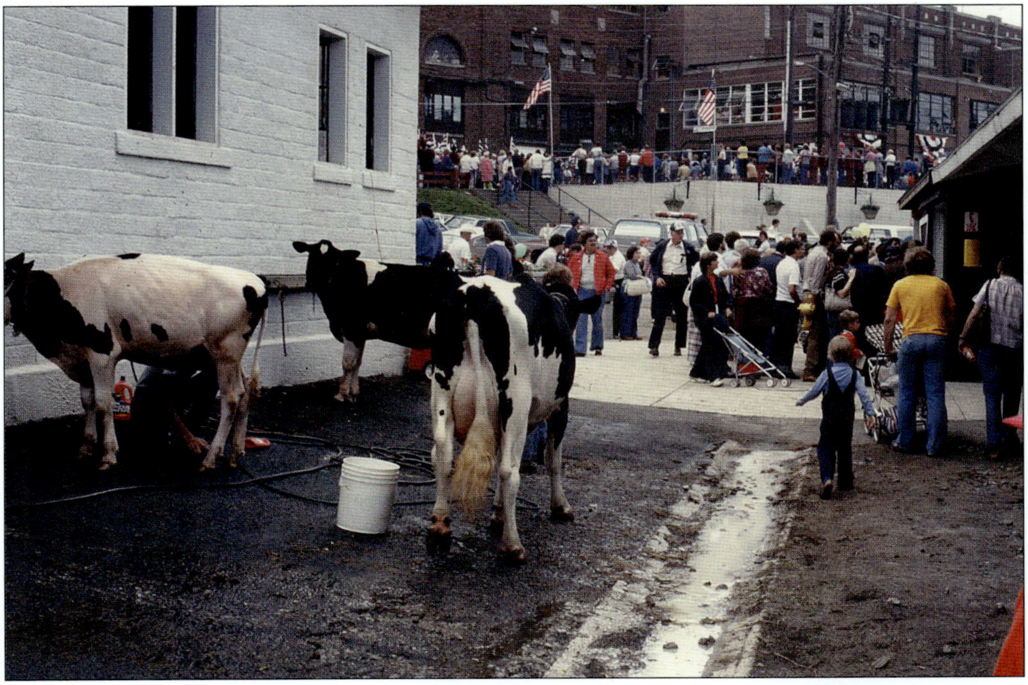

Three Holstein cows get a bath next to Barn 4 prior to milking at the Great Milk Show. Barn 4 was constructed in 1901 and removed in 2013 to make way for the Agriculture Discovery Center.

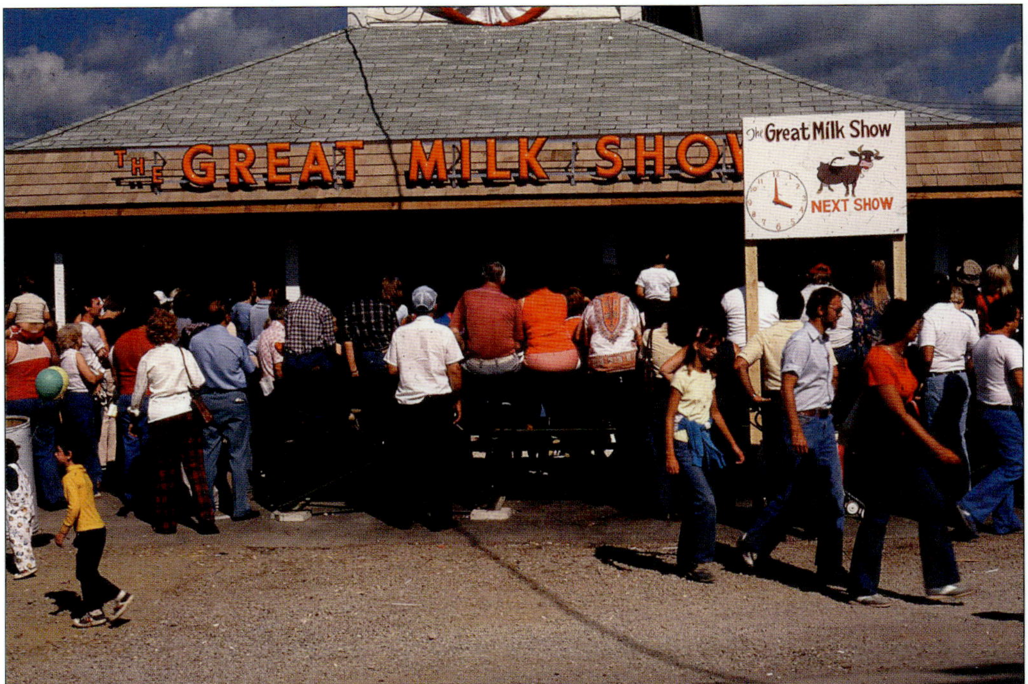

Located at the end of Barn 5, the fair's Great Milk Show allowed fairgoers to see cows being milked by modern methods. In 1994, the milking parlor collected 14,546 gallons of milk during the fair's run.

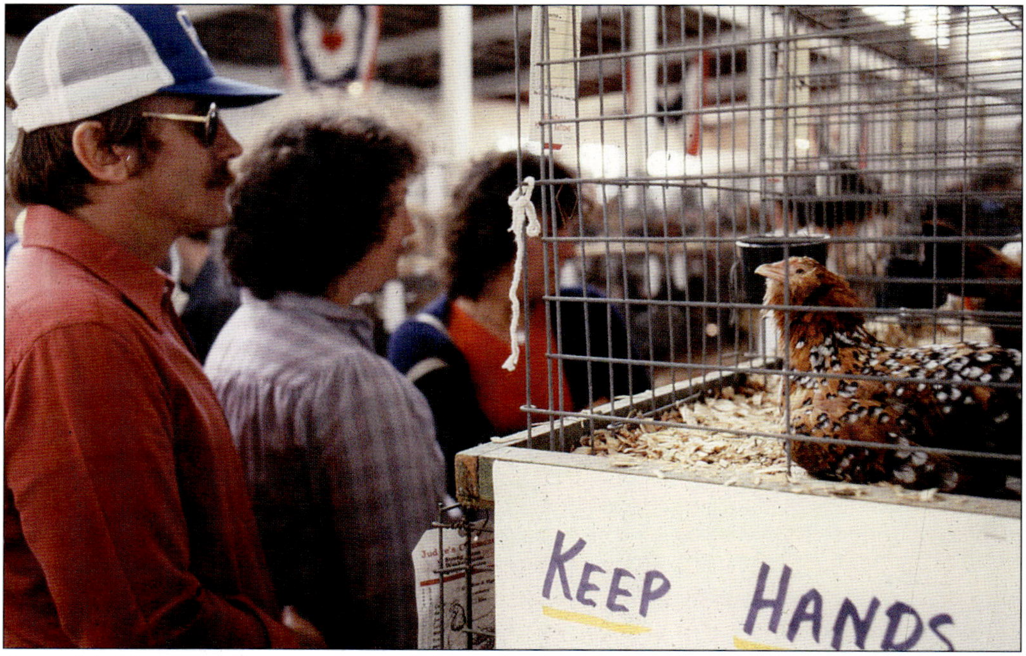

A speckled hen gets the once-over while on display inside the Poultry Building in 1981. The Poultry Building was located behind the Firemen's Building. During its lifespan, the building also housed exhibits provided by the Empire Sports Network/Adelphia Cable, automobiles, and the New York State Lottery.

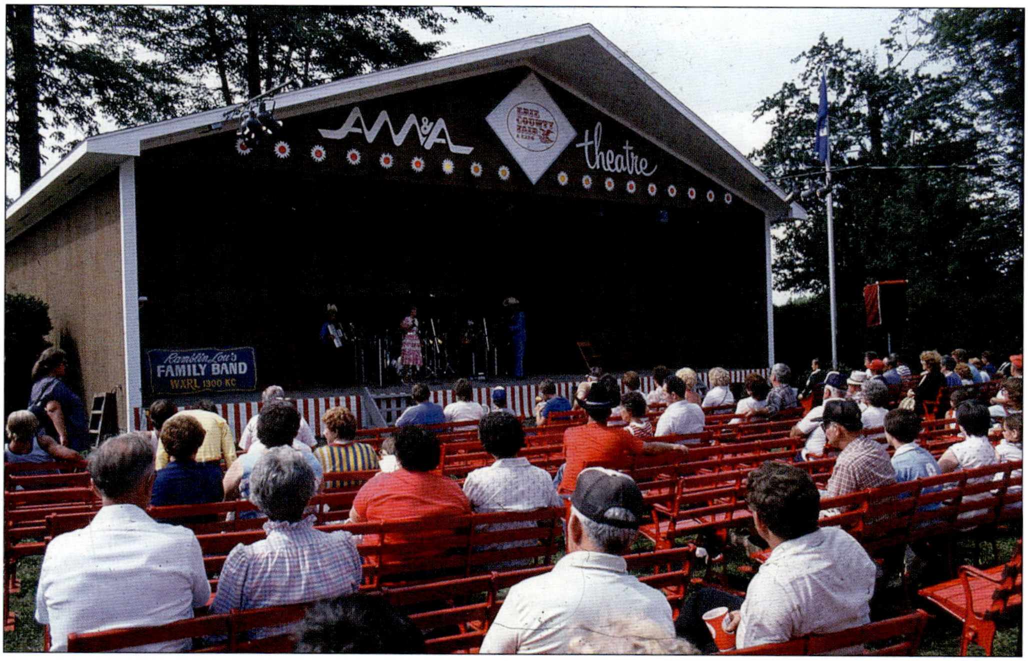

"Ramblin' Lou" Schriver and his Family Band headline the AM&A's Community Stage in 1983. Along with his wife, Joanie Marshall, Lou began performing at the Erie County Fair in 1965 with his band the Twin Pine Mountaineers. As his children came of age, he soon included his daughters Lori Ann and Lynn and son Lou Jr. in the act, and the "family band" was born.

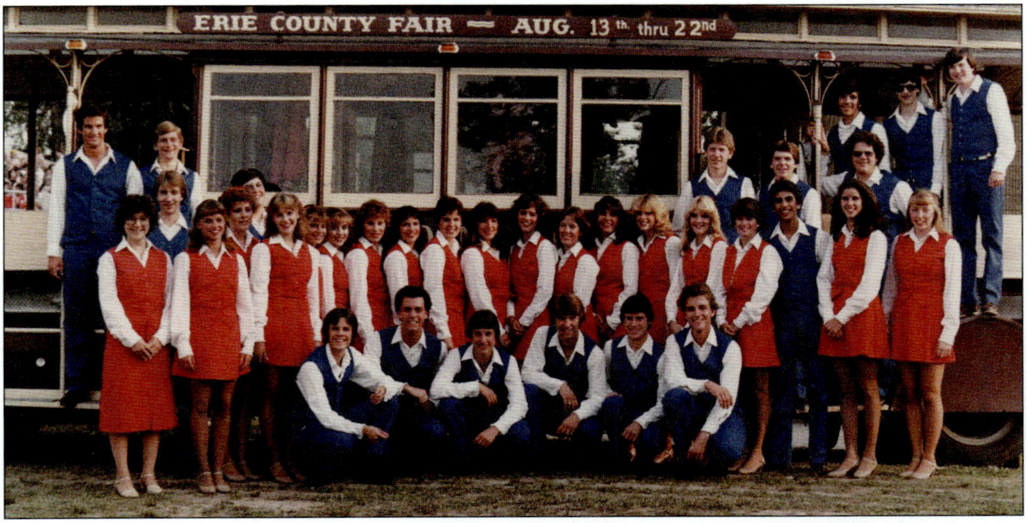

Created in 1981, the Spirit of Youth was a high-profile performance ensemble that became the public face of the fair at events across Western New York. Under the theme "That's Entertainment," the 1982 Spirit of Youth cast included, from left to right, (first row) Michael Rainforth, Patrick Herwood, John McCormick, Mark Wolfe, Kevin Bielmeier, and Joe Fredricks; (second row) Tina Scaglione, Dawn Church, Jackie Hearn, Cynthia Hiem, Janet Wojcik, Barbara Folts, Liz Horvath, Sally Mosey, Lynn Barrett, Melissa Quinn, Anne Glauber, Pam Cotter, Amy Powers, Sara Starling, Molly Stark, Carol Flanagan, Henry Menendez, Becky Murphy, and Louise Roemisch; (third row) Tony Dublino, Doug Welsh, Bill Jankowski, Scott Becker, Ken Farrell, Chris Zak, Eric Gustavel, Joe Bernard, John Hasselback, and Brian Coyle.

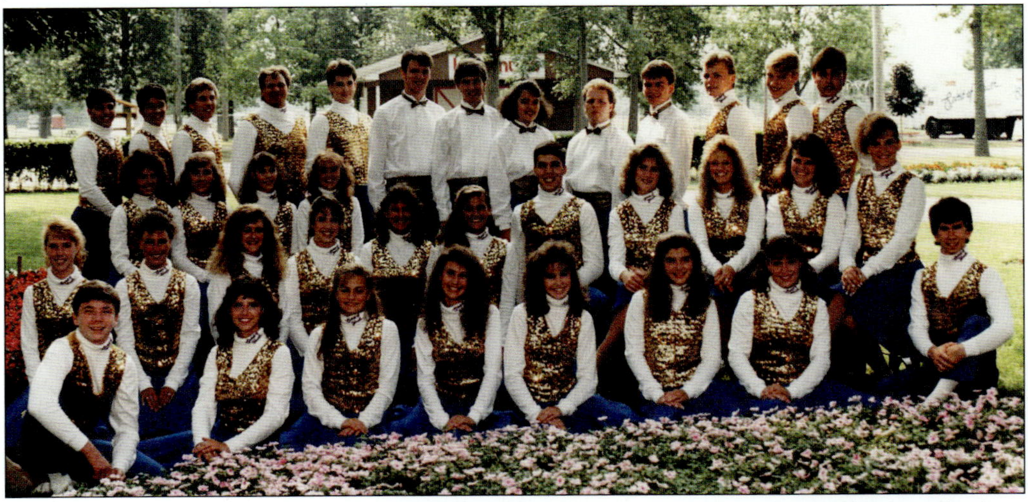

For 18 years, until the program was ended in 1999, the Spirit of Youth performed daily at the fair's Outdoor Stage. "Imagination" was the theme of the 1987 Spirit of Youth that featured, from left to right, (top row) Jeff Vogan, Danielle Berry, Lisa Guinta, Melissa Murphy, Gary Barrow, Kim Burczynski, Tim Graf, Kim Stearns, Andy Lawton, Joe Sonner, Jeff Lewis, and Chris Nowaczewski; (middle row) David Matwijkow, Jennifer Welsby, Jason Torres, Ken Bond, Nancy Grimes, Greg Stuhr, Ellen Shadle, Lisa Burczynski, Susan Burch, Colleen Dziak, Rene' Horbachewski, John Rozumalski, Bill Harmon, Colleen Marcello, Kari Anne Fiutak, and Dean Vallas; (bottom row) Rosalie Folts, Deborah Schmidt, Kathy Weese, Lori Bollomo, Amy Jurek, David Hurlburt, Brian Drajam, and Janet Caine.

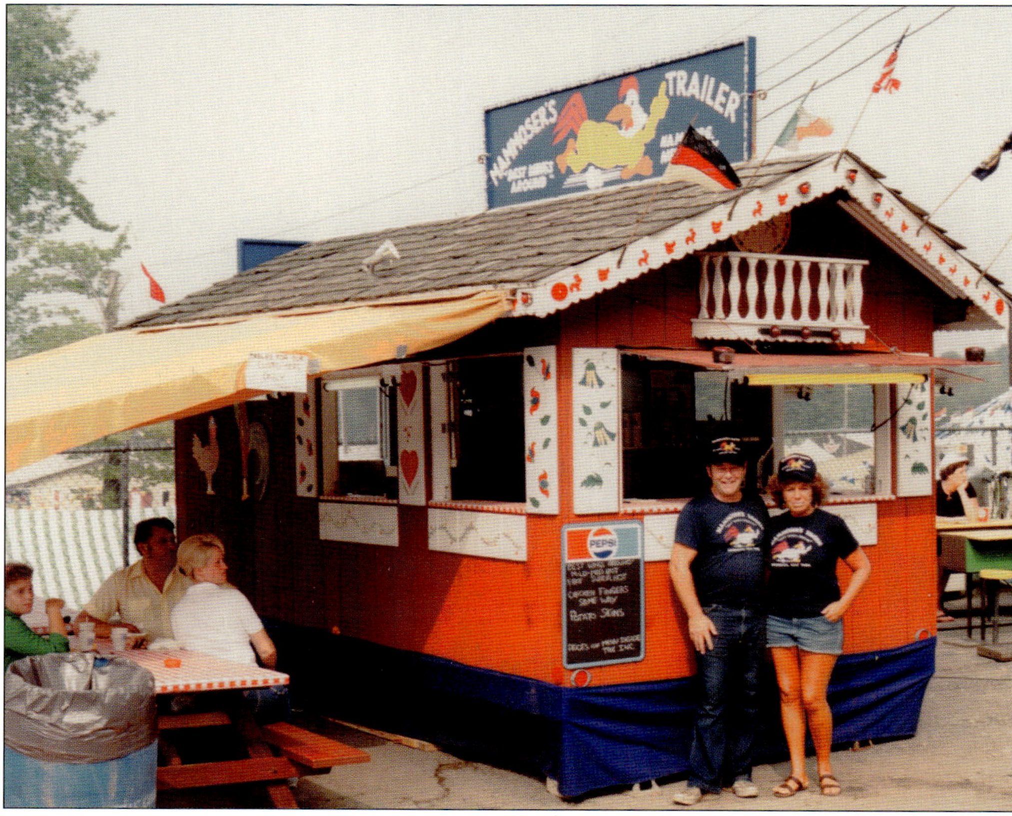

There is no doubt that Buffalo, New York, is the birthplace of the chicken wing. First served at the Anchor Bar in downtown Buffalo, wings can now be found in restaurants across the world. Mammoser's Tavern, located in the nearby Village of Hamburg, is known for its homemade wing sauces. This image from 1983 features Joe and Phyllis Mammoser posing in front of the Mammoser's trailer, located behind the Grandstand, featuring "hot," "extra-hot," and even "super-hot" wings.

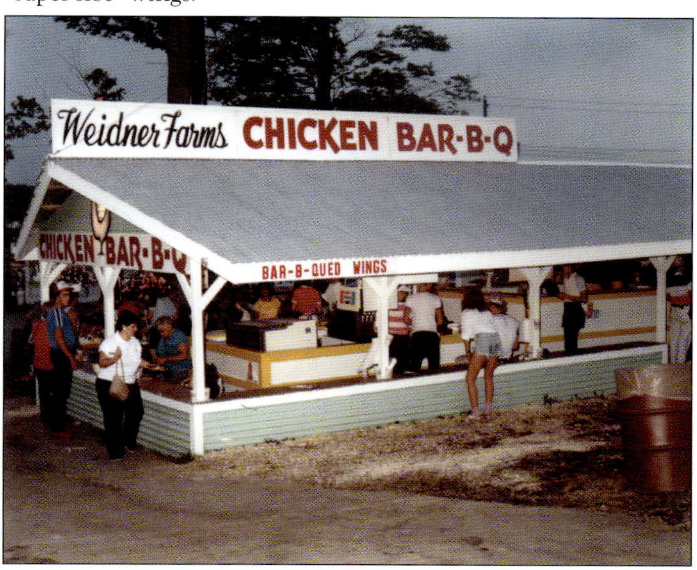

The Weidner Farms concession building is pictured in 1983. Originally a chicken farmer, Eden-based Bert Weidner began serving up his barbecue-style chicken dinners at the Erie County Fair in 1956. In 2016, current owners Charlie Gerber and his wife, Mary Weidner, celebrated Weidner's 60th anniversary on the fairgrounds.

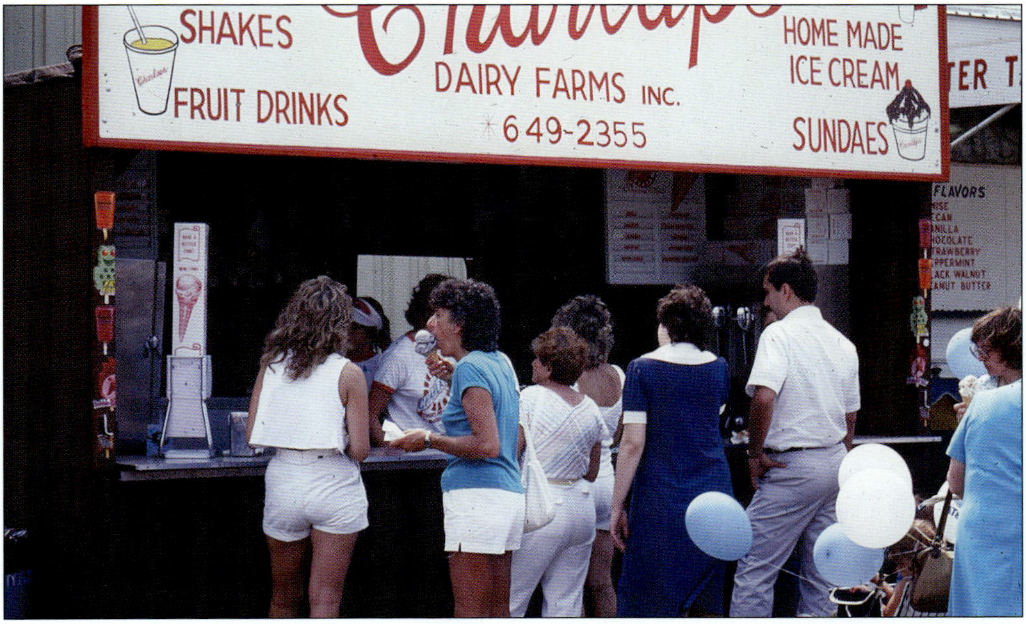

In 1961, dairy farmer Henry Charlap, along with his father, Nicholas, his uncle Leo Mrugala, and his brother-in-law Louis Fronczak, purchased an existing dairy in North Boston and began to make fresh dairy products using locally sourced milk. Originally just a rural farm and dairy, Charlap's soon became famous for its creamy, rich ice cream. Henry's son Nicholas took over the business in the 2000s and continued to expand the family business.

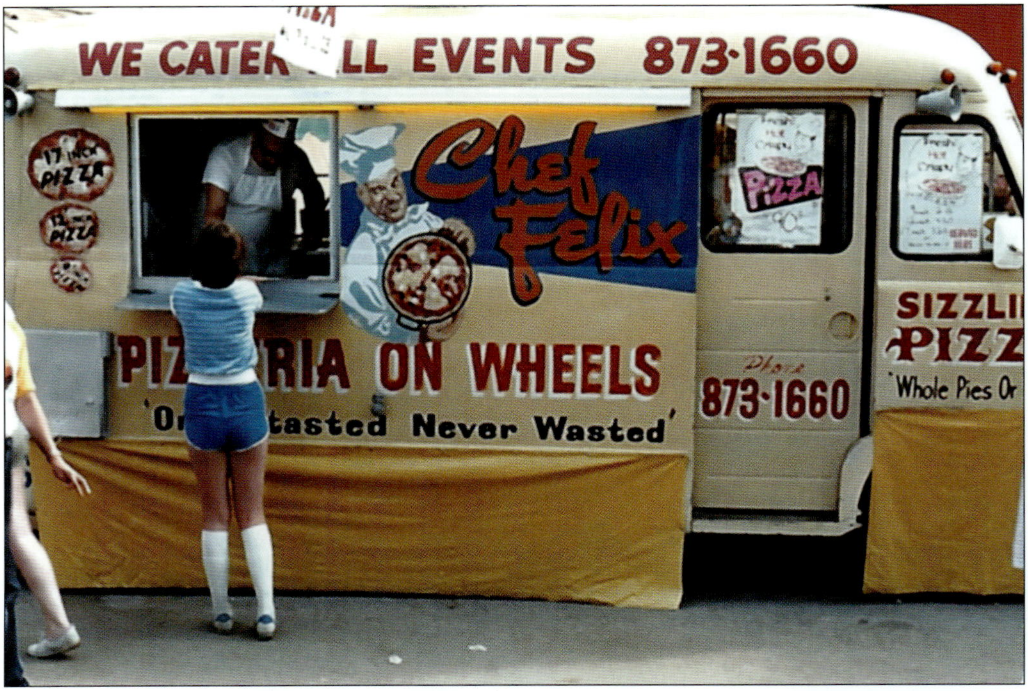

Felix Coniglio's bright yellow pizza truck was a fixture on the fair's food court from 1957 to 1992. In this picture from 1988, Chef Felix is serving up one of his fresh slices that featured oregano and other Italian spices.

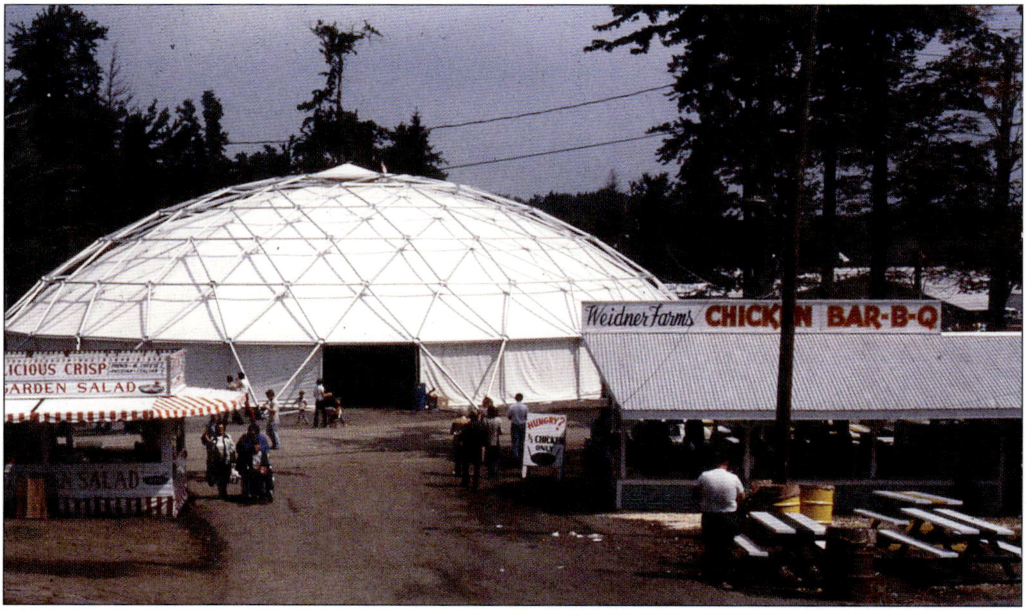

The Commercial Dome, located behind the Grandstand near the Conservation Building, hosted 57 vendor booths. It was one of two geodesic structures on the fairgrounds that were purchased from NASA in 1979 after use at the Kennedy Space Center in Florida. The structures were removed in 2003.

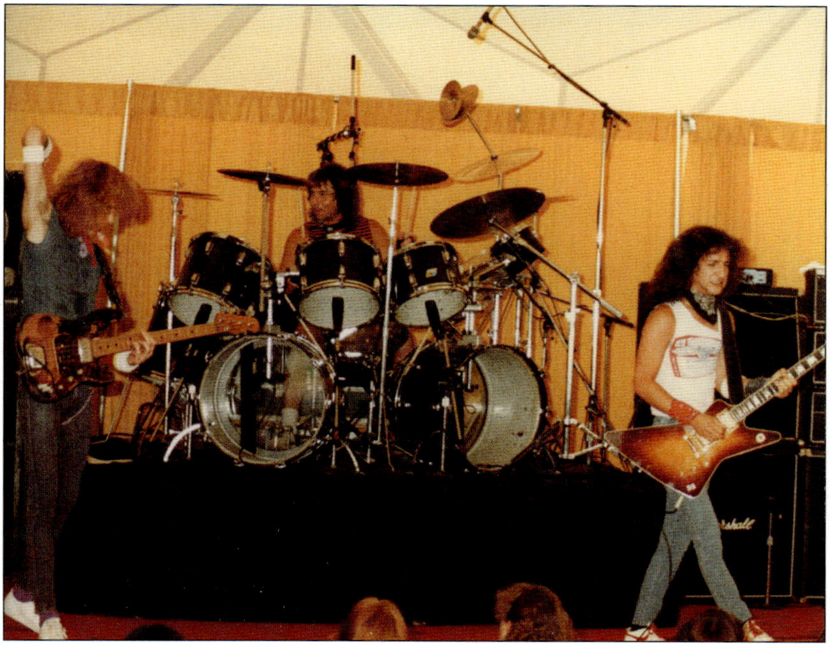

Buffalo rock band Talas performs under the Super Duper Music Dome during the 1983 Erie County Fair. The power trio was made up of Billy Sheehan on bass, Dave Constantino on guitar, and Paul Varga on drums.

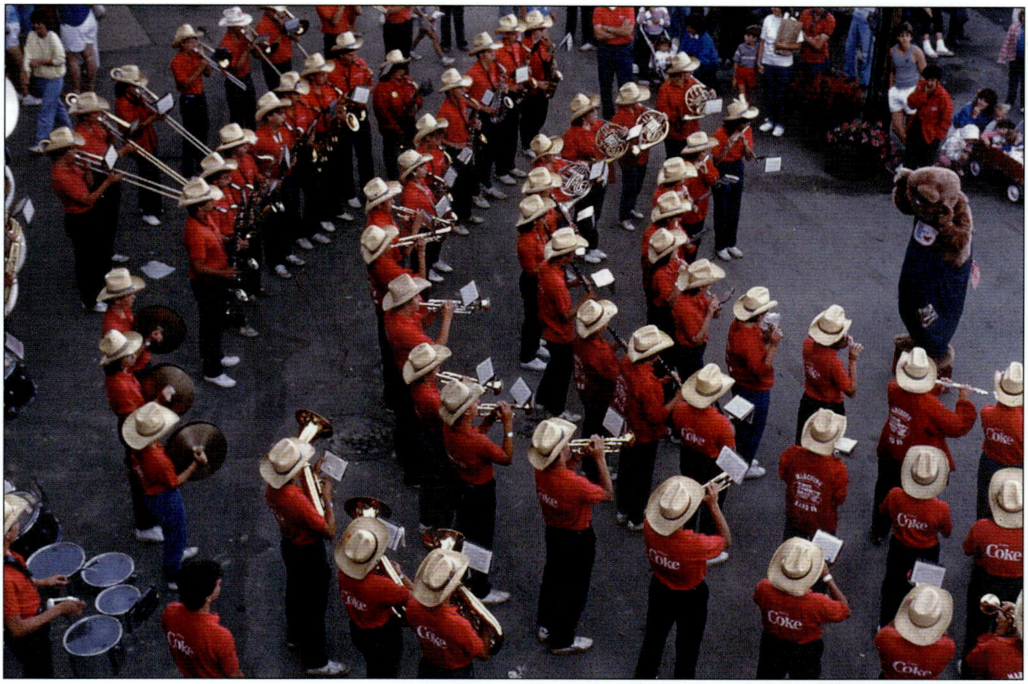

Over 100 members strong, the Erie County Fair Marching Band performs prior to the fair's daily parade in 1986. The band was founded in 1982 and features students from a variety of Erie County schools. The tradition celebrated 30 years in 2012.

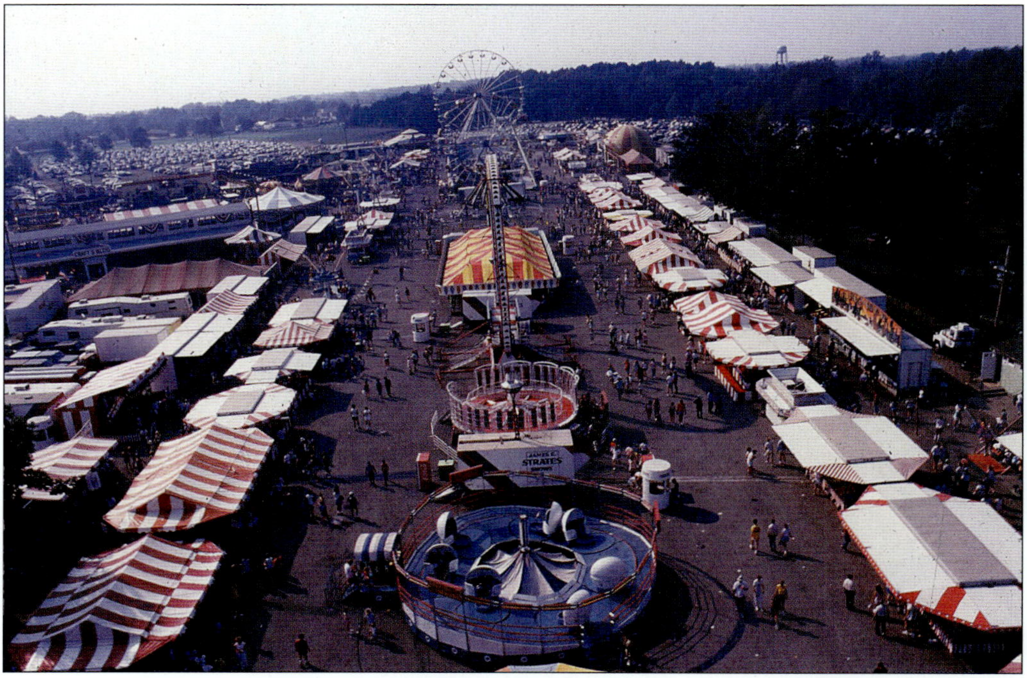

The brightest, lightest, most exciting place to be at the fair has always been the Strates Shows midway. This view of the midway was taken from the top of the Sky Wheel in 1987.

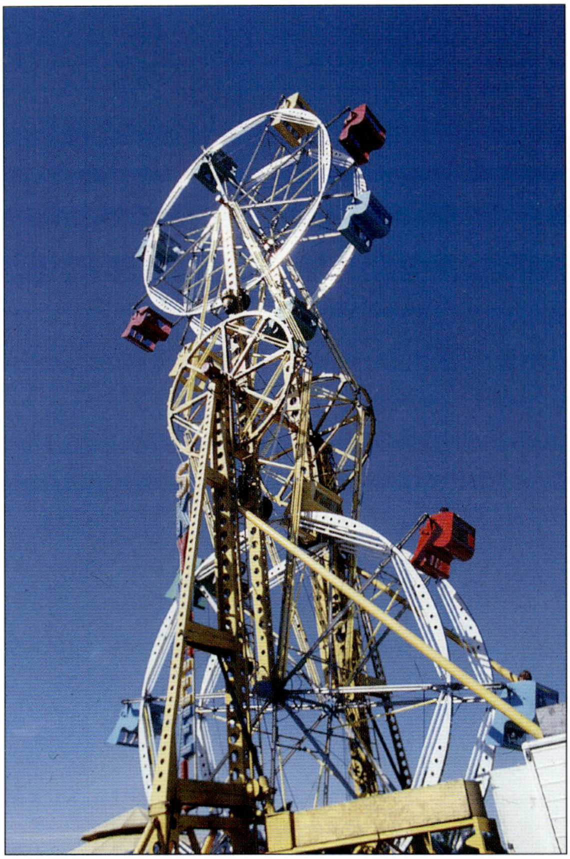

In 1960 the Allan Herschell Company of North Tonawanda, New York, purchased the exclusive rights to manufacture the 80-foot-high double Ferris wheel known as the Sky Wheel. Herschell secured the design from Curtis and Elmer Velare of Long Beach, California, who originated the basic design in the 1940s. The ride featured two traditional Ferris wheels attached to opposite ends of a large boom that rotated in the air. The Sky Wheel was a part of the Strates midway from 1963 to 1993 and again from 1996 to 1998. During its last three years at the fair, the ride was set up in Kiddieland.

The year 1987 marked the last appearance on the Strates Shows midway of its 1914 No. 28 Philadelphia Toboggan Company carousel (at the right). The ride entertained children at the Erie County Fair for over 40 years. In 2016, the Strates family donated one of the carousel's original horses for use in the fair's Heritage and History Center, located inside a renovated Octagon Building.

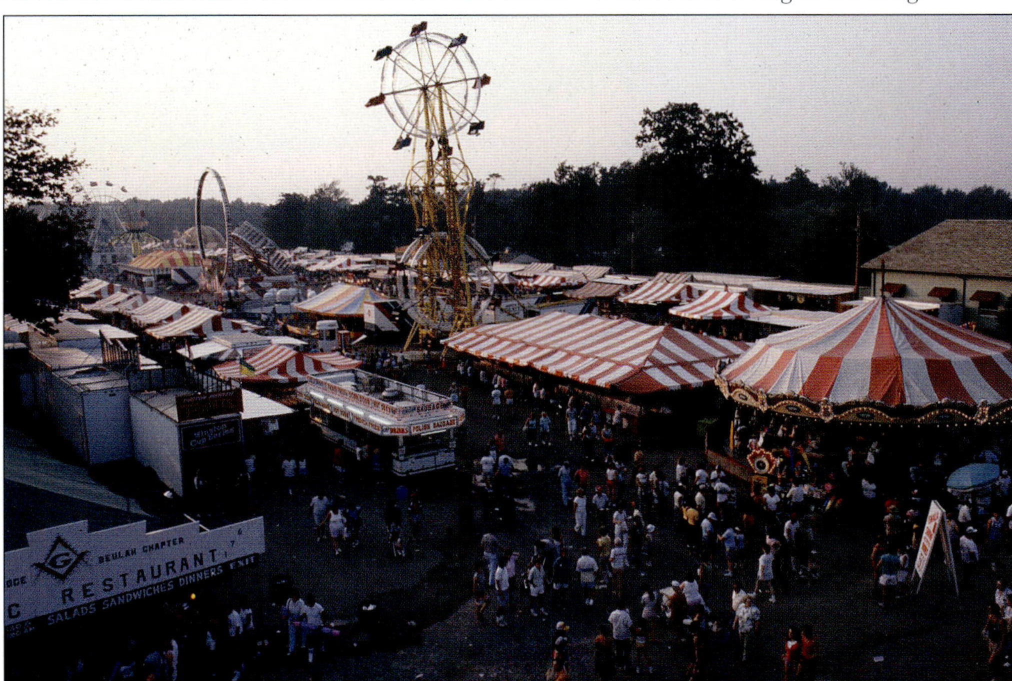

WXRL radio's Ramblin' Lou Schriver (left) shares a backstage moment with Boxcar Willie. Willie, whose real name was Lecil Travis Martin, brought his "old-time hobo" music to the Grandstand stage in 1984. Other featured entertainers in 1984 included Lee Greenwood, Ronnie Milsap, and Louise Mandrell.

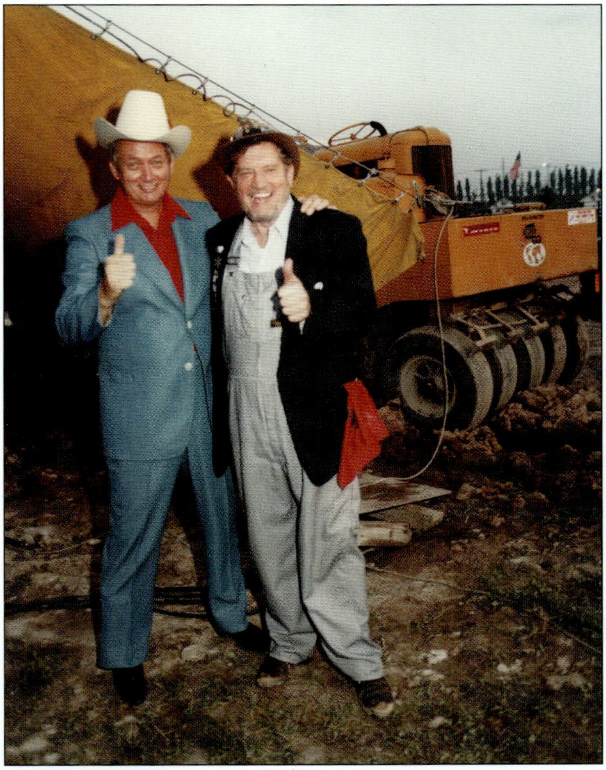

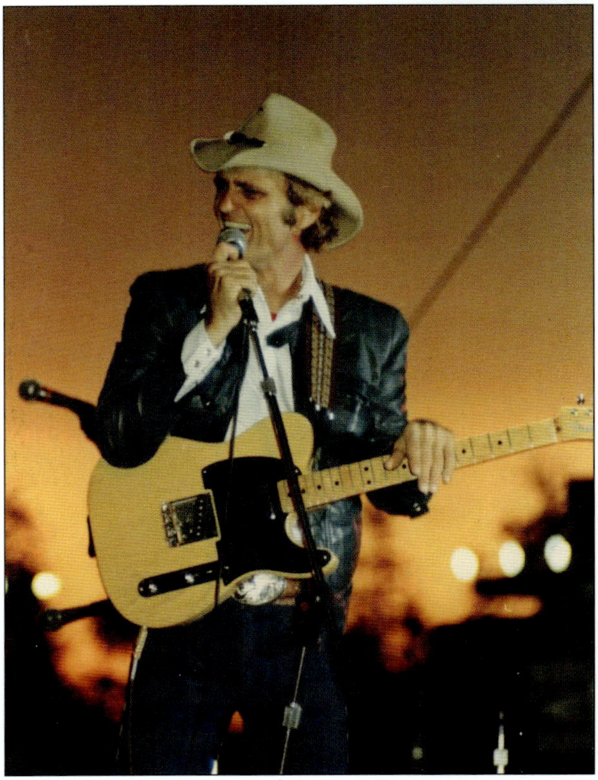

County music legend Jerry Reed plays his signature Fender Telecaster guitar during a 1981 performance on the Erie County Fair Grandstand stage. Reed was known as one of Nashville's greatest fingerpicking guitar players as well as an accomplished singer, songwriter, comedian, and actor. Reed stars alongside Burt Reynolds in the film *Smokey and the Bandit*.

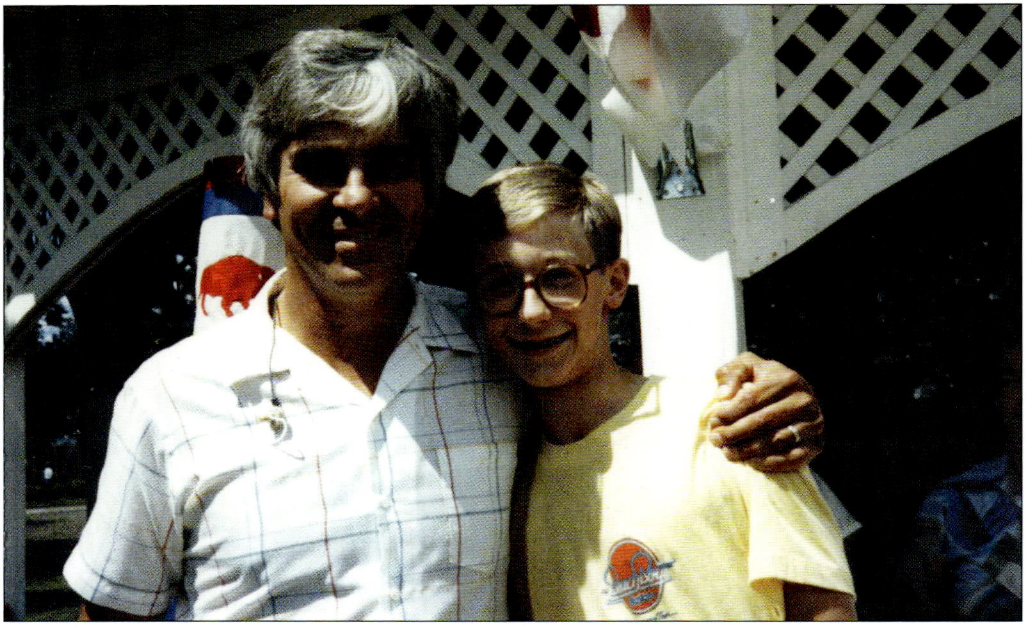

WKBW-TV weatherman Danny Neaverth poses with this book's author, Marty Biniasz, in front of the Channel 7 gazebo in 1986. A year earlier, WKBW-TV constructed the Victorian-style building in Slade Park as its permanent home at the fair. Neaverth spent over 40 years as a morning radio broadcaster in Buffalo, many of those years on WKBW radio.

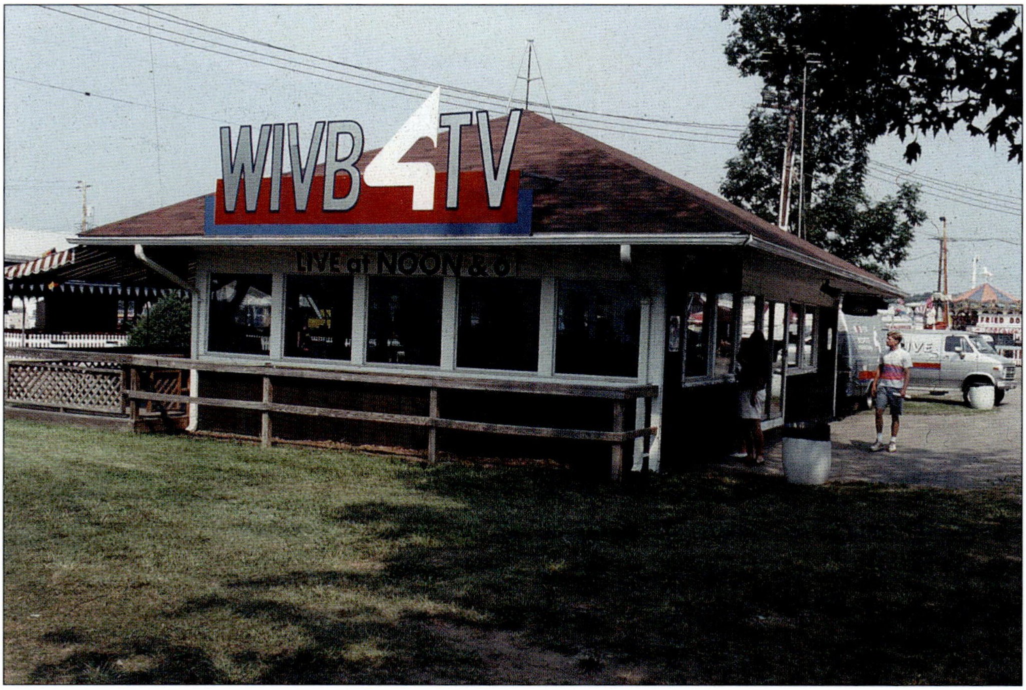

In 1985, WIVB-TV constructed a permanent studio on the Erie County Fairgrounds to originate its noon and 6:00 p.m. newscasts. The 24-by-40-foot studio featured windows on all sides to allow fairgoers to view live newscasts. Channel 4's Bob Koop, Carol Jasen, Van Miller, and chief meteorologist Don Paul were the featured broadcasters.

Five

The 1990s

America's County Fair

The Erie County Agricultural Society looked to greatly expand its geographic reach beyond the Buffalo-Niagara region as well as aggressively explore 12-month opportunities for use of the fairgrounds during the 1990s.

The theme "America's County Fair," first used for the sesquicentennial celebration in 1989, was adopted as a recurring slogan and used in conjunction with the fair name in 1990. The fair's 1991 theme, "Salute to Canada," was the first major effort to expand its marketing reach across the international border. It should be noted that in 2004, the recurring slogan was streamlined to "America's Fair" to position the Erie County Fair to a growing number of fairgoers in Canada and central New York State. In 2009, the fair dropped "America's Fair" to again focus its marketing efforts on its traditional Erie County Fair name.

Looking beyond the annual fair dates as a source of revenue, doors were opened on the new 74,000-square-foot, $4.5 million International AgriCenter in 1990. This multipurpose facility offered first-class exhibit space for consumer and business trade shows and events.

In 1992, Buffalo Raceway celebrated its 50th anniversary. Just two years earlier, the future of harness racing locally was insured as the Erie County Agricultural Society purchased the track's racing dates from Sportservice/Delaware North Companies, which had held the dates since 1968. Collectively, the trio made up of Buffalo Raceway, the AgriCenter, and fair would generate a combined attendance of over two million people annually to the fairgrounds. After $900,000 in track renovations and the stabilization of finances, revenue derived from the track contributed to the never-ending upkeep of the fairgrounds.

Expanding the fair from 10 to 11 days in 1993 resulted in another recording-breaking year. Total attendance reached 898,907. Another single-day attendance record was broken with 141,002 fairgoers on Sunday, August 15, 1993. The year 1995 was the first in the fair's history in which attendance reached the one million mark. The 11-day event welcomed 1,018,157 to the fairgrounds.

In 1999, a 75-year milestone with the James E. Strates Shows was celebrated by the fair. Back in 1924, the Strates family first brought its midway filled with rides, sideshows, and games to Hamburg for the Erie County Fair.

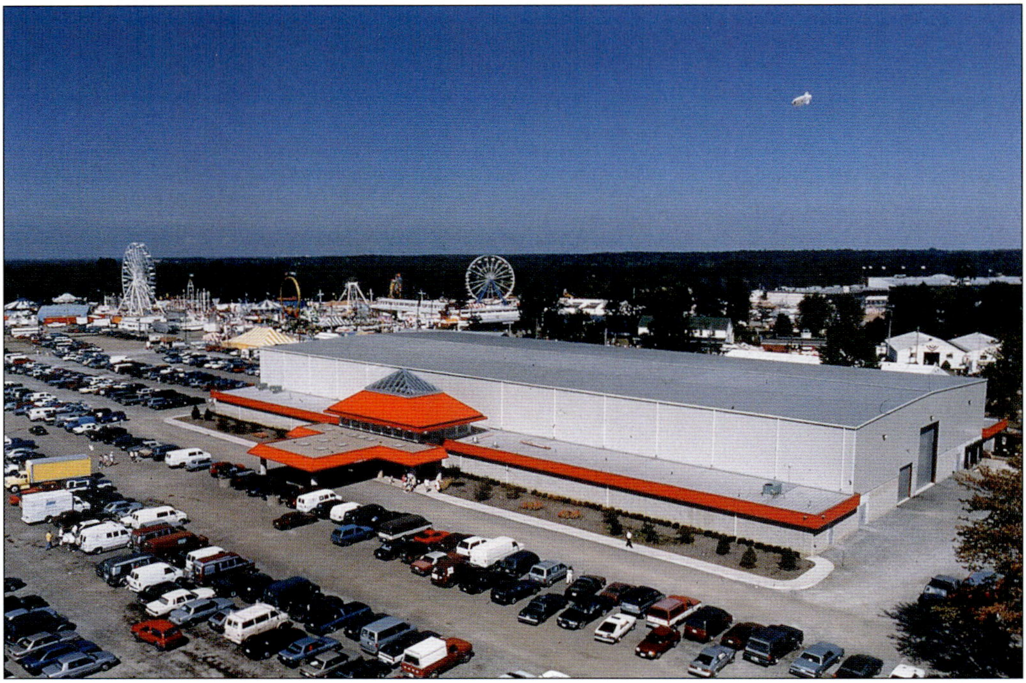

The opening of the 74,000-square-foot International AgriCenter in 1990 not only expanded the shopping choices during the fair, but also opened the Agricultural Society up to non-fair revenue the rest of the year. From trade shows to the Shrine Circus, the versatile event center became a year-round destination in Buffalo Southtowns.

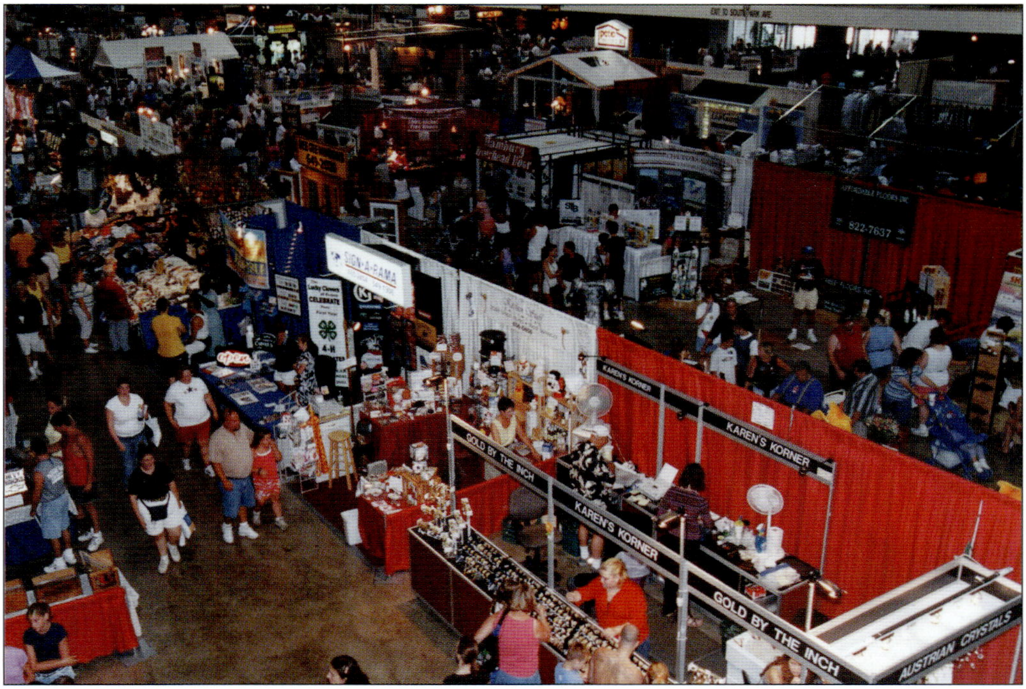

Everything from kitchen gadgets and hot tubs to telescoping flagpoles and toe rings could be found inside the International AgriCenter during the fair.

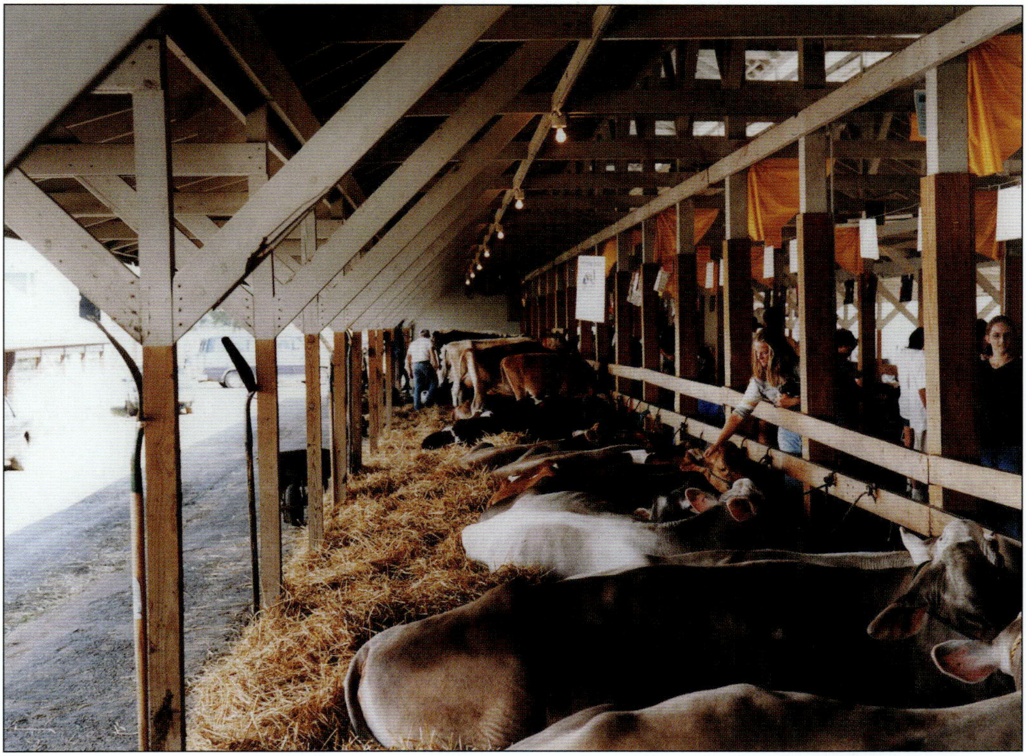

A gentle summer breeze drifts through the open-air floor plan of Barn 5. Originally constructed in the 1900s, the cattle barn was replaced by the Agriculture Discovery Center in 2014.

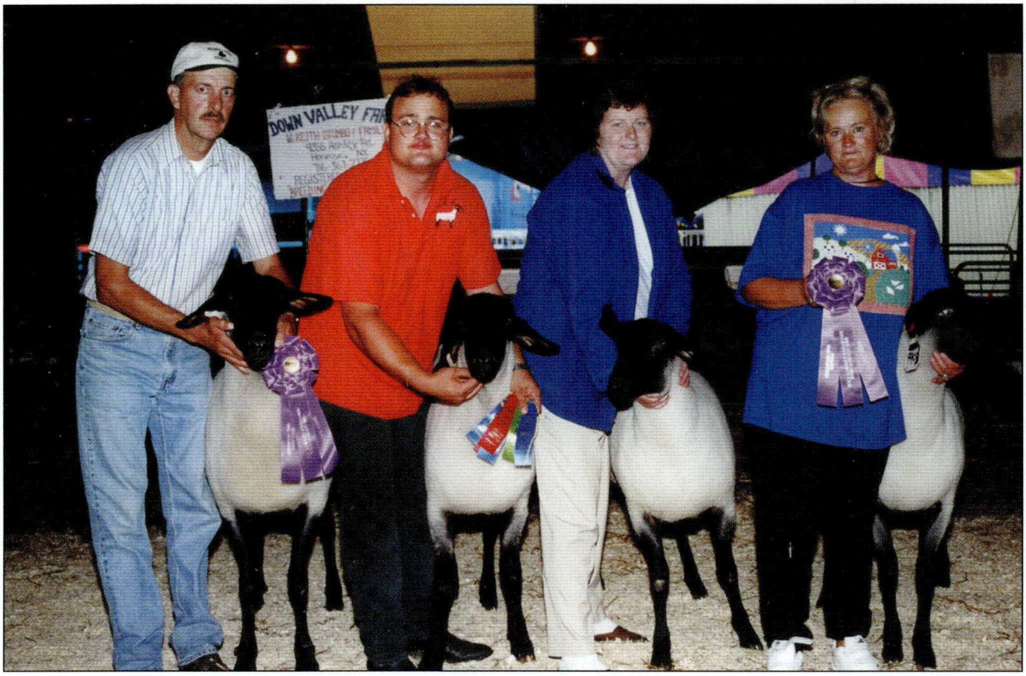

From left to right are Richard Feasley and his flock, including Dan Fitzpatrick, Peggy Galuski, and Linda Feasley along with the farm's yearling ewe, fall ram, fall ewe, and spring ewe.

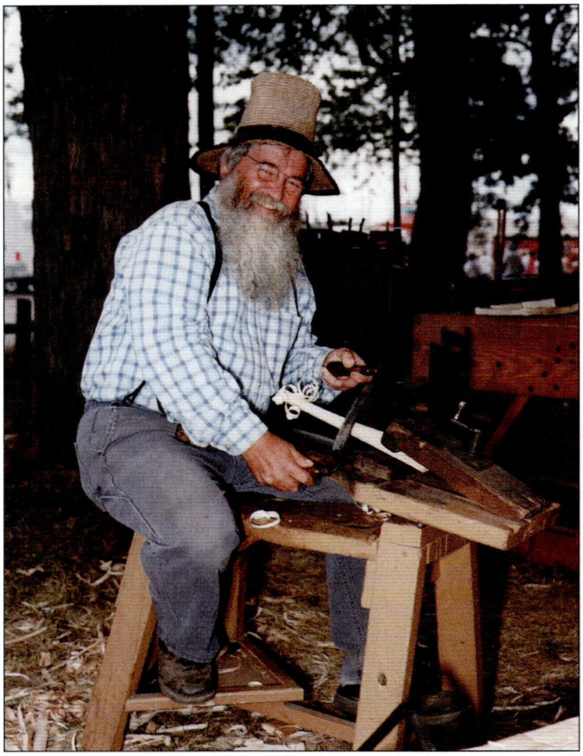

In 1994, Nick Nichols and his "old tool chest" could be found at a tree-shaded spot outside of the Historical Building. For nearly 25 years, Nick shared funny stories, jokes, and a wealth of historical information about vintage tools and traditional building methods as part of the fair's historical demonstration program.

Ringmaster Bill Carpenter invited children and their families to create memories during "The Backyard Circus" and "Midway Caravan." Props, costumes, and plenty of imagination were blended together to transform kids into animals and circus performers. Carpenter first brought his show to the fair in 1986 and was inducted into the Erie County Fair Hall of Fame in 2009. He retired from the business in 2012 and passed away in 2015.

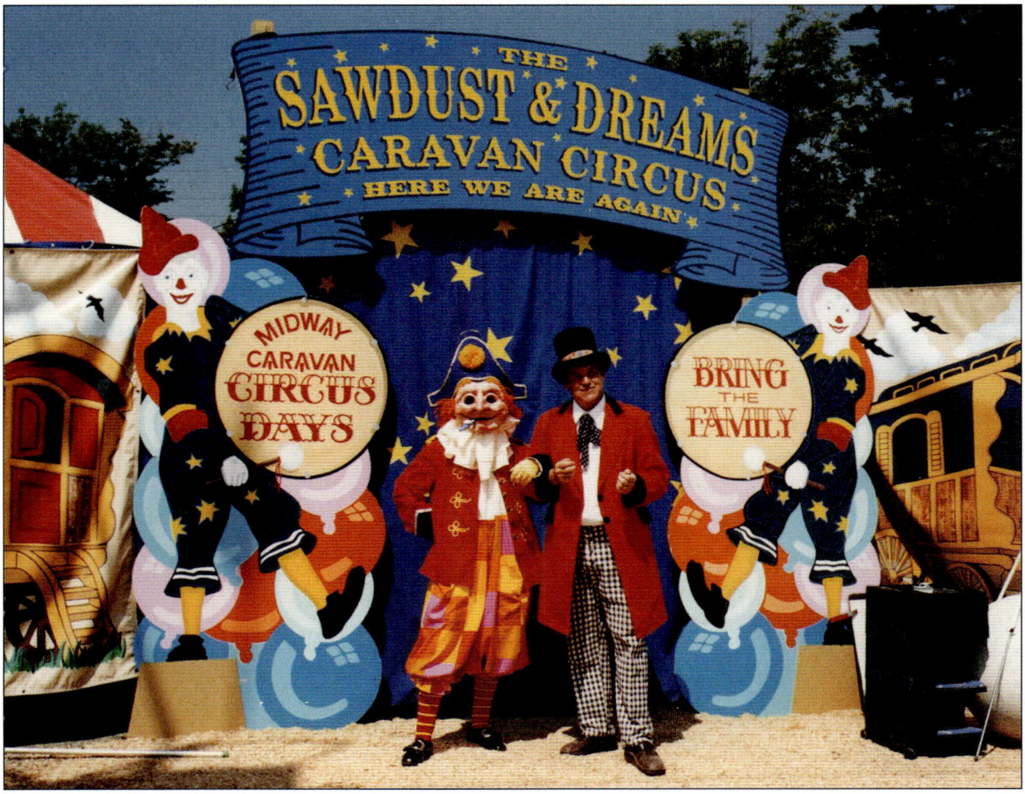

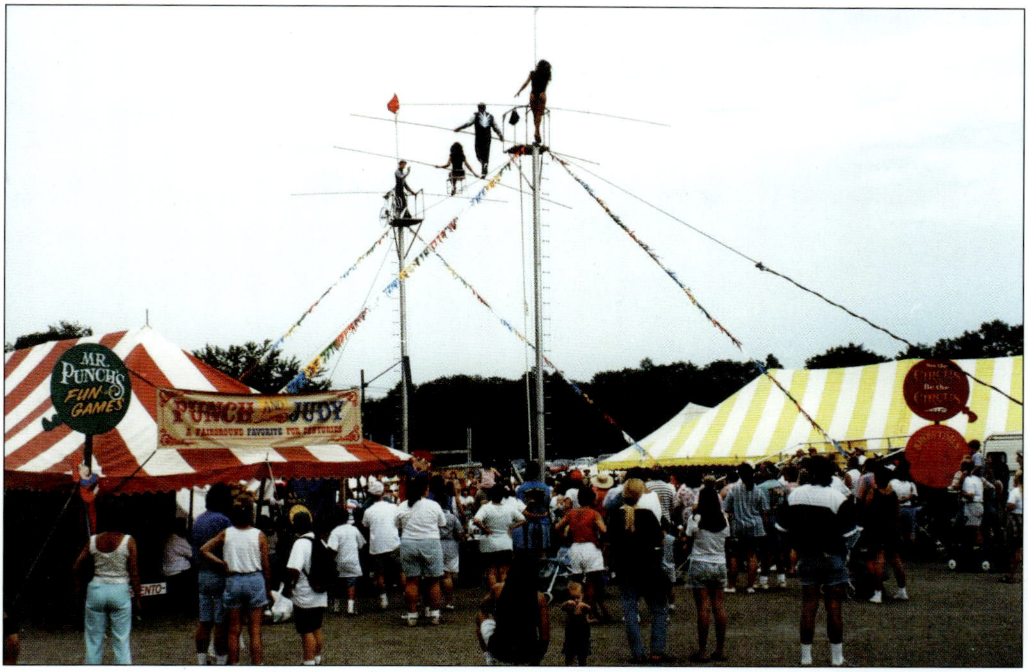

Members of the famous Flying Wallendas family perform during the 1995 Erie County Fair. The performance marked the Erie County Fair debut of 16-year-old Nik Wallenda. Nineteen years later, Nik would appear at the fair once again to attempt one of the longest skywalks of his career.

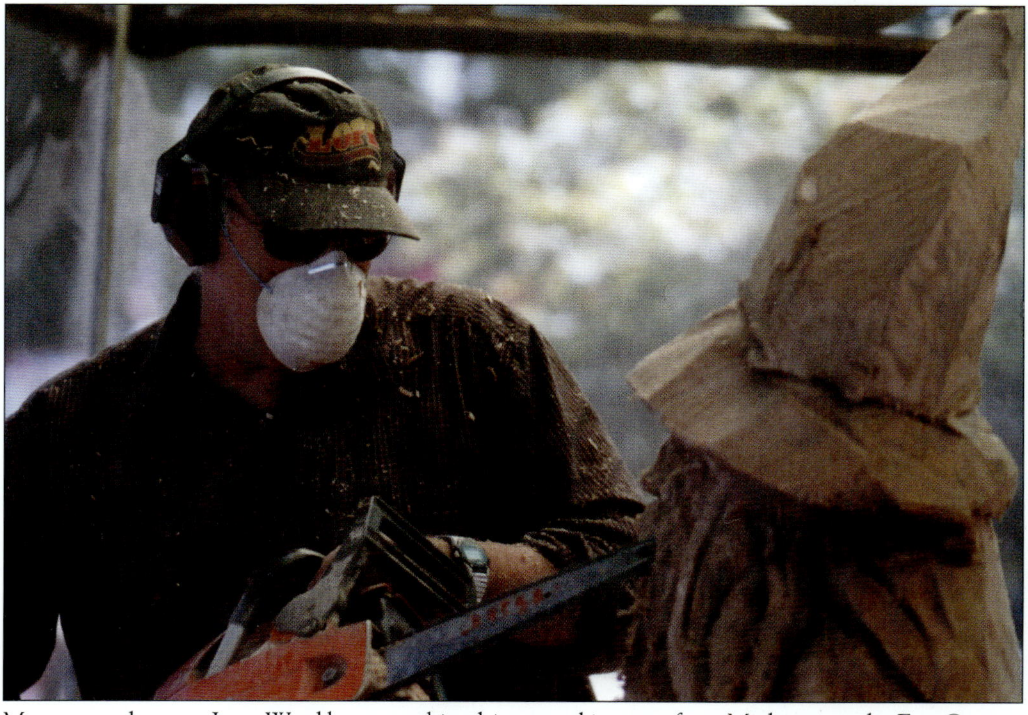

Master wood-carver Jerry Ward began making his annual journey from Michigan to the Erie County Fair in 1976. He is considered a pioneer of his craft for when he began using a chain saw instead of hand carving wood. Ward was inducted into the Erie County Fair Hall of Fame in 2011.

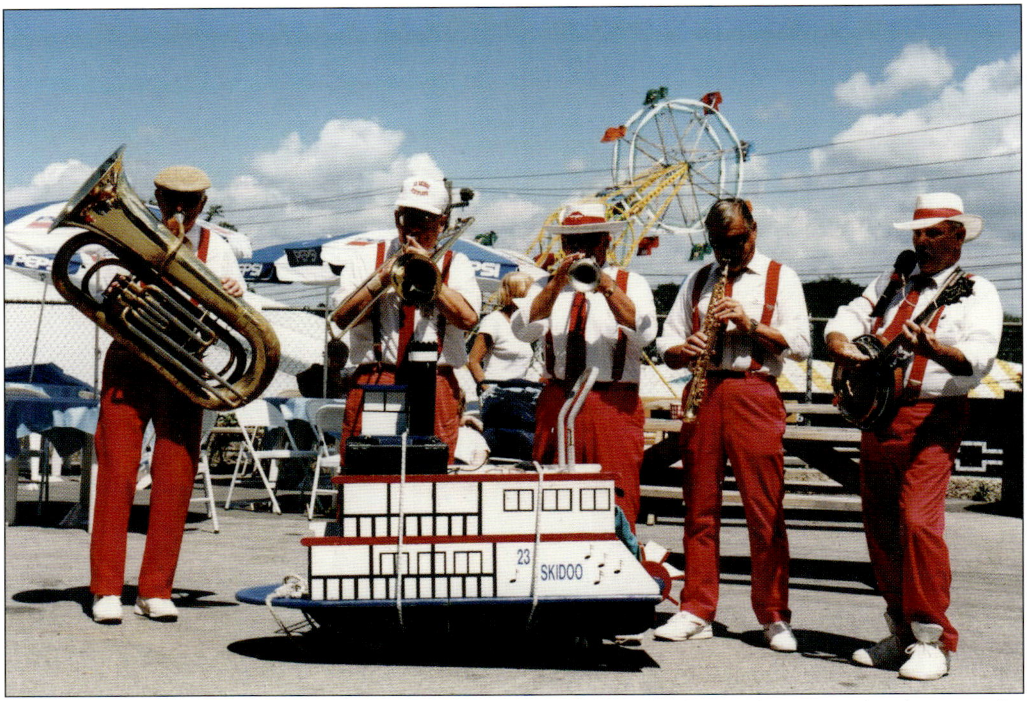

In 1986, Dick O'Dell's 23 Skidoo (pictured) took over the job of providing Dixieland jazz at the fair from the legendary Clayton Fatty band.

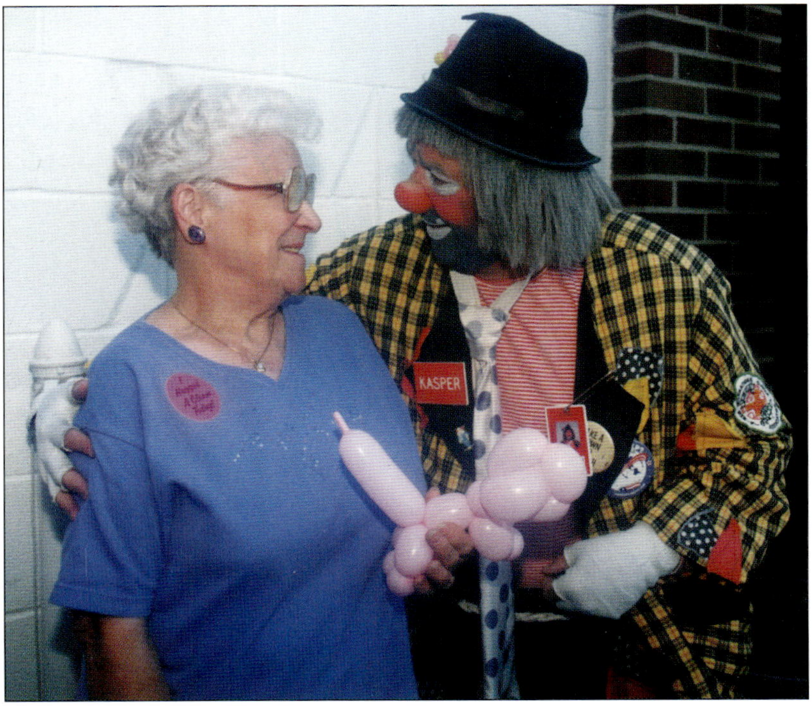

Don Heidenburg, known as Kasper the Clown, goofs around with Marie Backstorm on Senior Day in 1998. Heidenburg, a member of the Friends of the Fair clown group, was inducted into the Erie County Fair Hall of Fame in 2004.

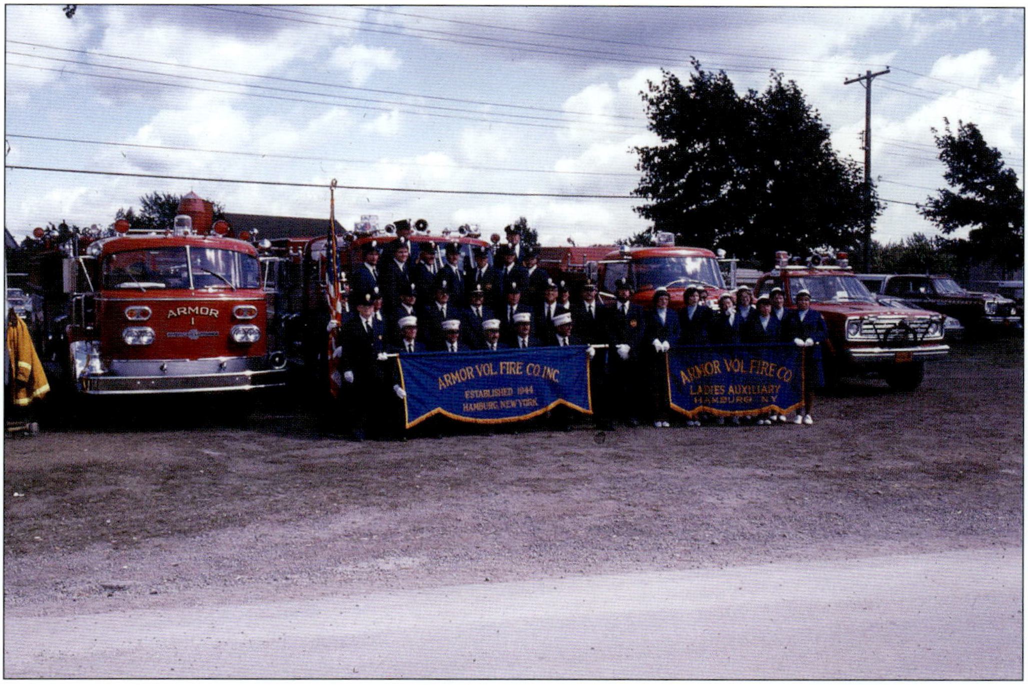

Since 1944, the Armor Fire Department has been providing emergency services to the Erie County Fair. As the fair's official fire department, Armor has its own fire station on the fairgrounds, located near Gate 6.

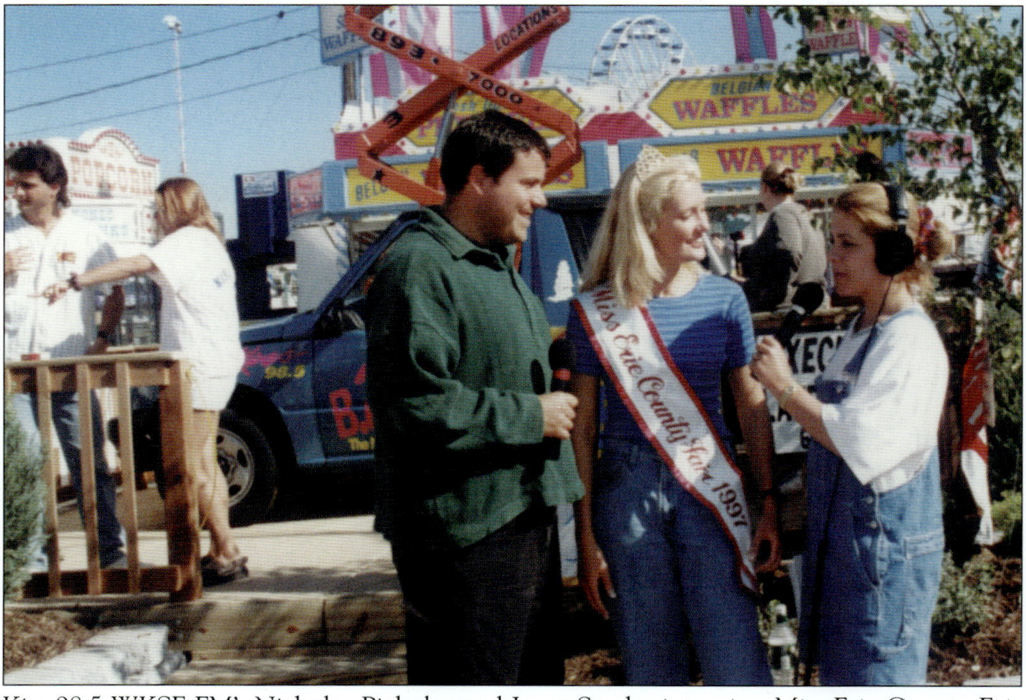

Kiss 98.5 WKSE-FM's Nicholas Picholas and Janet Snyder interview Miss Erie County Fair 1997 Ashley Sigrist during the radio station's infamous B.O. Geo contest. During the stunt, four contestants had to live day and night in a hot, stinky car for the entire run of the fair.

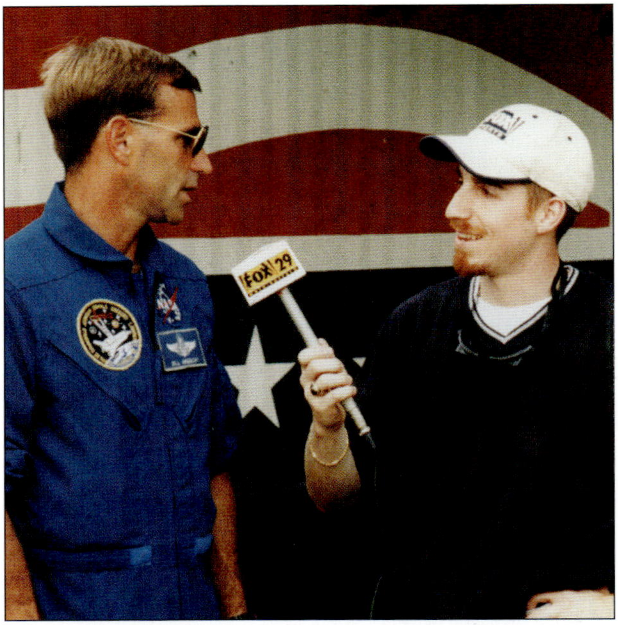

Under the theme "Out of this World," the 1998 fair featured a visit by NASA astronaut and Western New York native Lt. Col. William Gregory. As a space shuttle crew member, Gregory logged over 400 hours in space. In this image, Gregory is interviewed by WUTV's Craig Scime for his program *U's Place*.

Channel 4's Kevin O'Connell and Carol Jasen prepare to broadcast from the WIVB Erie County Fair Studios in 1990. Jasen had a legendary 23-year career in Buffalo, joining WIVB in 1979, when she became the first female anchor at Channel 4. O'Connell first joined Channel 4 in the mid-1970s and moved to WGRZ-TV in 1993.

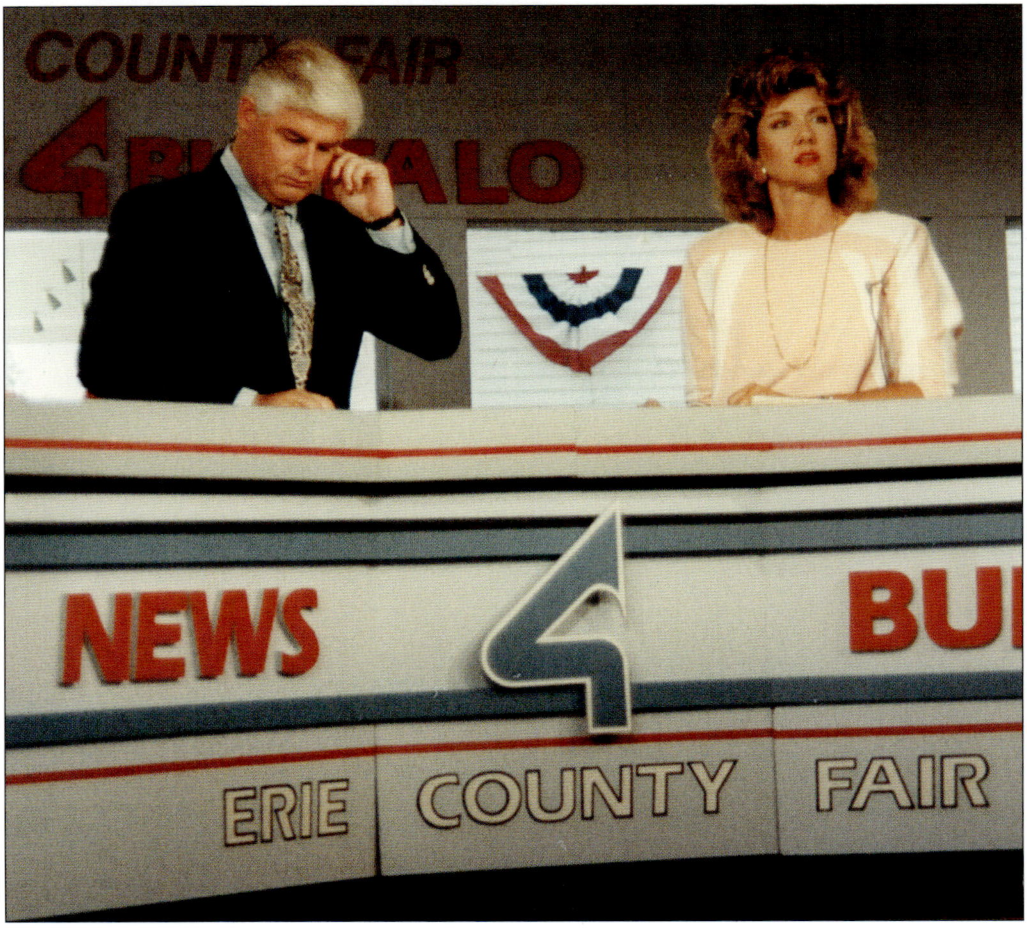

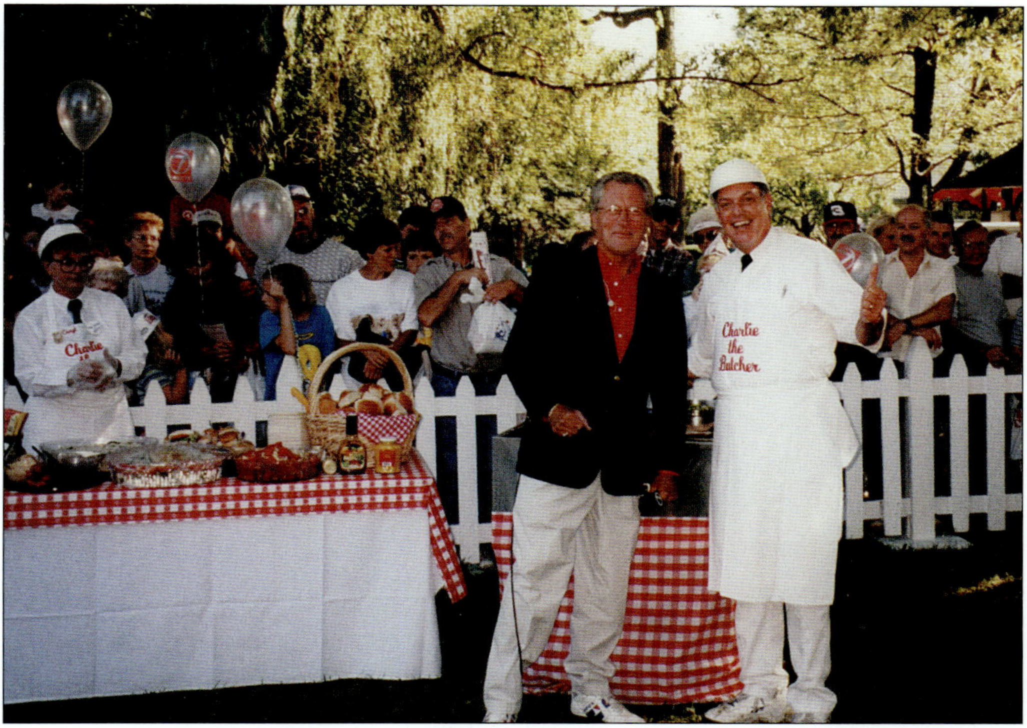

What is more Buffalo than beef-on-weck sandwiches, the "Commander," and the Erie County Fair? WKBW-TV's Tom Jolls interviews Charlie "the Butcher" Roesch during one of his many weather segments at the Channel 7 Gazebo in Slade Park. From 1965 to 1991, Jolls was host of one of the most popular kids' TV shows in Buffalo broadcasting history. In 1995, Jolls was inducted into the Erie County Fair Hall of Fame.

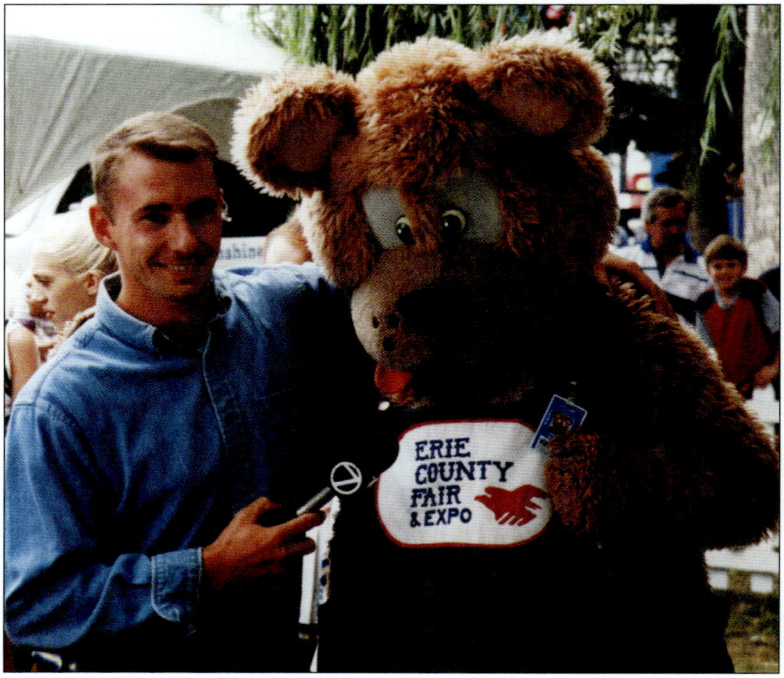

WKBW-TV meteorologist Andy Parker poses with Farley McFair the Fair Bear in 1999 at the Channel 7 Gazebo. After a stint at WGRZ-TV, Parker returned to WKBW-TV and broadcasted live from the fair in 2014.

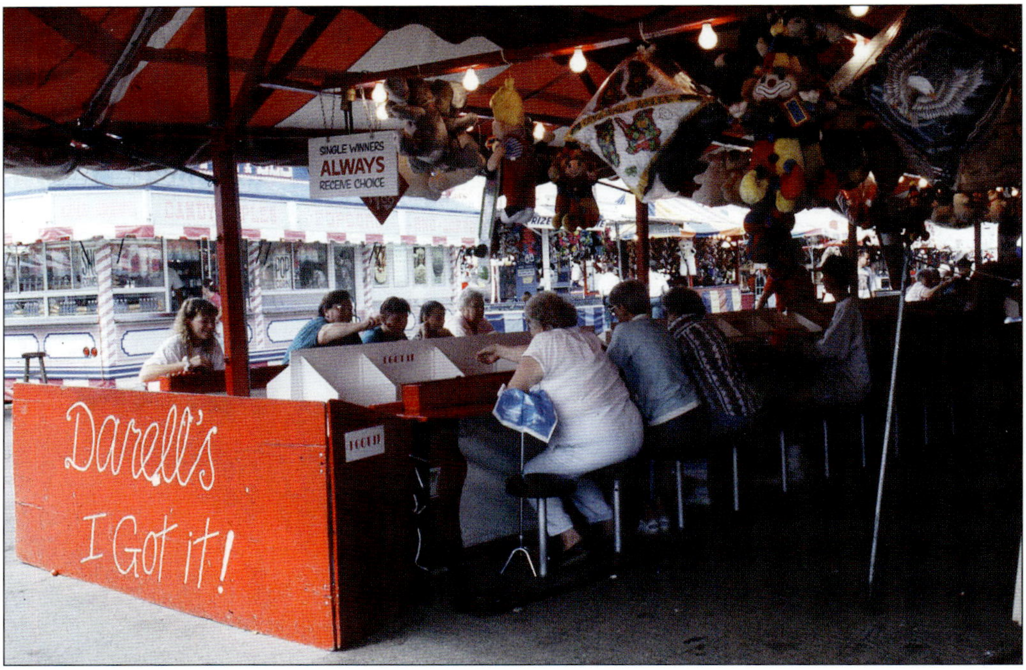

The tradition of throwing a pink rubber ball into a wooden bin and watching it bounce around until it rests was still popular in 1994. "I Got It" was invented by Orchard Park's Orrin "Peck" Catlin while he was a member of the Big Tree Fire Company. This image shows "I Got It" on the Strates Shows midway.

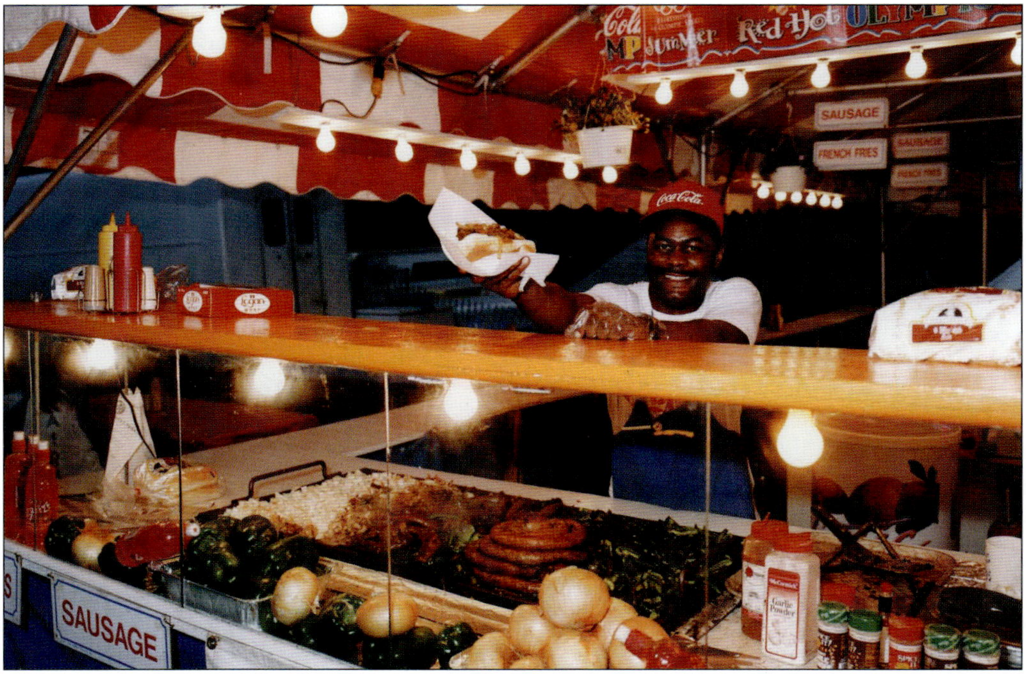

A fair tradition that teases the senses and can be found at almost every corner of the fairgrounds is the selling of freshly prepared Italian sausages loaded with peppers and onions. This picture features a stand run by Santillo's Concessions, which was founded in 1934.

During the 1990s, the third generation of the Strates family joined the business founded by their grandfather James E. Strates in 1923. James E. (left) and John E. Strates, pictured in front of the Wave Swinger, joined their father E. James Strates and siblings Susan Strates Magid, Sibyl Strates Doremus, and E. Jay Strates in keeping the carnival tradition going strong. The Wave Swinger ride first appeared in 1989, when it replaced the popular swing ride called the Yoyo.

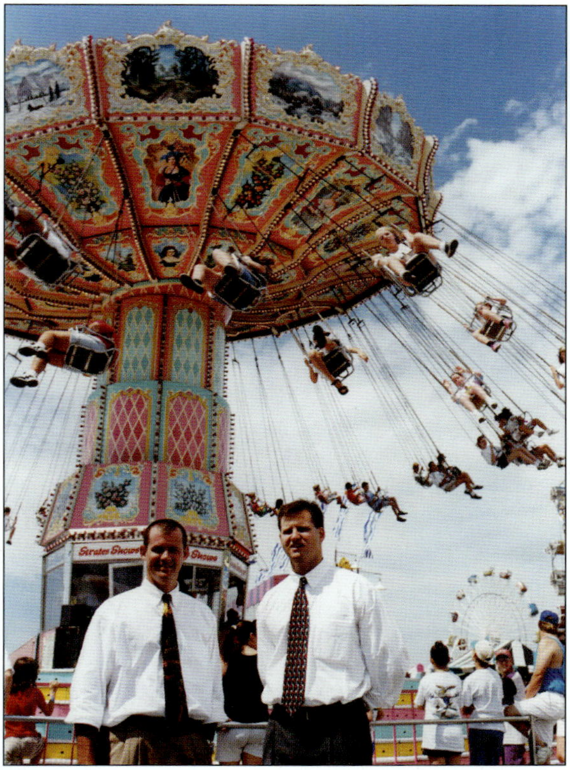

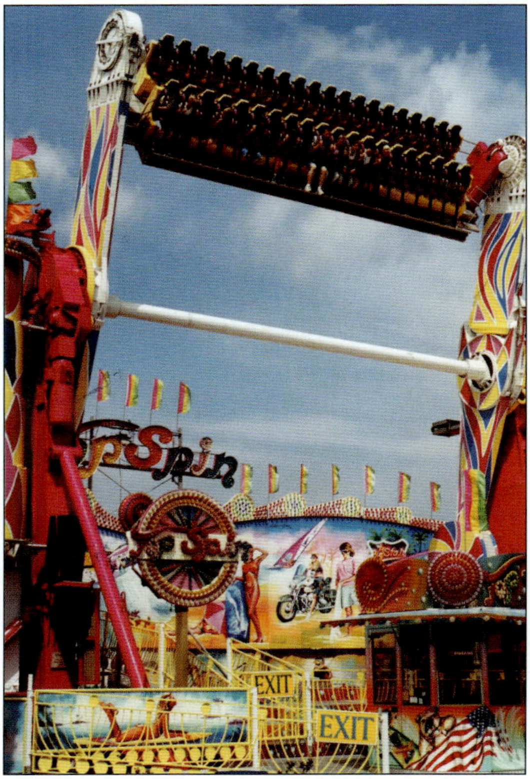

In 1997, the James E. Strates Shows added the Top Spin ride to its famous mile long midway. The multimillion dollar machine sent riders into a swing pattern of overhead loops and end-over-end spins, creating g-forces up to 4.0. Though it was normally relegated to amusement parks due to its size and weight, Strates Shows was able to transport the ride because it traveled by railroad.

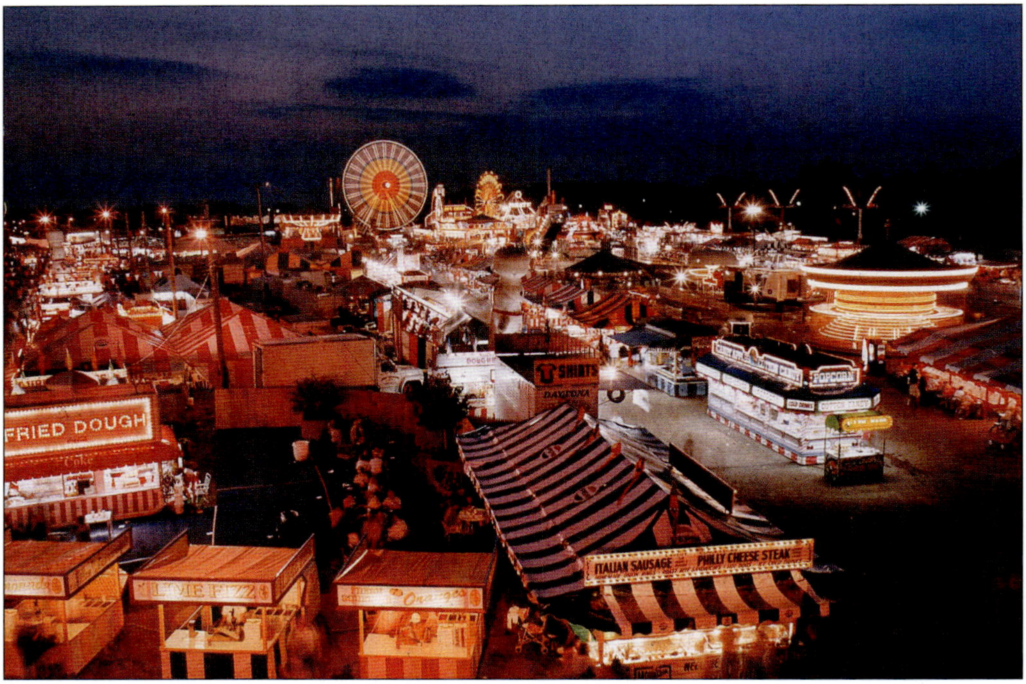

Since 1987, the Big Wheel has provided a dazzling backdrop to the Strates Shows midway. Taken from the roof of the Clubhouse, this panoramic view captures the magic of the midway in 1998.

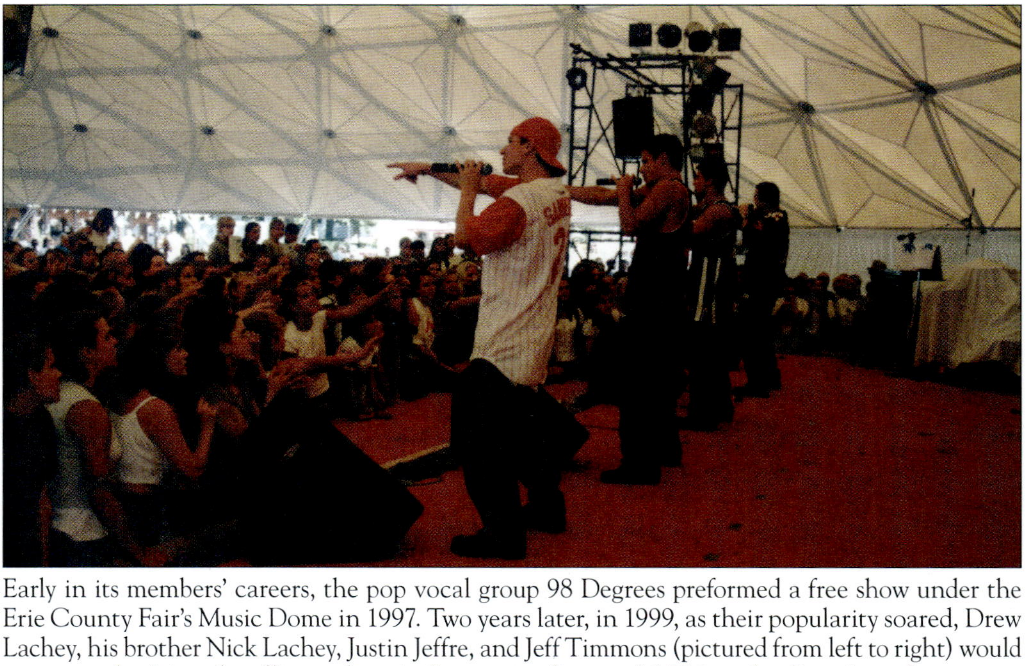

Early in its members' careers, the pop vocal group 98 Degrees preformed a free show under the Erie County Fair's Music Dome in 1997. Two years later, in 1999, as their popularity soared, Drew Lachey, his brother Nick Lachey, Justin Jeffre, and Jeff Timmons (pictured from left to right) would return to the fair to headline a show in front an audience of 9,000 in the Grandstand.

Six

The 2000s

Growing Strong

Challenges, opportunities, and new leadership awaited the Erie County Fair at the start of the millennium. With a family history at the fair dating back to the 1940s, Dennis Lang was appointed CEO/fair manager in late 1999. At that time, the fair faced a growing year-round infrastructure that included a collection of heritage buildings, barns that were no longer adequate for the proper housing and showing of animals, and utilities and sewers that needed updating.

In an effort to reverse the trend of decreasing revenue from pari-mutuel wagering at Buffalo Raceway, Fairgrounds Gaming and Raceway opened on St. Patrick's Day in 2004. Located inside a renovated Grandstand, the facility featured 996 video lottery terminals. In future years, revenue derived from the racino-style gaming would allow the society to embark on the biggest capital improvement campaign since the 1960s.

With animal comfort and safety a priority, the upgrading of livestock barns along McKinley Parkway that took place culminated with the opening of the Showplex Arena in 2010. Fairgoers welcomed new amenities that included upgraded parkland, with a new First Aid Building and lavatory complex in 2014. The Art Deco Firemen's Building, originally built in 1935, received a $600,000 restoration in 2012.

The importance of agriculture has changed dramatically over the past six decades. The region began to lose farmland in the 1950s when development pushed out from the city of Buffalo into first- and second-ring suburbs. According to Jessica Underberg, assistant fair manager and manager of agriculture, "98 percent of the public is not directly involved with agriculture. Our mission is to provide the vehicle where we can educate that 98 percent about what we do." To fulfill the society's mission and in celebration of the 175th Erie County Fair, the Agriculture Discovery Center opened in 2014. The building was the first structure on the fairgrounds dedicated exclusively to year-round agriculture education.

With the theme of "Growing Strong," the 2014 Erie County Fair experienced an all-time record-breaking gate attendance of 1,220,101, giving it the honor of being named the 10th-largest fair in North America. The ranking of fairs, based on attendance, includes all county and state fairs, exhibitions, and livestock and rodeo shows in the United States and Canada.

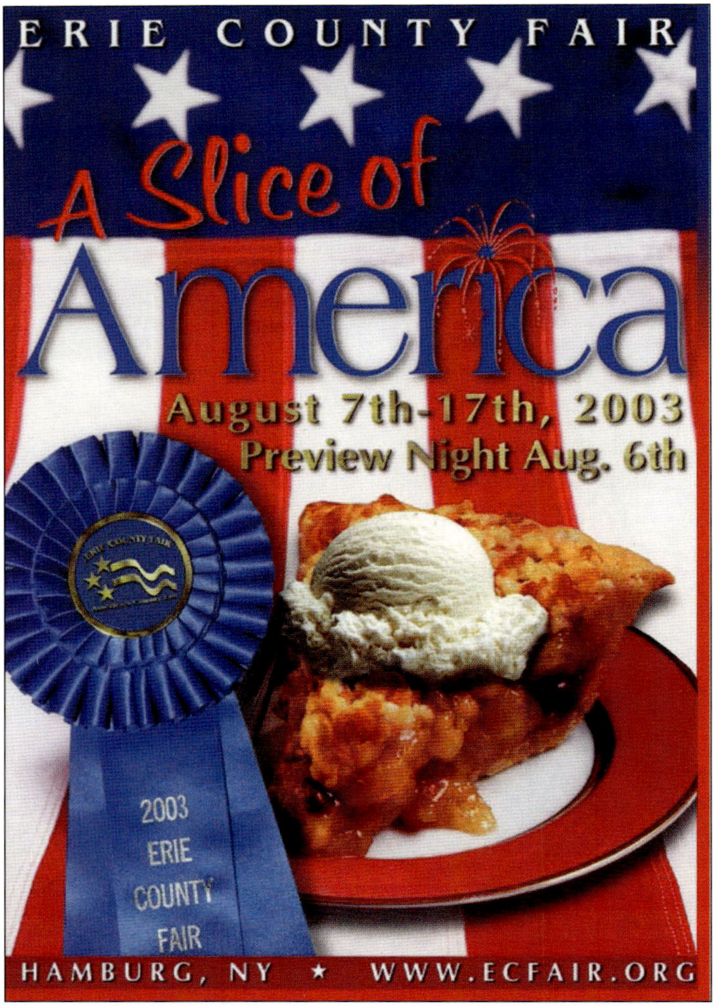

Following the terrorist attacks of September 11, 2001, people across America yearned for simpler times and traditions like those found at county fairs. With patriotism at an all-time high, CEO Dennis Lang asked the community in 2002 to "join us as we stand a little bit taller, sing a little bit louder and feel a little bit prouder when we come together and share the spirit of America." Again in 2003, patriotism was the focus as the fair served up a "Slice of America."

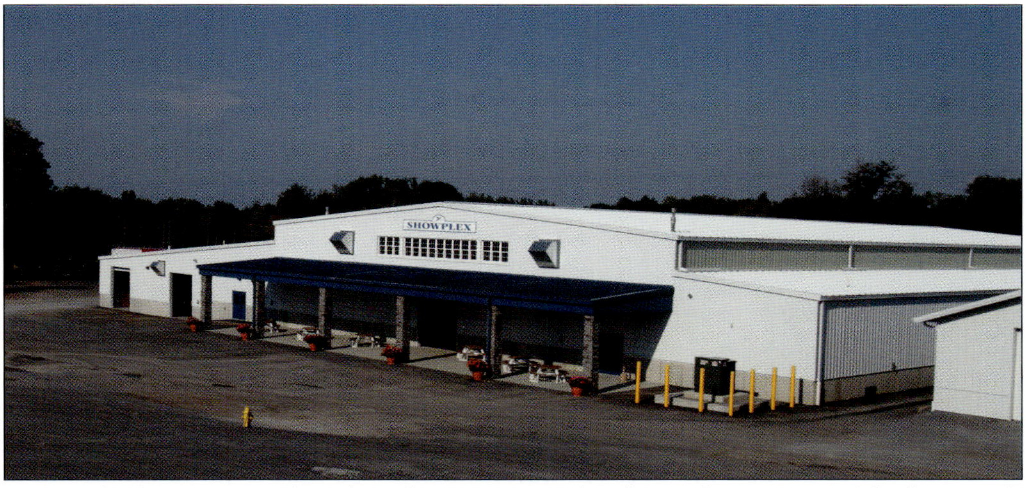

In 2010, the 52,000-square-foot Showplex arena opened in the northeast corner of the fairgrounds and featured a 125-by-225-foot show ring.

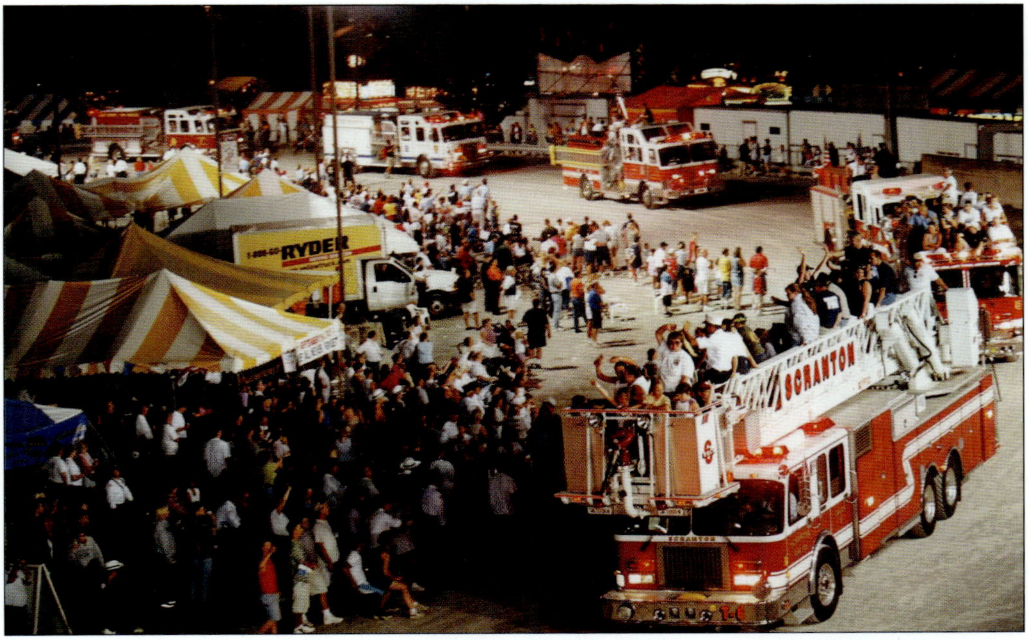

Firefighters Day is a long-standing Erie County Fair tradition that brings together first responders and their families for a day of reflecting, picnicking, and parading. Held the first Friday of the fair, the highlight of the festivities is the giant Firefighters Parade around the track, featuring a dazzling display of fire trucks and flashing lights.

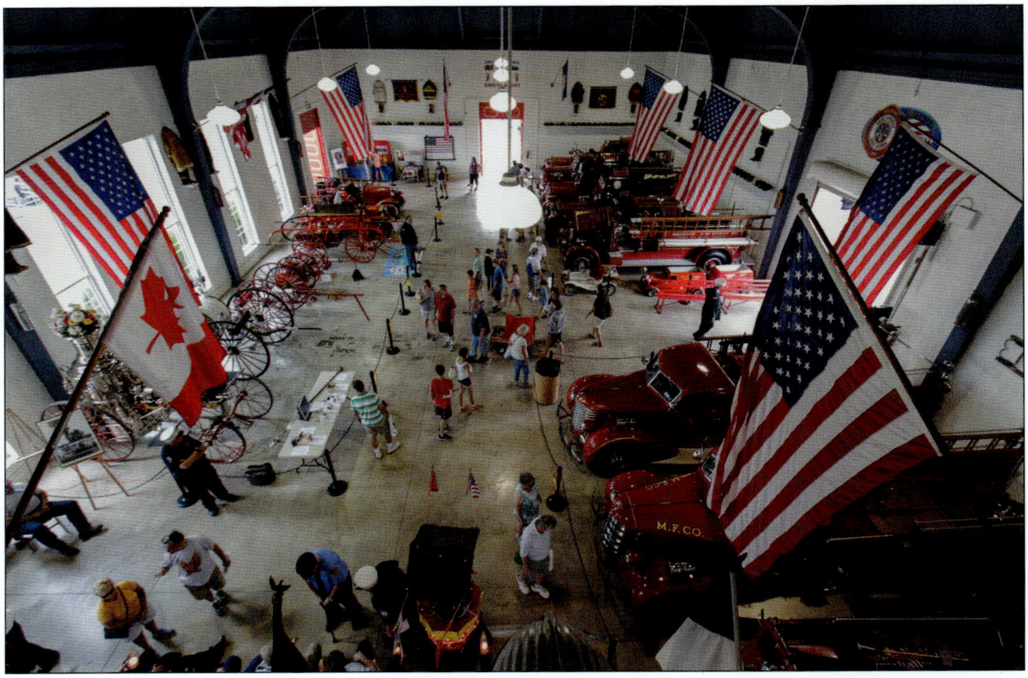

Since 1936, the Art Deco Firemen's Building has hosted educational display on fire prevention and housed both modern and antique firefighting apparatus. More importantly, the building serves as a memorial to the thousands of men and women who volunteer as first responders. In 2011, the structure was completely renovated at a cost of $750,000.

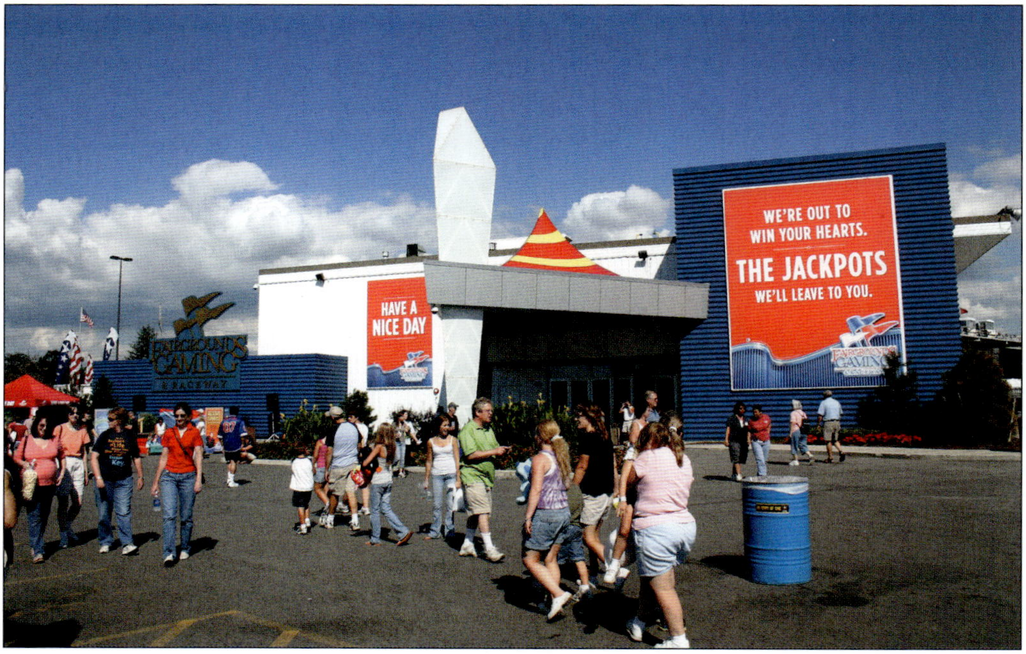

Fairgrounds Gaming and Raceway opened its doors on St. Patrick's Day 2004 inside the lower Grandstand. The facility featured 996 video lottery terminals in a racino-style environment. In 2010, the center moved to its own build adjacent to the Event Center near the South Park Avenue entrance to the fairgrounds.

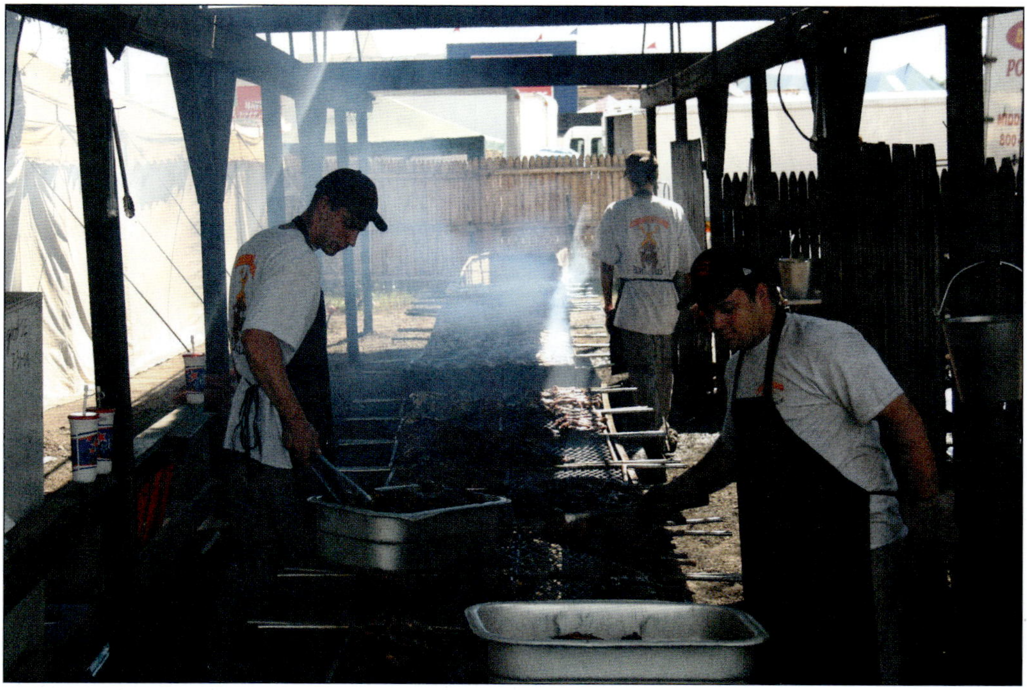

Smoke rising from the grills lifts the smell of barbecue chicken throughout the fairgrounds. Founded by poultry farmers Thomas and Eleanor Chiavetta, Chiavetta's celebrated 50 years of serving up chicken dinners to hungry fairgoers in 2007.

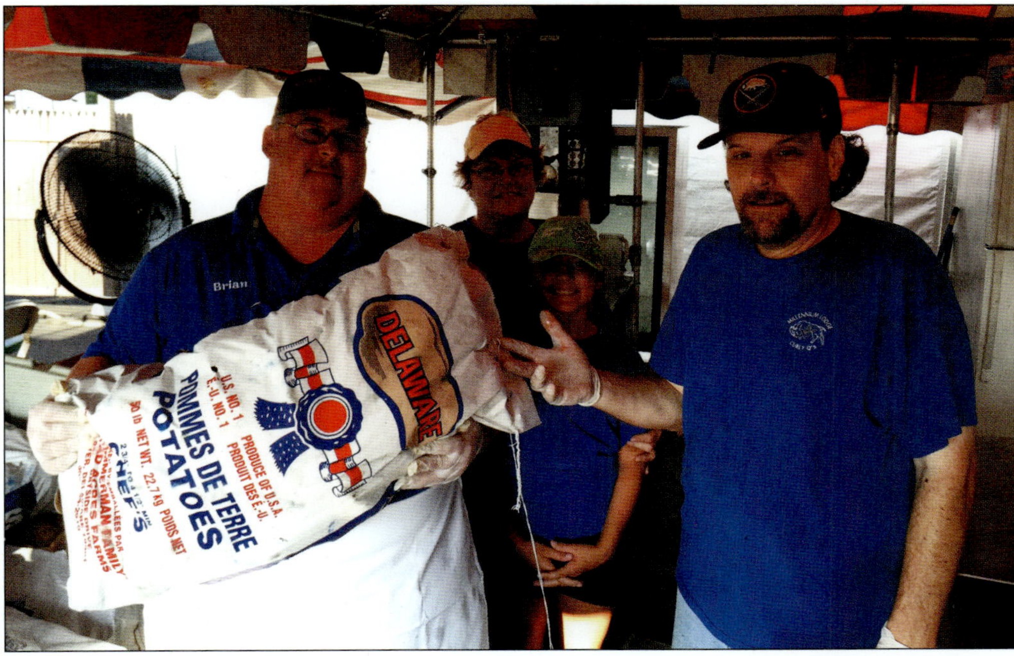

In 2013, members of the Millennium Lodge No. 1169 celebrated 50 years of suppling hungry fairgoers with fresh curlycue french fries. Volunteers arrive on the fairgrounds each day at 6:00 a.m. to prepare for hungry fairgoers. The lodge uses 15,000 pounds of potatoes during the 12 days of the fair as members serve up fresh-cut curlycue fries.

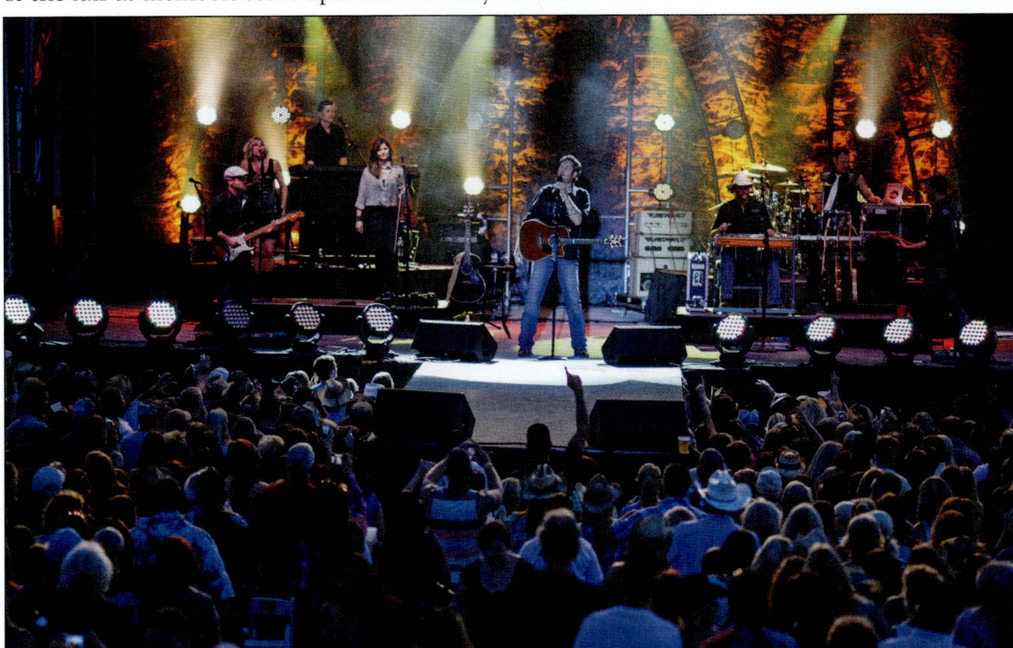

County star Blake Shelton performs to a near capacity Buffalo.com Grandstand crowd in the summer of 2012. Shelton, who stars as a judge on NBC's singing competition show *The Voice*, had fans rocking with a set that ranged from a cover of Bobby Brown's "My Prerogative" to his own hit ballad "She Wouldn't Be Gone."

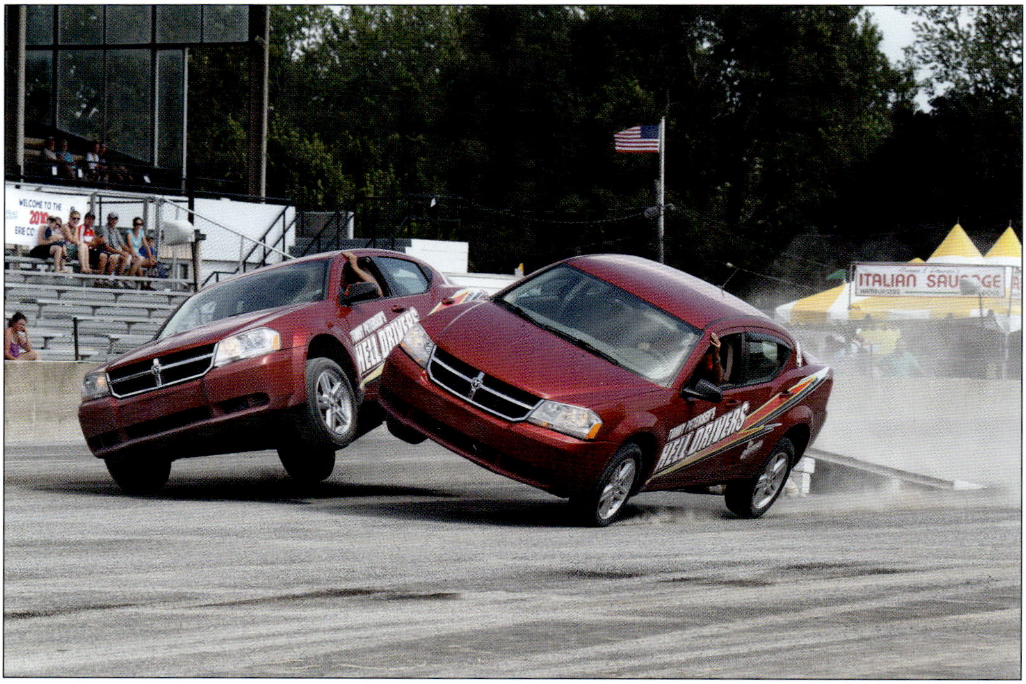

In the tradition of Grandstand shows from the 1950s and 1960s, Tonny Petersen brought his Hell Drivers show to the Erie County Fair in 2010. The 70-minute show featured an array of flaming cars, spectacular jumps, a parade of autos on two wheels, and the unforgettable head-on collisions.

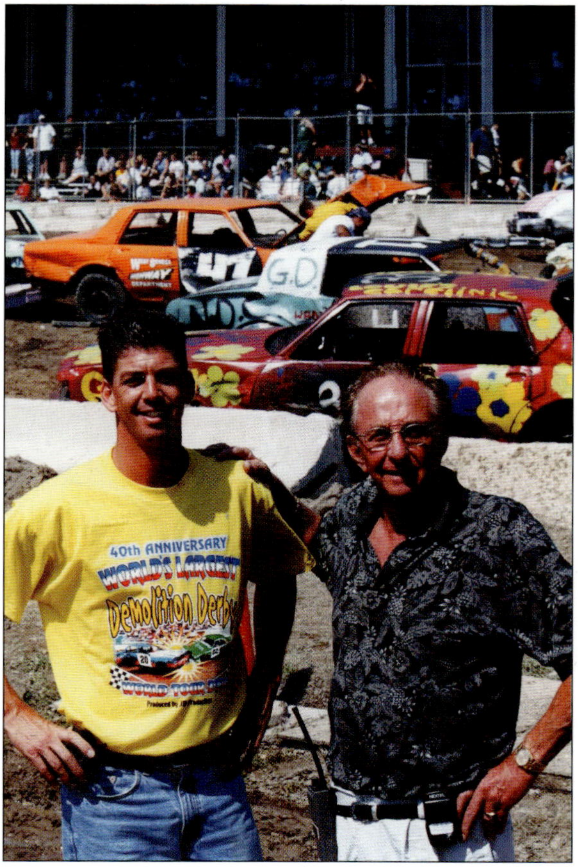

In 1963, W. Jay Milligan Sr. was asked to put on a demolition derby at the Erie County Fair. With success found in Hamburg, he soon was off producing demos and stunt shows at other fairs across the northeast. With W. Jay Milligan Jr. and Sr. at the helm, the World's Largest Demolition Derby attracts hundreds of cars annually to capacity crowds during the last day of the fair.

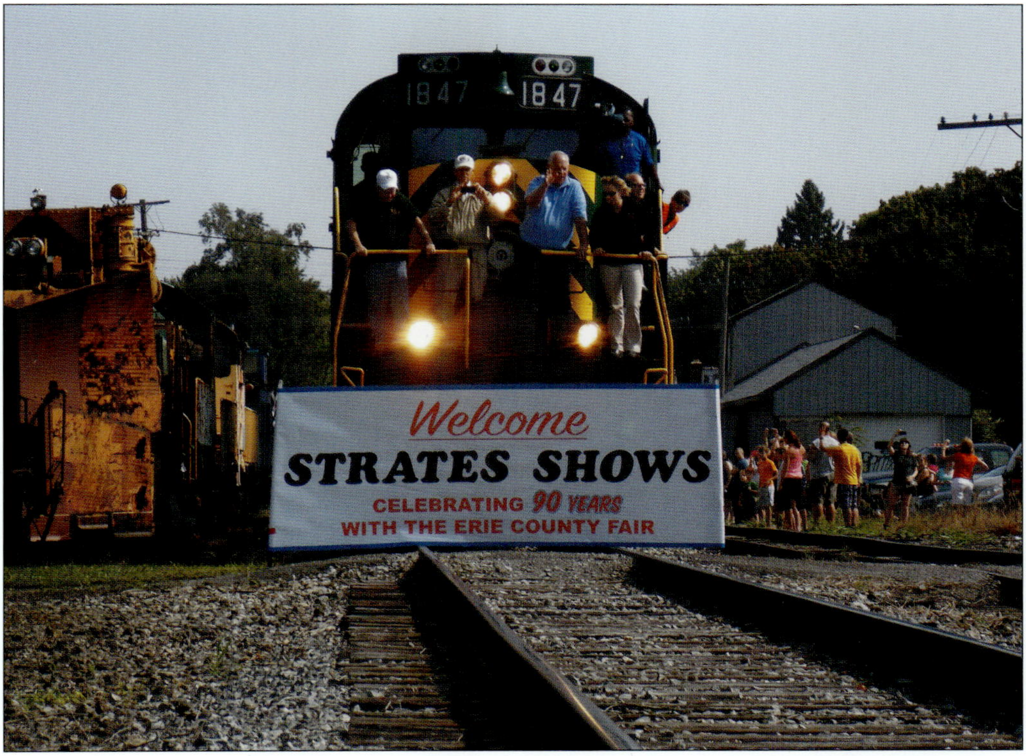

To commemorate the fair's 90-year partnership with the James E. Strates Shows, a celebration was held on August 1, 2014, at the former Erie Railroad Depot in the village of Hamburg. More than 800 people welcomed back North America's only remaining railroad carnival as two Buffalo Southern Alco locomotives crashed through a ceremonial banner. Eighty-three-year-old E. James Strates, president and CEO of Strates Shows, was on the front of the engine as it entered Hamburg.

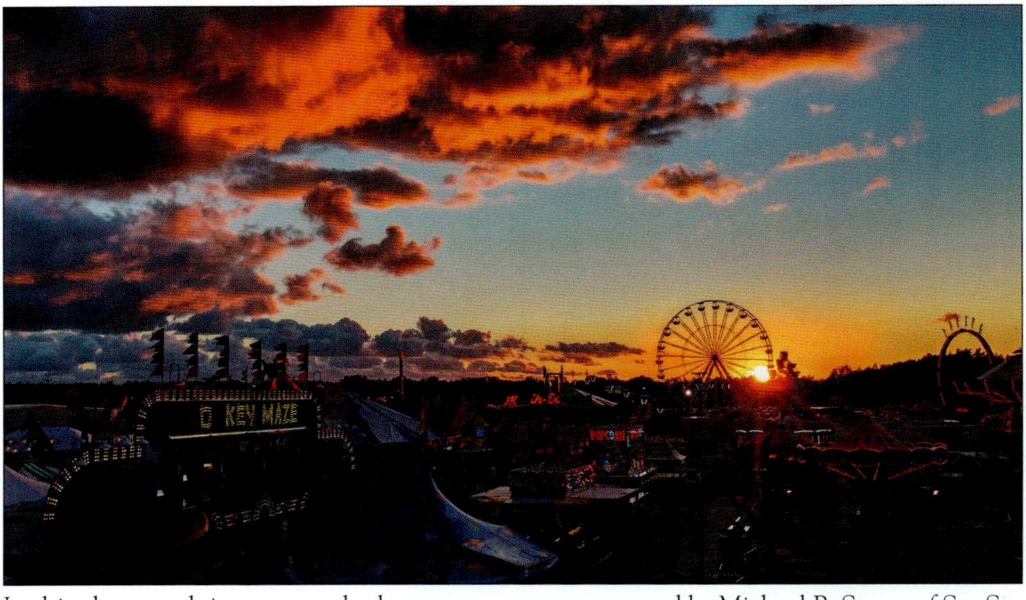

In this photograph is a spectacular late-summer sunset captured by Michael B. Stuart of Stu Stu Studio on August 14, 2014.

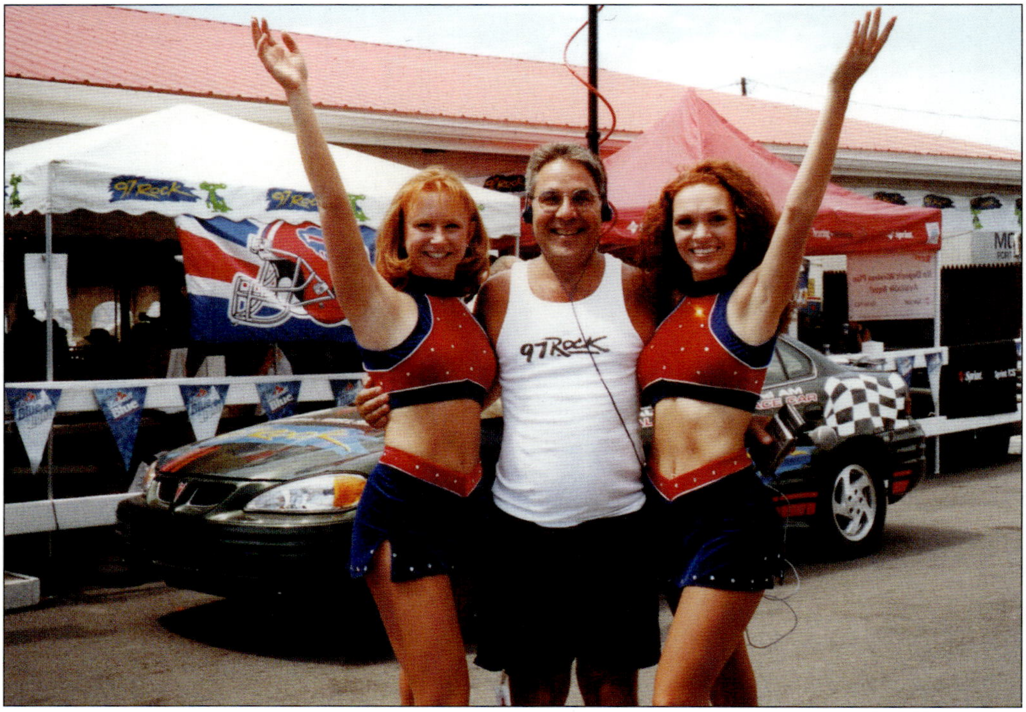

Carl Russo of 97 Rock is pictured with unidentified members of the Buffalo Jills during the 2004 Erie County Fair. A product of Buffalo's Westside, Russo began broadcasting live from the fair in the early 1980s. A Buffalo native, Russo started his radio career at WYSL-AM in 1979 and became a member of the legendary 97 Rock WGR-FM team in 1980. When the format was discontinued in 1985, Russo headed to stations in Indianapolis and Dallas before returning to Buffalo as part of the "new" 97 Rock in 1988. For his genuine love and ongoing support of "all things fair," Russo was inducted into the Erie County Fair Hall of Fame in 2013.

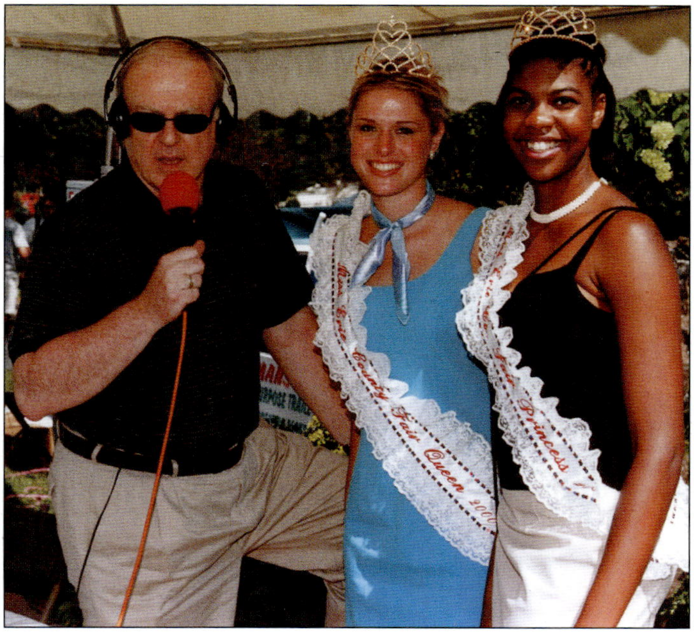

Oldies 104 WHTT's Tommy Shannon interviews the 2000 Erie County Fair Queen Summer Maue and Princess Kimberly Bowman. While on WKBW-AM and WGR-AM in the late 1950s and early 1960s, Shannon was one of the most popular media personalities during the golden age of Top 40 radio. In 1964, Shannon left his hometown of Buffalo to join CKLW-AM in Detroit, Michigan. He returned to Western New York in 1997 to join WHTT-FM, where he continued to entertain listeners until his 2005 retirement.

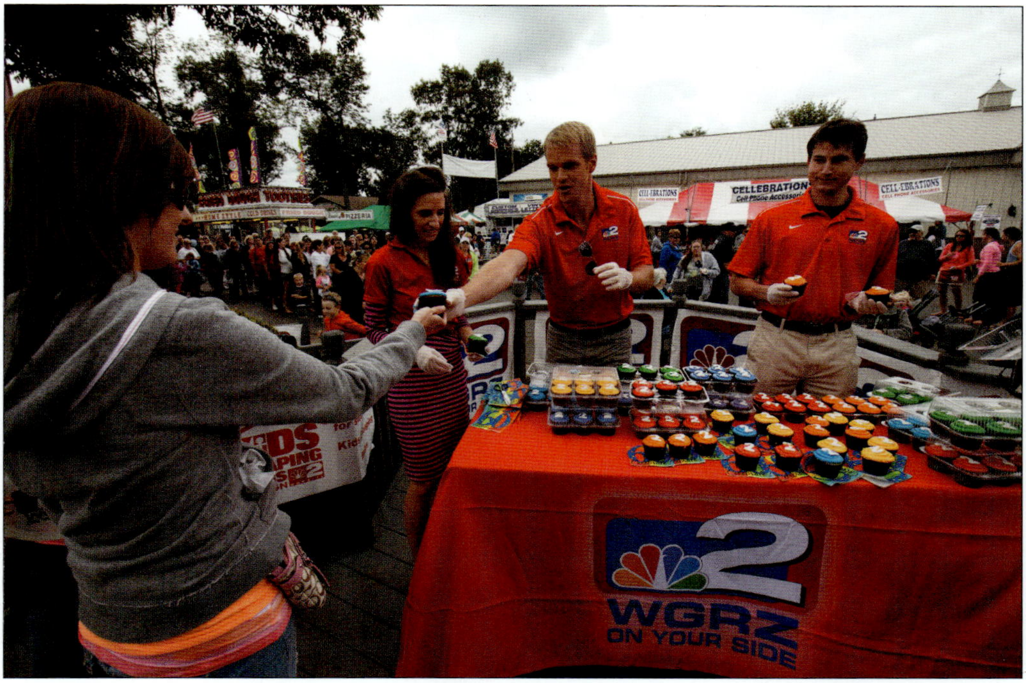

WGRZ-TV's Michael Wooten (left) and Danny Spewak help to distribute 222 gourmet cupcakes to celebrate Channel 2's 60th birthday in 2014.

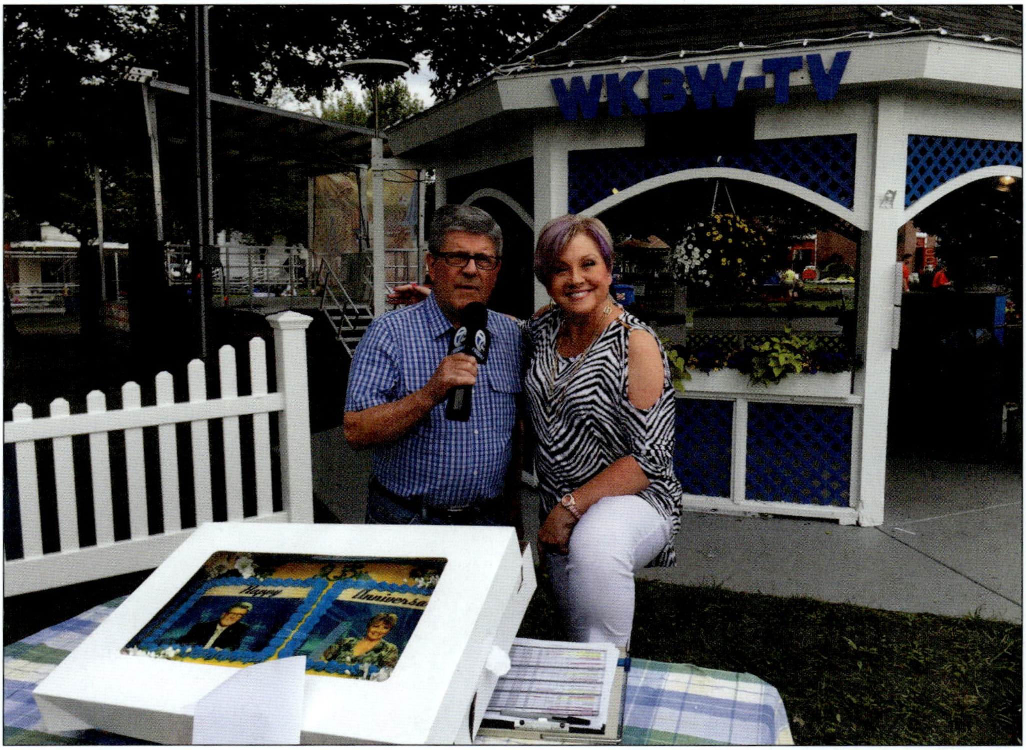

WKBW-TV's Linda Pellegrino and Jon Summers celebrate 25 years together on AM *Buffalo* during the 2015 Erie County Fair.

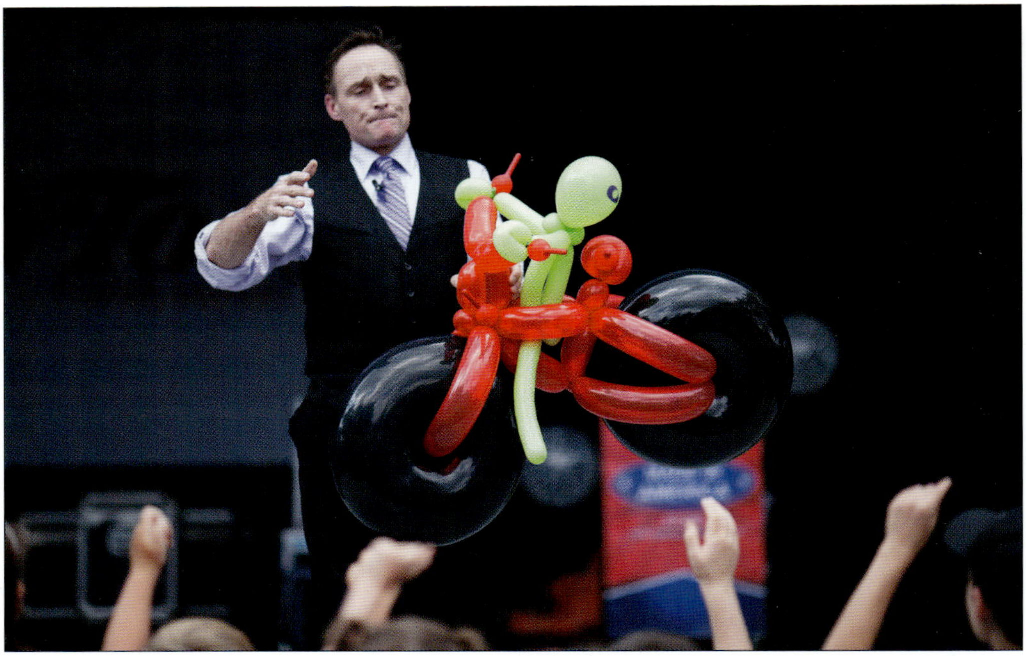

John Cassidy, known to fairgoers as the Bizarre Balloonologist, brought his mix of comedy, magic, and really weird stunts with balloons to the fair in 2006. During his career, Cassidy has held three Guinness World Records for his ability to inflate the most balloons in an hour and make the fastest balloon sculpture as well as the most balloon sculptures in an hour.

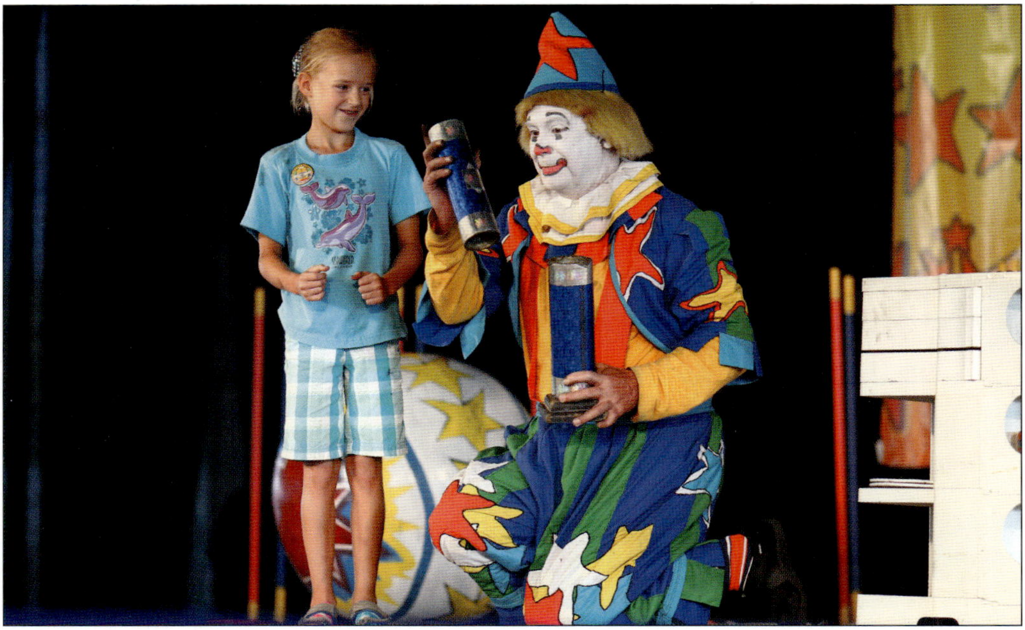

With a mischievous grin and a sparkle in his eyes, Gary the Silent Clown began entertaining Erie County Fair audiences in 1988. A graduate of Ringling Bros. and Barnum & Bailey Clown College, Gary has become a beloved tradition. Over the years, thousands of fair patrons have gone home at the end of "A Day at the Fair" with one of Gary's famous chalk sketches or balloon sculptures. Gary Girouard was inducted into the Erie County Fair Hall of Fame in 2010.

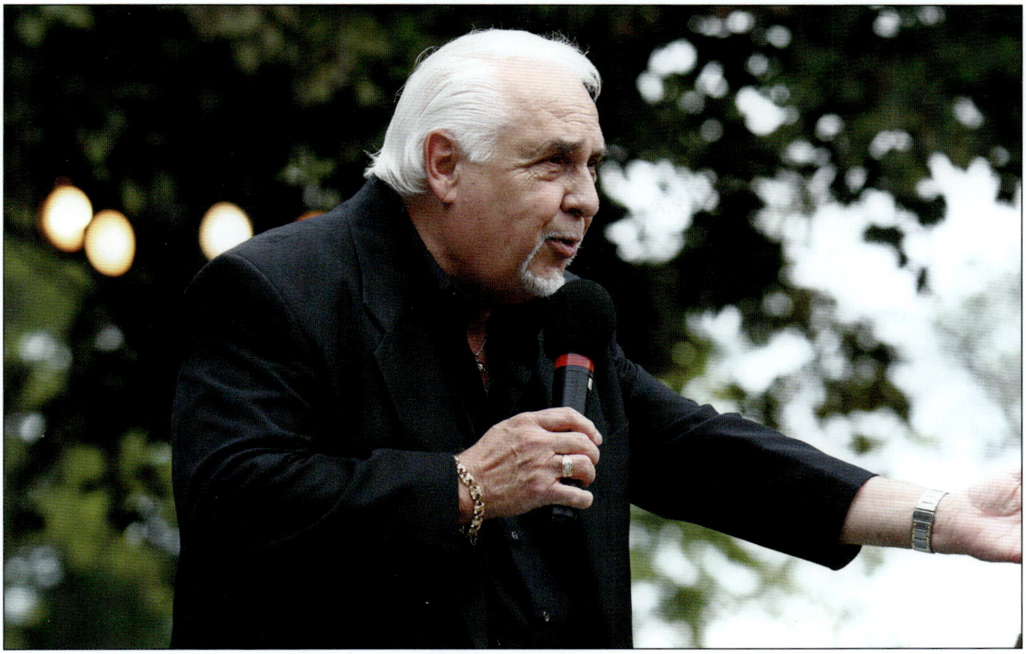

Master hypnotist Jerry Valley began entertaining fans at the Avenue of Flags Stage in 1994. Through the power of suggestion and a twist of comedy, he uses his unique talents to turn audience members into the stars of the show. Valley was honored for his years of service to the Erie County Fair in 2012.

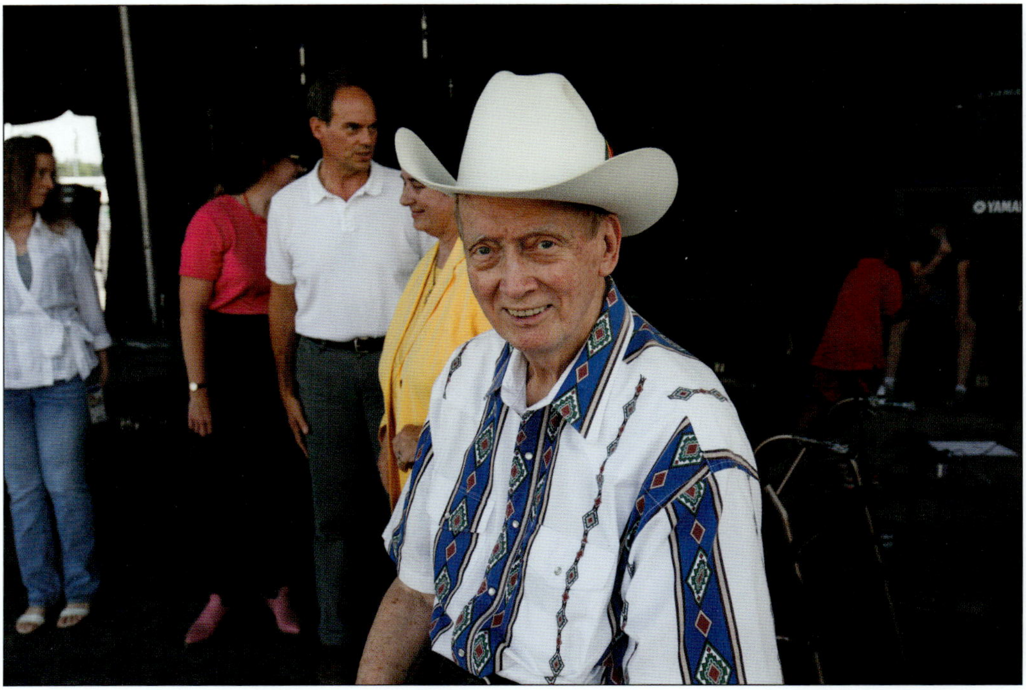

On August 9, 2014, the Erie County Fair paused to honor Ramblin' Lou Schriver on his 50th year of performing at the fair. A cornerstone of the fair's entertainment lineup, Schriver completed 51 years onstage in 2015 before passing away on January 17, 2016, at the age of 86.

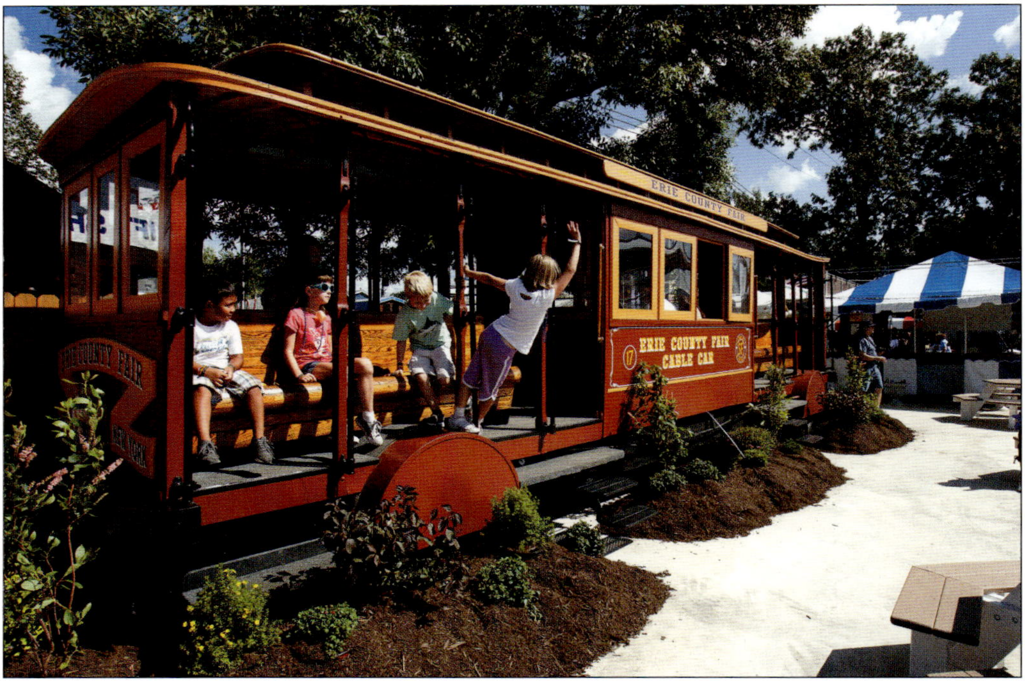

Purchased in 1962, the Erie County Fair's San Francisco Cable Car was the recipient of a major cosmetic restoration in 2009. Surrounded by landscaping, the trolley was put on public display near Gate 4 for all to explore.

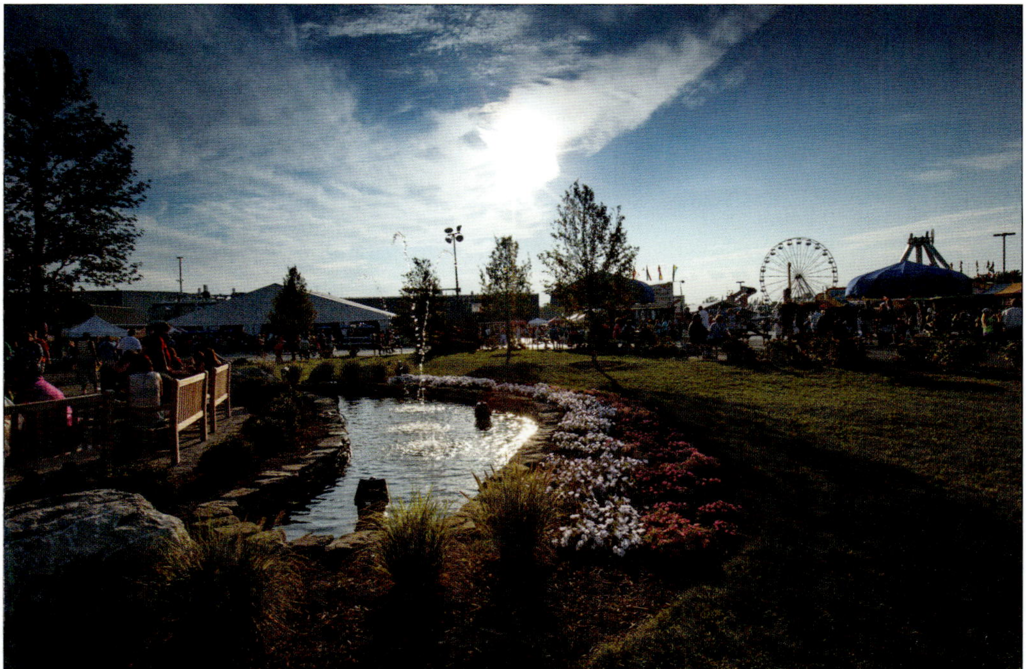

The fair dedicated Midway Park, located outside of the Firemen's Building, in 2014. The added green space features an annual display of colorful flowers and a leaping water feature.

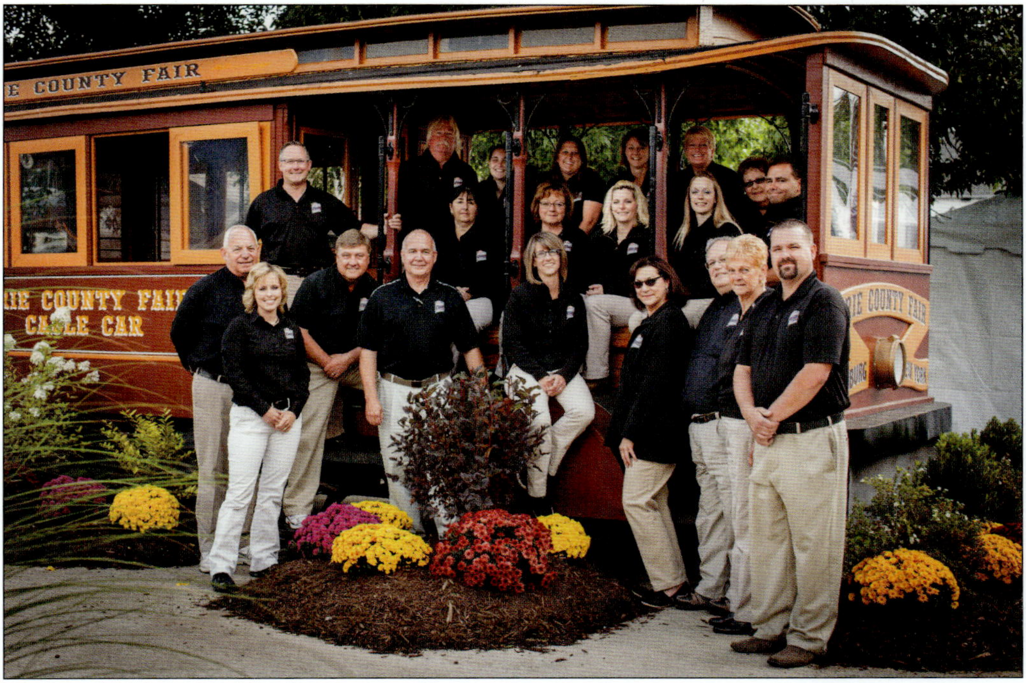

Pictured is the 2014 staff of the 175th Erie County Fair. They are, from left to right, (first row) Dennis Lang, Jessica Underberg, Jeff Horbowicz, Mike Bolas, Holly Smyczynski, Annette Mathews, Russ Marquart, Blanche McGiveron, and Jeff Rapini; (second row) Marty Biniasz, Concetta Sciolino, Susan Szymanski, Laura Kwilos, Paula Smith, Jean Bak, and Justin Iwankow; (third row) Gary Horton, Laura Woloszyn, Amanda Cammarano, Lynne Collard, and Jackie Cammarano.

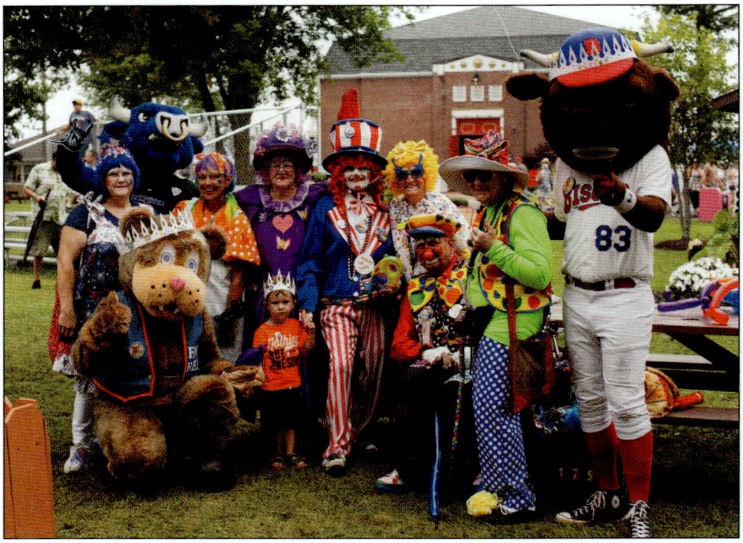

Members of the Friends of the Fair clowns corps, along with Buster Bison and the University at Buffalo's Victor E. Bull, celebrate Fair Bear's first birthday during a Slade Park party in 2015. Sporting an updated look, the tradition of the fair's mascot returned in 2014. The Friends of the Fair volunteer program was created by the agricultural society in 1987.

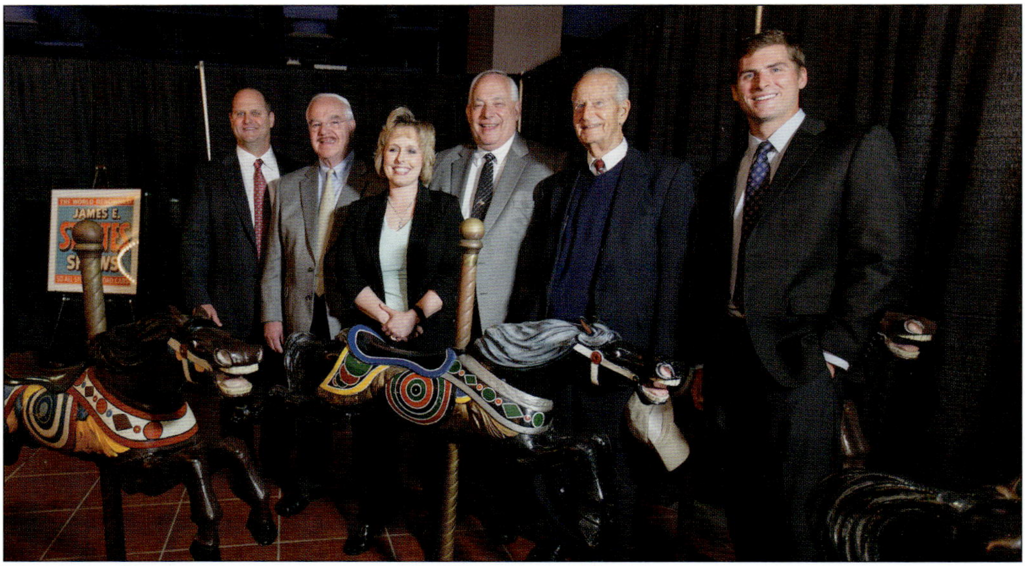

On April 29, 2016, the Erie County Agricultural Society announced that it extended its contract with the Strates Shows by 10 years to be its sole carnival provider. Three generations of Strates family members attended the contract signing. According to the Outdoor Amusement Business Association, the relationship between the Strates Shows and the Erie County Fair, which began in 1924, is the longest continuous run of any carnival in modern midway history. Pictured are, from left to right, John Strates; Joseph Solomon, chairman of the agricultural society; Jessica Underberg, assistant fair manager; Dennis Lang, fair manager and CEO; E. James Strates; and Nick Strates.

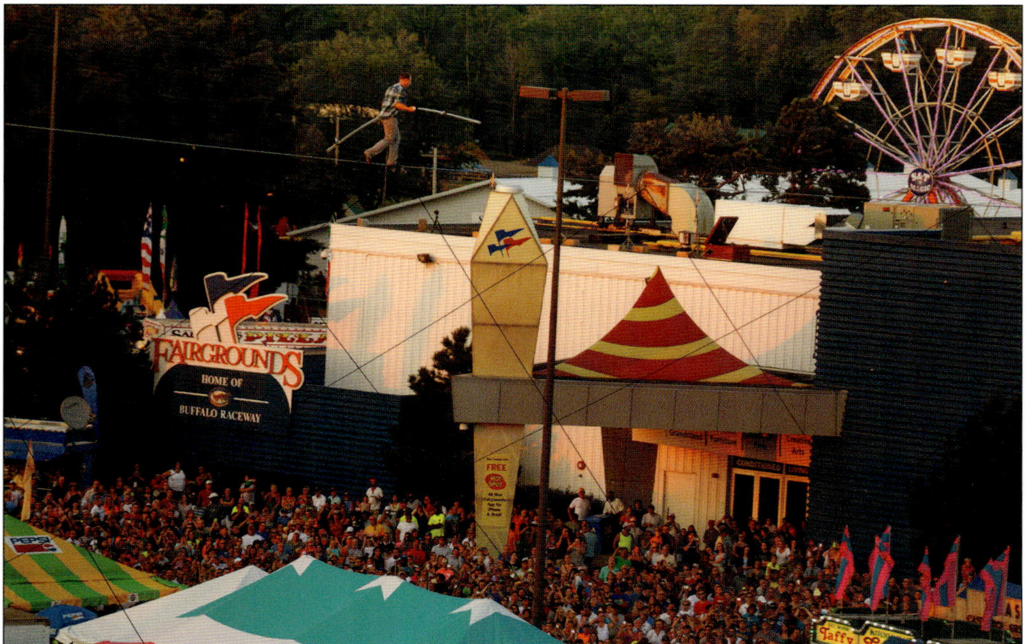

The Erie County Fair Skywalk on Sunday, August 9, 2014, was part of the fair's 175th celebration. At exactly 8:00 p.m., as the summer sun began to set, Nik Wallenda began his walk 125 feet above the fair on a wire measuring five-eighths of an inch in diameter.

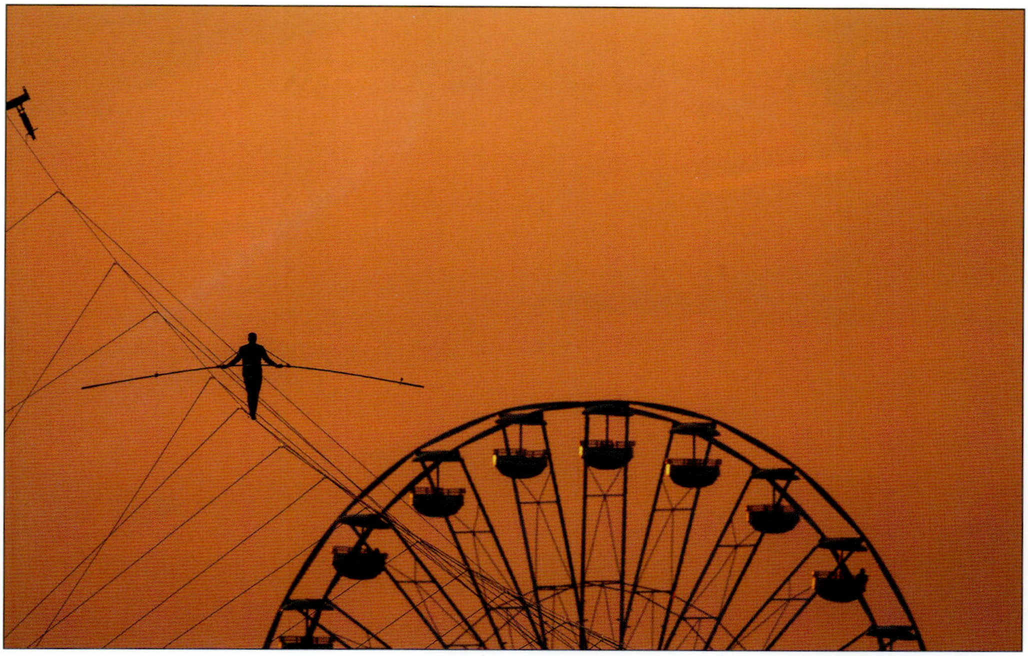

At a distance of 1,400 feet, the Erie County Fair Skywalk was longer than Wallenda's 2012 Niagara Falls Skywalk (1,300 feet) and just 100 feet shorter than his 2013 Grand Canyon crossing (1,500 feet). Wallenda's wire, whose route passed over the midway and ended in the Grandstand infield, was anchored by two cranes furnished by Clark Rigging.

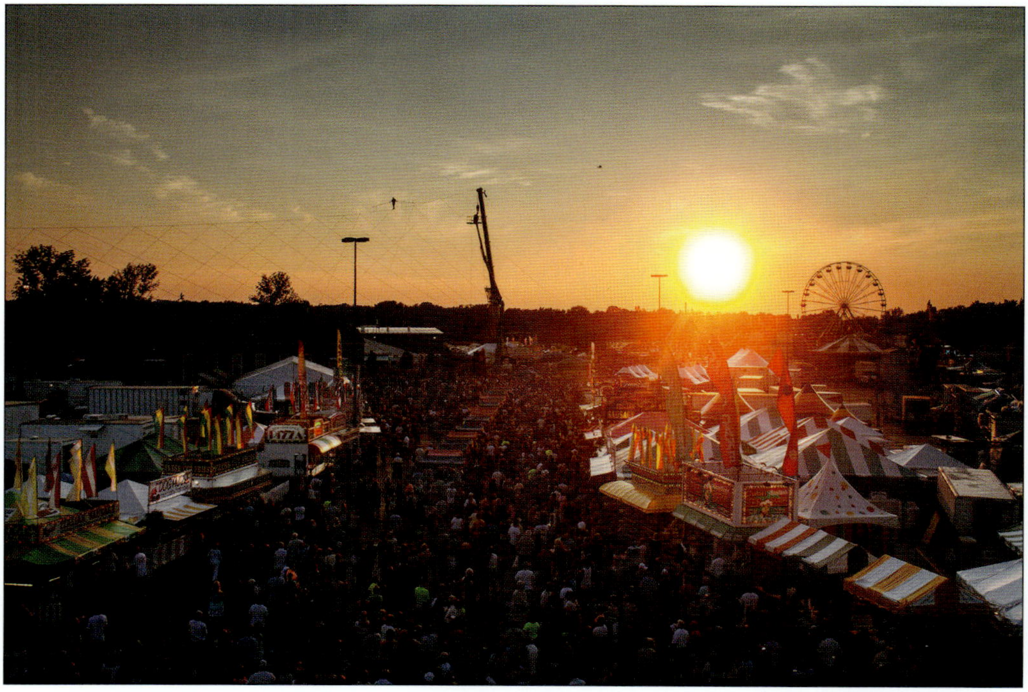

A crowd of 110,000 fairgoers was in attendance to witness the King of the High Wire's historic Erie County Fair Skywalk stunt. Upon completion, a flurry of fireworks welcomed Wallenda safely to the other side before he took to the Grandstand stage to address spectators.

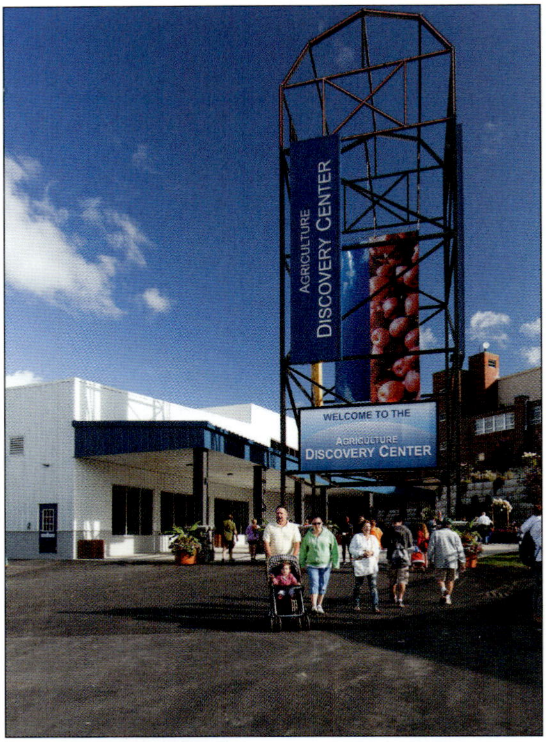

With its signature 65-foot Sky Barn tower and 60,000 square feet of display space, the Agricultural Discovery Center (ADC) opened its doors to fairgoers in 2014. The completion of the ADC was a signature element 175th Erie County Fair and signaled a long-term commitment by the Erie County Agricultural Society to support its core agricultural-based mission. During non-fair times, the ADC plays host to youth education programs, field trips, and events like the Western New York Farm Show.

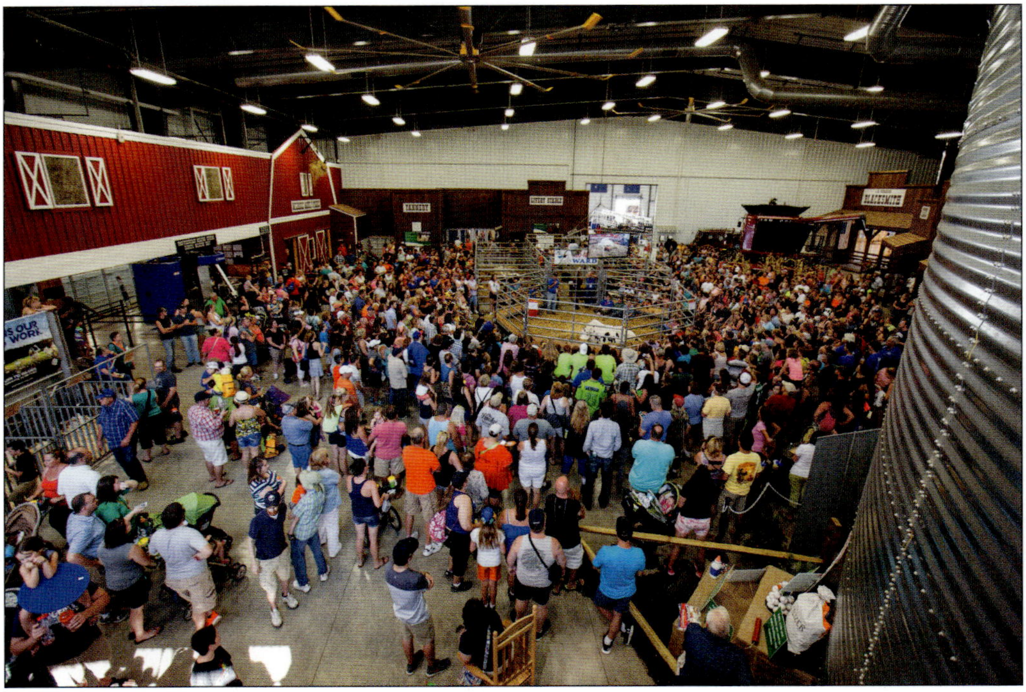

The Agriculture Discovery Center provides visitors with an up-close look at modern farming through exhibits like the demonstration of robotic milking technology and a ride inside a combine simulator. During the fair, visitors have a chance to see the birth of a live cow in the facility's Moo-Ternity Ward.

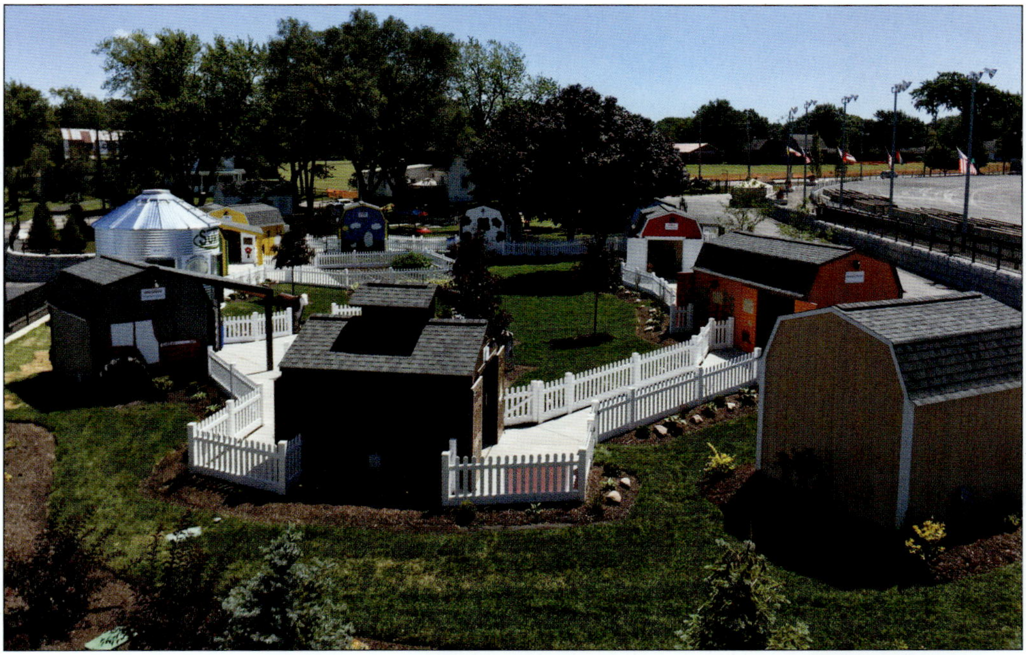

In 2015, the interactive Little Hands on the Farm was added to the fair's agricultural education offerings. Located in Baker Park, the children-sized farm features 10 barns, a produce garden, and a peddle-tractor track.

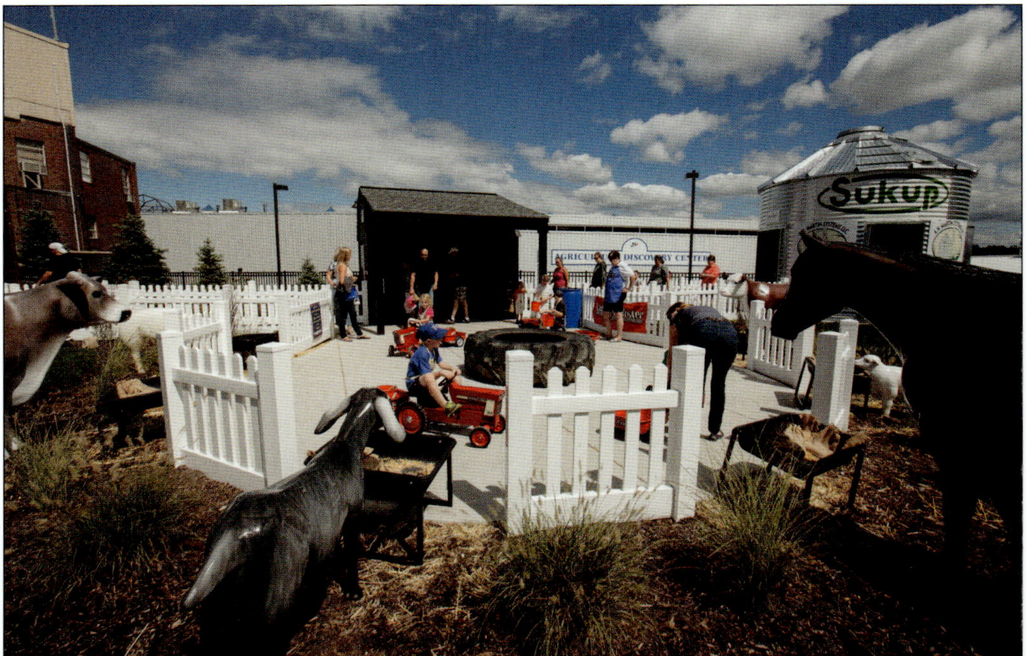

Activities featured at Little Hands on the Farm include grooming a mock sheep, gathering eggs, collecting grain from a grain bin, and peddling a tractor to feed the "animals." As participants travel from barn to barn completing the farm "chores," kids add their farm products to a basket and in the end sell their products at the farmers' market.